"The Christian faith teaches that death, the last enemy, has truly been defeated by Christ. In trying times such as these, the Church needs faithful Catholic academics such as the contributors to this work to engage contemporary problems with the enduring wisdom of the faith. This volume offers a timely message of hope to the ever-vexing problem of death. Priests and religious, students, and the lay faithful alike will find in these penetrating essays profound and clear answers to many common problems and objections to the faith that arise from the problems of death and suffering."

FRANK J. DEWANE
Bishop of the Diocese of Venice in Florida

Hope &
Death

Hope & Death

Christian Responses

EDITED BY

MICHAEL A. DAUPHINAIS & ROGER W. NUTT

EMMAUS
ACADEMIC
Steubenville, Ohio
www.emmausacademic.com

EMMAUS
ACADEMIC

Steubenville, Ohio
www.emmausacademic.com
A Division of The St. Paul Center for Biblical Theology
Editor-in-Chief: Scott Hahn
1468 Parkview Circle
Steubenville, Ohio 43952

Library of Congress Cataloging-in-Publication Data applied for.
ISBN: 978-1-64585-215-5 (hard cover) | 978-1-64585-216-2 (paperback) |
978-1-64585-217-9 (ebook)

Cover design and layout by Allison Merrick.
Cover image: *Resurrection of Lazarus*, graphic collage from engraving of Nazareene School,
published in The Holy Bible, St.Vojtech Publishing, Trnava, Slovakia, 1937

Table of Contents

Contributors

ROMANUS CESSARIO, OP is the Adam Cardinal Maida Professor of Theology at Ave Maria University in Ave Maria, FL. He holds an STD from the Université de Fribourg (1980), as well as an STL (1972) and STB (1970) from the Dominican House of Studies in Washington, DC. He previously earned a BA (1967) and MA (1969) from Saint Stephen's College. In 2013, Cessario was the recipient of the Sacrae Theologiae Magister, the highest honor bestowed by the Master General of the Order of Preachers. A specialist in Thomist theology, he is an author or editor of more than one hundred scholarly articles and over twenty books, including *Thomas and the Thomists: The Achievement of Thomas Aquinas and His Interpreters*, *Theology and Sanctity*, *Introduction to Moral Theology*, and *The Moral Virtues and Theological Ethics*. Cessario serves as Socio Ordinario for the Pontifical Academy of St. Thomas, Associate Editor of *The Thomist*, General Editor of *Catholic Moral Thought*, a multivolume series of textbooks, and Senior Editor of *Magnificat*.

MICHAEL A. DAUPHINAIS serves as the Fr. Matthew Lamb Professor of Catholic Theology and Co-Director of the Aquinas Center for Theological Renewal at Ave Maria University, Ave Maria, FL. He is the co-author of *Knowing the Love of Christ: An Introduction to the Theology of Thomas Aquinas*, *Holy People, Holy Land: A Theological Introduction to the Bible*, and *Wisdom from the Word: Biblical Answers to Ten Questions about Catholicism*. He has co-edited multiple books dedicated to Thomas Aquinas, including *Thomas Aquinas and the Crisis in Christology* and *Thomas Aquinas, Biblical Theologian*, and published numerous articles and chapters in books on moral, dogmatic, and biblical theology.

BRYAN KROMHOLTZ, OP is Academic Dean and Professor of Theology at the Dominican School of Philosophy and Theology in Berkeley, CA. He holds an STD and PhD from the University of Fribourg, an MA from the Graduate Theological Union at Berkely, an MDiv and BA from the

Dominican School of Philosophy and Theology, and a BSEE from Gonzaga University. His research interests include the teaching of St. Thomas Aquinas on the resurrection of the dead, St. Thomas Aquinas's eschatology and the role of beatitude in his anthropology, and the implications of eschatological beliefs for pastoral practice.

STEVEN A. LONG is Professor of Theology at Ave Maria University in Ave Maria, FL and Ordinarius at the Pontifical Academy of St. Thomas Aquinas in Rome. He holds a PhD from The Catholic University of America. He is particularly interested in the theology of grace, freedom, and law, and the historico-doctrinal disputes about this within Catholic theology and philosophy; natural law and moral theology, where he has defended classical Thomistic natural law; and metaphysics. Among his many notable publications are *The Teleological Grammar of the Moral Act* and *Analogia Entis: On the Analogy of Being, Metaphysics, and the Act of Faith.*

GUY MANSINI, OSB is the Max Seckler Chair of Theology at Ave Maria University in Ave Maria, FL. He entered the Benedictine Monastery of St. Meinrad in 1972 and was ordained in 1977. After philosophical studies at Marquette University in Milwaukee and theological studies at the Gregorian University, Rome, he taught at St. Meinrad Seminary from 1984 to 2016. While specializing in Christology and Ecclesiology, he has maintained a continuing interest in fundamental theological topics, especially Robert Sokolowski's "theology of disclosure."

ROGER W. NUTT is Provost of Ave Maria University, where he is also Professor of Theology and Co-Director of the Aquinas Center for Theological Renewal. He is the author of many articles and book chapters on Christology and Sacramental Theology. His books include *Thomas Aquinas: De Unione Verbi Incarnati*, *General Principles of Sacramental Theology*, and *To Die Is Gain: A Theological (re-) Introduction to the Sacrament of Anointing of the Sick for Clergy, Laity, Caregivers, and Everyone Else.* He is also co-editor of many volumes on the theology of St. Thomas Aquinas, including *Thomism and Predestination: Principles and Disputations*; *Thomas Aquinas and the Greek Fathers*; *Thomas Aquinas, Biblical Theologian*; and *Thomas Aquinas and the Crisis of Christology.*

TAYLOR PATRICK O'NEILL is Tutor at Thomas Aquinas College in Northfield, MA. His book *Grace, Predestination, and the Permission of Sin* was published in 2019 by Catholic University of America Press. His work has appeared in *First Things, The Heythrop Journal, Ecce Mater Tua, Reality: A Journal for Philosophical Discourse, Church Life Journal,* and the T & T Clark Companion Series, and his scholarship has been published by Sapientia Press and Ignatius Press. He is a founding member of The Sacra Doctrina Project.

MATTHEW J. RAMAGE is Professor of Theology at Benedictine College in Atchison, KS. His work has appeared in a number of journals, including *Nova et Vetera, Scripta Theologica, Cithara,* and *Homiletic and Pastoral Review,* as well as popular online venues such as *Strange Notions, The Gregorian Institute,* and *Crisis.* He is author, contributing author, or co-translator of a variety of books, including the monographs *Dark Passages of the Bible: Engaging Scripture with Benedict XVI and Thomas Aquinas; Jesus, Interpreted: Benedict XVI, Bart Ehrman, and the Historical Truth of the Gospels; The Experiment of Faith: Pope Benedict XVI on Living the Theological Virtues in a Secular Age;* and *From the Dust of the Earth: Benedict XVI, the Bible, and the Theory of Evolution.*

JOHN RZIHA is Professor of Theology at Benedictine College in Atchison, KS. He received his MA in theology from the University of Dallas (1998) and his PHD in theology from the Catholic University of America (2006). He has taught at Benedictine College since 2001. His area of expertise is moral theology, and he regularly teaches class in moral theology, Church history, bioethics, and Catholic social thought. He has written two books: *Perfecting Human Actions: St. Thomas Aquinas on Participation in Eternal Law* (CUA Press, 2009), and a handbook for moral theology called *The Christian Moral Life: Directions for the Journey to Happiness* (Notre Dame Press, 2017).

ANDREW D. SWAFFORD is Associate Professor of Theology at Benedictine College in Atchison, KS. He is general editor and contributor to The Great Adventure Catholic Bible published by Ascension Press and host of the DVD series (and author of the companion book) *Hebrews: The New and Eternal Covenant* as well as author and host of *Romans: The Gospel of Salvation,* both published by Ascension. He is author of *Nature and Grace, John Paul II to Aristotle and Back Again,* and *Spiritual Survival in the Modern World.* He holds a PhD in Sacred Theology from the University of St. Mary of the Lake and an MA in Old Testament & Semitic Languages from Trinity Evangelical Divinity School.

T. ADAM VAN WART is Assistant Professor of Theology and Director of Undergraduate Studies in Theology at Ave Maria University in Ave Maria, FL. He holds a PhD from Southern Methodist University, MTS from Duke University, ThM and MA from Dallas Theological Seminary, and BS from Texas Christian University. He is author of *Neither Nature nor Grace: Aquinas, Barth, and Garrigou-Lagrange on the Epistemic Use of God's Effects.*

JEFFREY M. WALKEY is Assistant Professor of Theology at Ave Maria University in Ave Maria, FL. He holds a PhD from Marquette University, MTS from Duke Divinity School, and BS from Purdue University. His interests include Thomas Aquinas, faith and reason, twentieth-century Thomism, the problem of God, modern atheism, apophatic (negative) theology, metaphysics, nature and grace, and the Divine Names tradition. He has published numerous articles in Thomistic theology.

WILLIAM M. WRIGHT IV is Professor of Theology at Duquesne University in Pittsburgh, PA. He is a specialist in New Testament studies with special focus on the Johannine writings. His interests also include the role of Greco-Roman rhetoric, literary criticism, and aesthetics in the Gospels, the use of premodern reception history as a theological and interpretive resource in light of the Catholic Ressourcement, and the theoretical underpinnings of biblical exegesis. He is the author of numerous articles and several books: *Rhetoric and Theology: Figural Reading of John 9* (Walter de Gruyter, 2009); *The Bible and Catholic Ressourcement: Essays in Scripture and Theology* (Emmaus Academic, 2019); and, with Francis Martin, *The Gospel of John* (Baker Academic, 2015) and *Encountering the Living God in Scripture: Theological and Philosophical Principles for Interpretation* (Baker Academic, 2019). He has been elected to the *Studiorum Novi Testamenti Societas* and serves on the U.S. Lutheran-Roman Catholic Ecumenical Dialogue. He is also a Lay Dominican.

From Here to Eternity:
Reflections on Death and the Afterlife in Light of the Resurrection of Christ

RANDALL B. SMITH
University of St. Thomas, TX

POPE ST. JOHN PAUL II began his great encyclical *Fides et Ratio* with the words "Know Thyself." "In different parts of the world, with their different cultures," he wrote, "there arise at the same time the fundamental questions which pervade human life: *Who am I? Where have I come from and where am I going? Why is there evil? What is there after this life?*" These are questions, says the pope, "which have their common source in the quest for meaning which has always compelled the human heart"—not just Catholics or Christians but all men and women throughout history and across all cultures.[1]

THE THREAT OF NOTHINGNESS: IS THERE ANY POINT TO LIFE?

Few things force us to face the question of "the meaning of things and of their very existence"[2] more powerfully and more insistently than having to consider the question of death, the possible end of our existence, and/or what might lie in store for us after this life. "Depend upon it, sir," said the

---

[1] Pope St. John Paul II, Faith and Reason *Fides et Ratio* (Sept. 14, 1998), §1. All quotations from papal encyclicals have been taken from the official English translations at the Vatican web site, www.vatican.va.

[2] John Paul II, *Fides et Ratio*, §1.

great Samuel Johnson, "when a man knows he is to be hanged in a fortnight, it concentrates his mind wonderfully."[3]

If all we have strived for, all we have learned and experienced, everyone we have loved, simply comes to nothing in the end, is there any point to life? To most people throughout history and across cultures, it has seemed as though we need some notion of life *after* death for this life to have any meaning.

INADEQUATE VIEWS OF THE AFTERLIFE

And yet, although it seems we need some notion of the afterlife to make this life meaningful, we also need a notion of the afterlife that does not itself make this life meaningless. If heaven is so wonderful, why not simply get there? Why are we wasting time here?

Does the picture we hold of the afterlife affirm what we take to be a noble human life, or does it rather contradict it? If we imagine a heroic life to be one in which we live chastely, defending the dignity of women, who could respect anyone whose vision of the afterlife was made up of the endless sexual conquest of virgins? If we think that a noble, flourishing human life is one devoted to the selfless love of others, what sense would it make to picture the afterlife as one in which we care nothing for those we left behind?

Some cultures and religious traditions have envisioned the status of the human person after death as involving a much *lower* level of existence. In Homer's *Odyssey*, for example, Odysseus meets the spirit of the Greek hero Achilles in the underworld and reassures him that he has become the most renowned among all the Greeks. Achilles tells him that he would rather be a slave for a poor farmer than ruler of all the dead.[4] Homer describes the souls Odysseus meets in the underworld as "shades" since they lack any substantial bodies. When Odysseus sees his mother, he tries to hug her, but his arms pass right through her. None of those whom Odysseus meets in the underworld are happy, satisfied, or at peace. They mostly want news of those who are still alive. We are left to wonder whether Achilles's heroic deeds might have been essentially meaningless.

The Roman poet Virgil has a slightly more agreeable idea about the afterlife. His hero, Aeneas, makes a journey to the underworld, like Odysseus, but what he finds there is much less grim. Although there are punishments

---

[3] James Boswell, *The Life of Samuel Johnson*, ed. David Womersly (London: Penguin Classics, 2008), 612.

[4] Homer, *Odyssey*, 11.488–91.

and torments for spirits who lived evil lives, those who lived noble lives enjoy the pleasures of the Elysian Fields.[5]

And yet, since they lack bodies, it is unclear whether they can feel the heat of the sun on their skin, smell the flowers and forest, or touch the grass—any of the experiences we associate with bodily existence. Aeneas does not seem to be able to hug anyone in the underworld either, although as a Roman Stoic, perhaps this did not seem like a great loss to him.

But was this mode of existence of persons in the Elysian Fields really better than the mode of existence of persons in this life? This is not entirely clear. One problem is that, given Virgil's admirable commitment to service on behalf of Rome, it is hard for him to tolerate the thought of noble Romans sitting around simply enjoying themselves in paradise in the afterlife because this would be at odds with the sort of life he wanted to inspire in his fellow Romans. We need a notion of the afterlife that does not involve an empty stream of essentially meaningless activities of the sort we would not respect here on earth and which we are convinced hold out little or no promise of making us truly happy. Would we enjoy games and pastimes in the afterlife while the people we love in this world continue to be subject to sorrow and suffering? We are bidden to "love our neighbor," but then in heaven, do we just forget them? And does that hope for life after death encourage us to be more complacent in the face of human suffering and ignore injustices in this life?

DOES HOPE FOR THE AFTERLIFE DIMINISH CONCERN FOR OTHERS IN THIS LIFE?

Two modern thinkers who believed this were the German Karl Marx (1818–1883) and the Frenchman Auguste Comte (1798–1857). Marx believed that hope for an afterlife robbed man of his only opportunity to be fully himself. The practice of worshipping an unreal Supreme Being, he claimed, alienated man from his better self. Those who suffered injustice patiently now in the belief that they would receive their reward later were having their sense of justice deadened by "the opiate of the masses."[6]

Auguste Comte believed that hope for the afterlife merely produced

---

[5] Virgil, *Aeneid*, bk. 6, esp. 6.268–800.

[6] Originally written in the Introduction to *A Contribution to the Critique of Hegel's Philosophy of Right* but first published in *Deutsch-Französische Jahrbücher*, February 7 and 10, 1844 in Paris. For this Introduction, see *Marx's Critique of Hegel's Philosophy of Right*, trans. Joseph O'Malley (Oxford: Oxford University Press, 1970) or the online version at https://www.marxists.org/archive/marx/works/1843/critique-hpr/intro.htm.

"slaves of God" and servants of the Church. In order to develop what was needed, namely "servants of Humanity," men had to turn away from the fictitious notion of a life after death and concentrate on this life.[7]

Perhaps we can agree that if these criticisms are correct—if Christianity causes people to devalue this life, if it causes people to have less concern for justice and the welfare of others—then Christianity would have a problem, not primarily because of these external critiques but because Christians would be holding a view of the afterlife that was inconsistent with its own stated principles. Having preached repeatedly that Christians have a special responsibility to exhibit a "preferential option for the poor," if Christians then held a view of the afterlife that resulted in a diminishment of that care and concern, Christian doctrine would be in conflict with itself, quite independent of anything Marxists or other secularists might claim.

REINCARNATION?

But let's return to the *Aeneid* for a moment. Aeneas's father, Anchises, seems happy and satisfied when Aeneas meets him in the afterlife, but he shows Aeneas the place where many other souls are readying themselves to be reincarnated into new bodies.[8] Does Anchises himself yearn to return to an embodied state? Virgil does not tell us. But it is interesting to note that the narrative of the story depends on him *not* being reincarnated. A key step in the process of reincarnation is that souls must cross the River Lethe, the "river of forgetfulness," before they get their new bodies. If Anchises had crossed that river, he would not remember his own son, and he could offer him no wise advice. However much Anchises had loved Aeneas before, however much he had been devoted to him in this life, this connection would be broken and lost forever once he crossed that river.

This lack of identity of the self—the loss of all wisdom gained, all memory of the people one loved—is especially telling because what disturbs people the most about the prospect of death is the fear that they will lose their connection with their loved ones. It is not without reason that in all the most famous stories about the afterlife—in Homer, Virgil, and Dante—the most frequent request souls make is to get news about those they have left behind.

The second problem with reincarnation, however, from the Christian perspective, is that it encourages the view that our bodies are essentially

---

[7] See Henri de Lubac, *The Drama of Atheist Humanism*, trans. E. Riley, A. E. Nash, and M. Sebanc (San Francisco, CA: Ignatius Press, 1995), 172–73, esp. nn101–3.

[8] Virgil, *Aeneid*, 6.703–24.

meaninglessness to our personal identity. On this view, bodies can be switched out without violation to one's "identity." And not only one's body but also one's memories and most treasured relationships—all these are to be jettisoned as so much excess baggage in order to "liberate" the self. Perhaps this is why so many modern people find this view appealing.

DEATH AS LIBERATION? WHAT IS "LIBERATED"?

Let me suggest that a person's notion of the afterlife reveals a great deal about what they think makes life meaningful. A person who thinks *intellect* is the most essential element of our humanity will likely believe that *intellect* is what survives death. And vice versa, if a person believes it is *intellect* that survives death, this is likely because he believes that *intellect* is the most essential element of our humanity. We leave behind sense experience, appetites, passions, and physical intimacy, "transcending" them, it is said, as we move into realms of pure intellection.

The question we must ask, however, is whether pure *intellection* is the sole and/or most important part of our human identity and whether a life made up solely of intellection, lacking, for example, all physical intimacy, would be a *higher* mode of existence or a much diminished one.

DEATH IS THE ENEMY

But let us turn now to the Christian message. The first thing we should notice is that, in the Christian Scriptures, death is not pictured as a release or a liberation. Death is the enemy. So, for example, in the Book of Wisdom, we read:

> God did not make death, and
> he does not delight in the death of the living.
> For he created all things that they might exist,
> and the creatures of the world are wholesome,
> and there is no destructive poison in them;
> and the dominion of Hades is not on earth.
> For righteousness is immortal. . . .
> For God created man for incorruption,
> and made him in the image of his own eternity,
> but through the devil's envy death entered the world.[9]

---

[9] Wis 1:13–15; 2:23–24.

HEAVEN REVEALED IN AND THROUGH THE RISEN CHRIST

There are numerous images in the Scriptures meant to suggest something about heaven: it is said to be "the new Jerusalem," a city whose buildings and streets are made of precious stones. But these images are meant to be taken figuratively, suggesting a reality that is largely beyond our understanding.

Thus the clearest and most definitive revelation of what "heaven" is has been given to us, I would suggest, in the person of the risen Christ. St. Paul describes the proclamation that Christ has risen from the dead in a famous passage in 1 Corinthians 15 as "of first importance" (v. 3). And he goes on to complain that, "if Christ is preached as raised from the dead, how can some of you say that there is no resurrection of the dead? But if there is no resurrection of the dead, then Christ has not been raised; if Christ has not been raised, then our preaching is in vain and your faith is in vain" (vv. 12–14). Indeed, "if for this life only we have hoped in Christ," says Paul, "we are of all men most to be pitied" (v. 19). "But in fact," adds Paul immediately, "Christ has been raised from the dead, the first fruits of those who have fallen asleep" (v. 20). For Paul, this is the heart of the Gospel. Hence it is no accident that each of the four Gospels culminates in the story of Christ's death and Resurrection.

But we turn now to another famous passage—this one from the Gospel of John—in which Jesus promises that in his Father's house "are many rooms" and that he must go to "prepare a place" for us (John 14:2; see also v. 12). In John's Gospel, this passage comes during the Last Supper, not long after Jesus has washed the disciples' feet. "Let not your hearts be troubled," he tells them; "believe in God, believe also in me. In my Father's house are many rooms; if it were not so, would I have told you that I go to prepare a place for you? And when I go and prepare a place for you, I will come again and will take you to myself, that where I am you may be also" (vv. 1–3). But then Thomas says to him: "Lord, we do not know where you are going; how can we know the way?" (v. 5). To which, Jesus answers with the famous admonition: "I am the way, and the truth, and the life; no one comes to the Father, but by me" (v. 6). But then Philip speaks up and says: "Lord, show us the Father, and we shall be satisfied." To which Jesus answers: "Have I been with you so long, and yet you do not know me, Philip? He who has seen me has seen the Father; how can you say, 'Show us the Father'? Do you not believe that I am in the Father and the Father is in me?" (vv. 8–10).

Note the association here with the afterlife and entering the Father's house (in which there are "many rooms") and the further association of this union with the Father with our union with Christ. Christ is, in one sense, the way to the Father, but in another sense, he and the Father are one. So to be united to Christ is to be united to the Father. Or to put this another way, the way to be united to the Father is to unite ourselves to Christ, who himself is from the Father and returns to the Father. In uniting ourselves to Christ, we enter into the threefold communion of love shared between the Father, Son, and Spirit.

It is an important refinement of our conception of the afterlife to realize that "heaven" is not merely a place like the Elysian Fields in Virgil's *Aeneid*; "heaven" is a name we give to our union with God after death, when we will enjoy the "beatific vision"—that is to say, when we will share with God so great an intimacy that it is said we will see God "face to face," the way lovers stare into each other's eyes.[10]

Toward the end of Mark Twain's comic tale "Eve's Diary," Adam—who had at first been resistant to Eve, this strange, somewhat distressing new creature who invaded his space—upon her death, laments at her grave: "Wheresoever she was, there was Eden."[11] Twain's "Diary" is meant to be a comic love story, not profound theology. But it poses for us the important question: Is paradise primarily a place or a person? If we can say, with Mark Twain's Adam, that it is primarily a person to whom we are connected in love, then perhaps it should not be so hard for us to accept in faith that heaven is not primarily a place but a Person. And that Person is Christ, who sends the Holy Spirit to pour the love of God into our hearts and so bring us into a more perfect union with his Father (see Rom 5:5).

WHO CAN SEE GOD AND LIVE? RESURRECTION AND THE TRIUNE GOD

But we are still left with a bit of mystery, are we not? Christ tells his disciples that he will be crucified, that he must leave them, but that he will send the Holy Spirit to help and guide them after his death. Why, then, does he stop off on the way back to his Father to spend some extra time with the disciples—forty days, in fact?

Certainly Christ's Resurrection appearances after his death had a great deal to do with revealing his victory over death and the fidelity of the Father to his Son's sacrifice on the Cross. But *along with* revealing this crucial truth, we might suspect there was something going on here since he appeared multiple times over a full *forty* days before "ascending to the right hand of His Father."

Jesus had never been given to bouts of histrionic miracle-making to

---

[10] See 1 Cor 13:12.

[11] This is the last line in "Eve's Diary." It is said that Twain wrote it about his own wife, who had recently died.

reveal his power during his life. If he had simply wanted to show himself as "God," he could have "come down off the cross," as his antagonists tempted him to do. Indeed, if he had wanted to "prove" that he was God, he could have shot fifty feet up in the air and spun around in mid-air while shooting laser beams out of his eyes. That's the kind of ending you want as a kid. But (a) Christ did not choose to do this, even though the Apostles likely would have been highly relieved if he had, and (b) if he had done this, what kind of "God" would he have been revealing himself to be? The kind of pagan god everyone expected him to be? The kind of god to whom people give sacrifice so that they can gain power?

But what if the "God" he was trying to reveal himself to be was the kind of God who wasn't asking for human sacrifice but was willing to make himself the sacrifice? How else than by dying would he reveal his message that we have to die to "self" and to selfishness in order to rise in "life"? How else would he show mortal, suffering human beings that he would be *with them* at the moment of their death? How else to demonstrate to suffering, mortal human beings that he *understands* our suffering and was not asking of us anything that he himself had not suffered? How better to show them that death need not be, as it so often seems, a final, obliterating end, but that it might be, in union with his death and Resurrection, a purgation and beginning of a new resurrected life?

But what else? If he is "the first fruits" of what we, too, will enjoy, what does Christ reveal to us in his Resurrection appearances? Two things, in particular, I would suggest. First, he shares fully in the Father's power and glory and enjoys full communion with him. And second, though united fully with the Father and the Father's glory, Christ retains his personal identity. This is still the same man the Apostles knew and loved, the man with whom they ate, slept, and suffered.

What is promised to us, then, by the risen Christ, who is the "first fruits" of what we, too, will enjoy, is that, like Christ and with Christ, we can, after death, be united fully with God and share in the eternal communion of love shared between the Father, Son, and Holy Spirit. But also—and this is important—we will be united to God in such a way that *we will not lose our personal identity*. The "I" that I am will remain and not be lost like a drop of water returning to the ocean.

But what makes us be so presumptuous to imagine that it is possible to be united with *God*—that infinite Being beyond all our comprehension— and not be swallowed up like that drop of water returning to the ocean? The ultimate basis of that faith is founded upon the revelation that the Father, the Son, and the Holy Spirit can be perfectly united *in* God as perfectly *One*, and yet not lose their separate "person-hood." Their distinct person-hood does not make impossible their true union as one God; and yet their unity also does not dissolve their distinctness *as three Persons*. They are a perfect unity in diversity and a perfect diversity in unity.

This, then, is how *we* can hope in faith that we, too, can be united to God and not lose our person-hood: because this is what Christ reveals to us in his Resurrection appearances: he is the fruit of the promise of the Triune God, a perfect communion of Persons in One, extended to us in and through the Person of the Son incarnate.

"BE NOT AFRAID": RECOGNITION AND THE RESURRECTION APPEARANCES

The descriptions we find in the Gospels of the Resurrection appearances can be puzzling. They are obviously trying to express something ineffable, something they cannot quite capture. On the one hand, the Gospel writers go out of their way to indicate that Christ could *not* have gotten into the room *bodily*. The doors and windows were all locked, they insist, hence when they saw him, they assumed what most of us would assume: it's a ghost! But having gone out of their way in one direction, the Gospel writers then go out of their way to insist on the opposite: that he was *there bodily*. Jesus calms them, saying, "It is I myself. See, put your hands in the nail marks in my hand and in the hole in my side." They *touch* him. He *eats* with them. These are things you cannot do with ghosts. Anyone who has seen comic ghost cartoons knows that ghosts don't eat or drink. The liquid goes in but then pours right out. Ghosts cannot *touch* people.

And yet, having gone out of their way to insist that Jesus was there with them in the room *bodily*, the Gospel writers then tell us that he simply disappeared, leaving them to wonder again, "Did we just imagine that? *Was* it a ghost?" Indeed, the apostle Thomas, who was absent when Christ comes the first time, is so skeptical about what the others tell him that he says he will not believe it unless he is able to put his hand in the nail marks and in the hole in Christ's side for himself. And a week later, he does. Jesus still has the wounds from the Crucifixion. He addresses Mary and the others in identifiable ways as *the same person he was before the Crucifixion*.

We say that Christ's presence among the Eleven in the Upper Room was a *glorified* presence, but this does not mean he was any *less* present to them than during life; rather, he became even *more* present to them. He reveals even more fully who he truly is: the only begotten Son of the Father. But this revelation was not accomplished through some sort of disembodied presence, as though he were present only in their memories or present merely "spiritually." He revealed himself to them in and through his risen *body*.

And yet Jesus's bodily existence does not suffer the same limitations as ours. We are limited by time and space. But the risen Christ transcends these limitations. He can be with his disciples on the road to Emmaus and in the Upper Room at the same time. He can be present at the times and places of his choosing, with those who need him most at that moment. But note, he is not conjured up like a demon or a ghost. He appears when and where he chooses and stays only as long as he is needed.

This is the same Jesus who died on the Cross, not some phoenix that has risen from his ashes. Consider, for a moment, how the story of the Resurrection appearances might have been told differently. A "divine being" made of light, glowing like gold, might have shown up in the Upper Room with the Eleven to calm their fears, saying, "Be not afraid. I am the divine being who existed in the man you knew as Jesus. With his death, I have been released, and now I go to be with my Father and your Father in heaven." If *that* had been the story, that would be the kind of afterlife we knew we were being promised. It would have been the kind of story that a good Neoplatonist might have respected. The body is a shell hiding an angelic being, and with the death of the body, the angel is released and goes to a "higher realm." Many people think this is what Christianity teaches.

But the truth St. Paul proclaimed was quite different; it was something he himself understood would be a "stumbling block to Jews and folly to Gentiles" (1 Cor 1:23). For St. Paul, the "good news" was the resurrection of the *body*—not merely Christ's body, but ours. Christ's Resurrection is the promise, the first fruits, of the "general resurrection" that will be for all the faithful.

THE GENERAL RESURRECTION AND THE RESURRECTION OF THE BODY

Christianity is a very fleshy religion, a characteristic that often in history has made it seem absurd to those with a gnostic "spiritualist" bent. Christianity, in accord with the Jewish creation account, affirms that the material world is "good, very good." The Christian creed includes the affirmation that the Word became *flesh* in the Incarnation of God's Son. And its notion of the afterlife is that we will enjoy a *bodily* resurrection. Properly understood, then, the Christian view of the life after death would not cause one to diminish the value of the human body or, by extension, of our other material connections in this life, especially our connections to other people and the particular communities into which we are born or to whose good we have devoted ourselves.

As St. John Paul II emphasized in his *Theology of the Body*, our communion with others is achieved in and through the *body*. The Christian teaching about the resurrection of the body assures us that we will not be denied the benefits of our bodily existence after death. Things like taste, touch, and hearing are functions of a body: feeling the softness of skin, tasting the sharp yet bitter combination of salt and tequila in a margarita or the musky flavor of some barbequed ribs, feeling the warmth of a hot shower in the morning—all these depend on having a *body*. Ghosts don't hug, as Odysseus found out when he attempted to embrace his mother in the underworld.[12]

But the *way* we are embodied at present in this life comes with restrictions. The problem we have now is that when we are with our friends in New York, we cannot be with our friends in San Francisco. And when we are with our beloved grandparents, we usually cannot also be with our beloved grandchildren. We are limited by time and space. To be free of those restrictions, but not as a ghost or a memory, is the promise of the glorified body. It is the promise Christ *shows* us when he reveals himself to the women at the empty tomb and the disciples on the road to Emmaus and to the Eleven in the locked Upper Room. It is the promise realized every day around the world when the *one* crucified, risen Christ makes himself present in the Eucharist in Chicago and Tokyo and St. Petersburg and Berlin and in cities and hamlets around the world, as he has been doing for centuries and will do until the end of time.

We should not think of heaven as just a place, as though dying and going to heaven were something like losing your job and having to leave your friends and move to Cleveland where you don't know anyone. Heaven is a loving communion of persons. You enter into an eternal communion of Trinitarian love. United with the living, risen Christ, we do not love this world and the persons in it less; we can love them even more perfectly, more divinely.

THE COMMUNION OF SAINTS

What if, instead of losing our loved ones, we could be even more intimately present to them, help them more fully, and love them more selflessly? For many people, that would be a comforting thought. And this is the significance of the doctrine of the communion of saints. We believe that Christ

---

[12] See Homer, *Odyssey*, 11.204–22.

lives and that he continues to watch over us, sending his Holy Spirit to guide and strengthen us. When those we love were alive, we sometimes asked them to pray for us, knowing they would precisely because of their love for us. The Christian promise is that this sort of love can never die.

Thus the Christian view of the afterlife neither negates the value of this life nor proposes an activity for those in the next life that those of us in this life would find essentially empty and meaningless. We are bidden in this life to give ourselves over to the love of God and neighbor. The activity we are promised we will be engaged in the next life is an even more perfect love of God and neighbor. We are bidden to *care* for the world, especially for the poor and those in need. This is not some "dirty work" we need to do until we are released from the "burden" in the next life. The next life is the life of infinite care, when we will be able to see all people with the eyes of divine love, not with the limited perspectives we now have.

The hope of entering the communion of saints in union with God the Father, Son, and Spirit, should not make us *less* concerned to love and care for our neighbors in this life. It should make us *more* concerned for them, *eternally*, so to speak. The Catholic view of the afterlife does not *negate* the importance of this life; rather, it encourages us to see that all our actions and all the connections we make in this life remain meaningful eternally. If we devote ourselves to the love of God and neighbor, then, as St. Paul assures us, no power in heaven or on earth, neither death nor life, can separate us from that love (see Rom 8:39). The good news of the Gospel is this: start living the heavenly life *now*, and God will see to it that you never have to stop.

Hope & God

PART ONE

Acts 17 and the Integral Structure of Christian Hope

GUY MANSINI, OSB
Ave Maria University, FL

BECAUSE THE DESPAIR human beings naturally find themselves in is complex, Christian hope must be similarly complex in order to respond to it. There is, first of all, despair over the evil we suffer, the evil that happens to us and that culminates in death. Try as we might technologically and after the pattern of Prometheus to turn fire to our protection from outrageous fortune and to the furtherance of health and the enhancement of life, in the end, we die. Second, there is despair over our moral failure and fragility. Try as we might to install the virtues in our moral action following the pattern of Aristotle's *Ethics*, we rarely attain to more than continence. Moreover, even the virtuous man can be surprised by fate and reduced to a moral condition unworthy of his former aristocracy, thence to an unfortunate and ignoble death. The prospects for virtuous communities are at least as bleak as the prospects for virtuous individuals.

Finally, and third, there is that deepest wound to our being, the suspicion that, after all, we are but orphans in a vast universe. Congruent with this suspicion that the universe is impersonal and cares nothing for our desires or our fate, all we may aspire to, beyond some temporary promethean mastery of the conditions of life, is a titanic but of course futile resistance to the entropy of things. We may look to be Ahab, Melville's Ahab, and strive to plant a harpoon in the faceless brow of the whale. But that will not relieve us of the knowledge that the ways of the world cannot be bent to our advantage by either prayer or sacrifice. Moby Dick hears no prayers and accepts no sacrifice and neither does the universe.[1] Neither, then, properly, can we be even orphans because the sky never was father to us nor nature ever mother.[2]

Christian hope must address all three of these grounds of despair. And so it does, as we know. The point of this essay is that our hope does so only in addressing all three together, all at once, and that this must necessarily be the case.

* * * * *

In Acts 17, St. Paul addresses the Athenians at the Areopagus. He informs them, first, that the God they do not know but for whom they have an altar is the creator of heaven and earth and all the things therein (v. 24). Second, he tells them that the times of ignorance are over, and that now all men everywhere are to repent (v. 30) because the day of God's judgment has been fixed (v. 31). The time of ignorance of the true God is over, for Paul has just made him known, and men are to repent of their religious errors and faults in worshipping idols and human representations of the divine (vv. 24b–25a, 29).[3] Third, Paul tells the Athenians that we know the day of judgment has been fixed because the one by whom judgment will be executed is a man whom God has raised from the dead (v. 31).

Now it turns out to be the case that unless we can repent and unless we have faith in the resurrection of Christ and therefore in our own resurrection, we cannot come to acknowledge God as the Creator of heaven and earth, of all things visible and invisible. In other words, these three things in the speech at the Areopagus are not loosely tied together but tightly bound up with one another. Thus, the answer to our moral fragility contained in the command to repentance before a God who judges us and can forgive,

---

[1]   In the novel, the power that governs and dooms all things has no face, and neither does the whale (see chapters 76 and 86 together). The rain falls on the good and the wicked alike, and whaling leaves some men whole and some men lame, not because of the providence of God but because of the mindlessness of the world order—because of its disorder.

[2]   There are countless expressions of modern nihilism. A good old standard can be found in W. T. Stace's "Man Against Darkness," in *The Meaning of Life*, ed. E. D. Klemke (Oxford: Oxford University Press, 2000). The essay first appeared in 1948.

[3]   That it is religious error and faulty religious practice that is the object of repentance is the teaching of the Venerable Bede, *Ancient Christian Commentary on Scripture, New Testament V: Acts*, ed. Francis Martin (Downers Grove, IL: InterVarsity Press, 2006), 218b. In the same vein, see Luke Timothy Johnson, *The Acts of the Apostles*, Sacra Pagina Series, vol. 5 (Collegeville, MN: The Liturgical Press, 1992), 317.

the answer to our mortality contained in the news of the resurrection of the body, and the answer to the question of our identity, sons and daughters of the God who creates heaven and earth, are given together; the answer to one cannot be given independently of the answers to the other two.

That repentance for sins is possible, in the sense that we have hope for the remission of our sins, is of course a function of Good Friday. That Jesus was raised from the dead is the news of Easter. So, otherwise stated, the claim is that knowledge of and confession of the Paschal Mystery is a necessary condition of coming to acknowledge God as the Creator of heaven and earth. Since the Incarnation is the culmination of God's revelation of himself that begins with the promise to Abraham, then the claim is that the revelation of the Incarnation (and so also of the Trinity) is a necessary condition of coming to acknowledge God as the Creator of heaven and earth.

To repeat and paraphrase, the vicarious satisfaction of Christ for our sin, which grounds the possibility and necessity of repentance, and the Resurrection of the God who has been made man and which gives assurance of the efficacy of the Cross—I am saying that these two things are necessary for the manifestation of God as Creator. At least, they are necessary for his manifestation as Creator in *our* world, which is to say, necessary for his manifestation as Creator in a fallen world. Derivatively, then, the two things—repentance and faith in the Resurrection—turn out to be necessary for the subsequent rational manifestation of God as Creator of the world. That is, the Incarnation and *supernatural* revelation are necessary conditions for that *rational* manifestation of God as Creator of which the First Vatican Council speaks in *Dei Filius* (chapter 2), of which St. John Paul II speaks in *Fides et Ratio* (§22), of which the *Catechism of the Catholic Church* speaks (§§31–36), all of which *magisterial* teachings presume to tell us nothing but what St. Paul teaches in the first chapter of Romans on the rational clarity with which God is *naturally* known, in which he repeats what the Book of Wisdom teaches in the Old Testament (ch. 13).[4]

In the expression just given it, the claim advanced here may seem contradictory and unorthodox. It may be helpful to locate it relative to two other important positions on the issue of the relation of the natural to the supernatural knowledge of God. Certain radical Protestants claim that God is known only, uniquely, by his Word, by the Word of revelation that is to be received in faith. There is no other way whatsoever to come to the knowledge

---

[4] As necessary conditions, the Incarnation and its revelation may be remote from one wondering about God today, and they do not imply that faith is a necessary condition of arriving at the natural knowledge of God. Still, they have historically to have been given if there is to be a natural knowledge of God as first principle and last end of the universe.

of the true God except in his personal speaking to us, and natural theology is impossible. That is not the claim of this essay.

Again, second, many Catholics suppose that the possibility of exercising the light of reason so as to come to a natural knowledge of God as first creative cause and last end of the universe is an absolute possibility in that the light of reason is always "on" and we are ever surrounded by "the things that have been made," and such that there are no important conditions on this exercise, either no important moral conditions or no important cognitive conditions. I consider this position, at least in the stark way I have just described it, to be naïve, apologetically misleading, something that confounds the task of evangelization, something ill-suited to sharing our Christian hope.

What I am affirming is something between the two barely sketched positions just mentioned. The claim is that there are supernatural conditions that must be fulfilled in our fallen world in order to realize the possibility of coming to know God by an exercise of our natural reason. This thesis is similar to a claim that Robert Sokolowski makes in *The God of Faith and Reason*, to the effect that the exercise of the natural light to come to the knowledge of God depends on the distinction between God and the world having been *already* introduced into the world by revelation.[5] What I am affirming, however, is perhaps more detailed than what Msgr. Sokolowski would maintain, and I don't want to enlist him as an authority for what the remainder of this essay argues. The thesis of this paper is also akin to the position of Jean Luc Marion, according to whom natural knowledge of God does not precede revelation but is encompassed in it and enabled by it.[6]

Evidently, I do not think that any authoritative teaching of the Church requires one to assert the possibility of an absolute and unconditioned exercise of reason that affirms the existence of God. The teaching of the Church certainly requires us to affirm that the exercise of our natural reason can come certainly to affirm the existence of God. However, the Church teaches this truth, as it were, abstractly. It teaches it as a religious truth. It teaches it vaguely.

Abstractly—the First Vatican Council teaches the *de iure* possibility of coming to know God by the natural light. It does not specify the conditions of realizing this possibility but recognizes that there are conditions.[7] As a

---

[5] Robert Sokolowski, *The God of Faith and Reason: Foundations of Christian Theology* (Notre Dame, IN: University of Notre Dame Press, 1982), 114–15

[6] Jean Luc Marion, *Givenness and Revelation*, trans. Stephen E. Lewis (Oxford: Oxford University Press, 2016), 28.

[7] Marcel Chossat, SJ, "Dieu (Connaissance naturelle de)," *Dictionnaire de Théologie Catholique*

religious truth—the *deputatio de fide* at the Council expressly recognized the connection between knowing God by the natural light and the moral consequences of that knowledge, maintaining that this connection is so well known as not to need to be stated: "No person can incline to God, the author of nature, as to his natural end, without knowing at least his principal obligations to God."[8] Fergus Kerr paraphrases: "No one can know of God as *finis* without acknowledging his or her obligations to worship God, obey God's commandments and so on."[9] Vaguely—the Council does not maintain that one comes to know God as Creator where creation is taken strictly as *creatio ex nihilo* nor necessarily as the principle and end of *all* things whatsoever, nor as "in fact and *by right* the unique eternal principle of all that is not him."[10]

That the Council allows for a certain vagueness about the idea of God as the "principle" of all things reflects the fact that the Bible does not expressly teach the doctrine of *creatio ex nihilo* in so many words. The Bible certainly implies this doctrine.[11] But the intellectual conditions for formulating it just as such did not exist until the second century AD.[12] For Justin Martyr, the Incarnation and the Resurrection of Christ imply the omnipotence of God.[13] God's unconditional omnipotence, however, implies *creatio ex nihilo*, as Theophilus of Antioch saw and asserted in contrasting the Bible's account of creation with the surrounding pagan theories of some divine formation of the world out of a pre-existing and eternal matter.[14]

It is perhaps important to note the exact weight the Council gives its teaching that God can be known as principle and end by the light of natural reason from the things that have been made (see the first canon of chapter 2). It does not teach this as a dogma of faith, the denial of which would be heresy, but as a certain truth that is at least necessarily connected with what is revealed. This is to be concluded from the fact that the canons are

---

4:826, 828; Bernard Lonergan, SJ, "Natural Knowledge of God," 117–33 in *A Second Collection*, ed. William Ryan, SJ, and Bernard Tyrrell, SJ (London: Darton, Longman & Todd, 1974), 133. See also CCC §37.

[8] Quoted by Chossat, "Dieu," 824.

[9] Fergus Kerr, OP, "Knowing God by Reason Alone: What Vatican I Never Said," *New Blackfriars* 91 (2010): 215–28, at 221.

[10] Chossat, "Dieu," 837–38.

[11] Robert M. Grant, *Miracle and Natural Law in Graeco-Roman and Early Christian Thought* (Amsterdam: North-Holland Publishing Company, 1952), 136–37. He thinks it is implied by Second Isaiah and Genesis (136–37).

[12] Gerhard May, *Creatio Ex Nihilo: The Doctrine of "Creation out of Nothing" in Early Christian Thought*, trans. A. S. Worrall (London: T & T Clark International, 2004), xii.

[13] May, *Creatio Ex Nihilo*, 127–29.

[14] May, *Creatio Ex Nihilo*, 161, 180

understood to repeat in negative form what is positively asserted in the chapters, and the positive assertion of chapter 2 that its associated canon mirrors is that the Church "holds and teaches" (*tenet et docet*), not that she believes and confesses (*credit et confitetur*) that God can be known by the natural light. For the Council distinguishes a primary and secondary object of its teaching authority, and indicates these objects by the distinct notions of "believing" and "holding" something to be true—believing by faith, holding by reason what follows from faith.[15]

* * * * *

The thesis put forth here sometimes takes Catholics, and especially Catholics who are partial to the thought of St. Thomas, by surprise. This is, in turn, astonishing because while the Scriptures are very clear about the native capacity of the human mind to come to the knowledge of God from the things that have been made (Romans, Wisdom), they are equally clear about the necessity for revelation for human beings to come to the *actual* knowledge of God—about the necessity of revelation to come to the knowledge of God *at all*. Before turning to Acts 17, let us fire off a few preliminary salvos, softening up the beach before landing the marines.

First, the *de facto* ignorance of God on the part of pagans or Greeks is clearly asserted in the New Testament. There is 1 Peter 1:14: "Do not be conformed to the passions of your former ignorance." There is a similar assertion in Ephesians 3:18–19. There is also 1 Corinthians 1:21: "In the wisdom of God, the world did not know God through wisdom." The world, the *Greek* world, did not, in fact, know God through the wisdom it actively cultivated (v. 22). "Did not know God"—this seems perfectly straightforward. It is rather part of God's wisdom according to St. Paul that the Gentiles first come to know God through Christ, "the power of God and the wisdom of God" (v. 24).

Second, however, the New Testament does not assert pagan ignorance as a brute fact but asserts it as a fact the explanation of which we know. This explanation is contained in Romans 1 as well as in the Book of Wisdom.

---

[15] Ioachim Salaverri, SJ, *De ecclesia*, in *Sacrae Theologiae Summa I: Theologia Fundamentalis* (Madrid: BAC, 1958), nos. 909–13. It is worth noting as well that Vatican I did not identify knowing God through created things with the cosmological argument and forbore to equate "knowing" with "demonstrating." These are identifications made in the Oath against Modernism of 1910. See Kerr, "Knowing God by Reason Alone," section III. It is not defined, therefore, that the exercise of the natural capacity to know God from the things that have been made is discursive or syllogistic. See Chossat, "Dieu," 846–47. Nor, of course, is the ontological argument of St. Anselm excluded.

Notwithstanding the native ability of man to come to know the power and deity of God, "clearly perceived in the things that have been made" (1:20), men "exchanged the glory of the immortal God for images resembling mortal man or birds or animals or reptiles" (1:23; see Wis 13:10–14:21 on the origin of idols and false gods). The voluntary nature of this turning from the light is emphasized, for St. Paul next reports how men are punished for this sin of self-blinding: "Therefore God gave them up in the lusts of their hearts to impurity" (Rom 1:24; see vv. 25–32; see Wis 14:21–31). By their sin, men turned off the natural light; it is not turned back on except under a supernatural condition which Paul specifies: "But now the righteousness of God has been manifested apart from the law" (Rom 3:21)—that is, it is manifested by Christ, by the redemption he works, apprehended through faith in him (vv. 22–26).[16] God is manifested, note, only in manifesting his righteousness that justifies us in our repentance, something also said at the Areopagus.

* * * * *

Now let us turn back to Acts 17, which comprises an assertion of the existence of God, a call to repentance for sin, and the news of Jesus's Resurrection, the man who will judge the world.

PAUL'S FIRST STATEMENT: GOD IS THE MAKER OF HEAVEN AND EARTH

The assertion of God's existence is more than a bare assertion, of course, for it includes a statement of the world's cosmological relation to him and the ethical and religious relation of all men to him. It does this in three movements, none of which are arguments although each one of which suggests an argument for God's existence.[17]

First, the world and everything in it, both the heavens and the earth, are conceived as something that needs a maker (Acts 17:24a). From this Paul concludes to his transcendence of the world: God does not live in shrines made by man, and he is not served by man as if he needed anything (17:24b–25a).[18] Rather, he is the giver of life and breath and of all

[16] Marion, *Givenness and Revelation*, 63. The truth that should have shone for us in creation gives way to revelation.

[17] The three movements suggest, in order: (1) the argument to a first cause from the contingency of the world and the things therein; (2) the argument from providence; (3) the argument from conscience.

[18] For a survey of pagan religious and theological opinion in the first centuries after Christ,

good things (v. 25b). A second movement indicates the providence God exercises over all the nations, a providence available to pagan inspection, the knowledge of which has an important ethical-religious implication. God determines allotted periods and boundaries for the nations of man, Paul says, with such orderliness that men *should* seek him in the hope of finding him—even if they in fact do not find him (v. 27). This is similar to the witness Paul tells the people at Lystra that God gave to himself in the rains and fruitful seasons of the earth (14:17). There follows a third movement, a statement of the closeness of God to men: we live and move and have our being in him, for we are his offspring (17:28). Just because we are his offspring, just because we can be reasonably conceived as his offspring, we are bound to him much more closely than other created realities. Moreover, as his offspring and as having our being in him (v. 28) and so made in his image, we ought not think of him as material. Rather, if we are his offspring precisely as seekers of the truth about ourselves in seeking him (v. 26), that is to say, if we are his offspring precisely in virtue of our mind and mindfulness, then he is above human representation in gold or silver (v. 29).

It seems relatively easy to see that the knowledge that God is our Creator leads to the acknowledgment that we ought to repent of the moral fault we commit which then shows up as sin in his sight, for if he is the Creator and giver of all good things, he gives also the natural law that is a standard of conduct for all (see Rom 2:14). The duty of repentance follows from the knowledge of God as our end, which is implied in saying that we should seek after him (Acts 17:27) and is coordinate with the worship of the divine that is the context of the whole discourse (vv. 22–23). Furthermore, unless the true God is Creator, the Resurrection of Christ and our own resurrection will not in the end be conceivable. There can be a new creation only if there was a first creation.

It is the dependence of acknowledging God as Creator on grasping at one and the same time the call to repentance and the news of the Resurrection that is more difficult to show, and to that I turn.

PAUL'S SECOND STATEMENT: IT IS NOW TIME TO REPENT

Unless we repent, we cannot come to the rational knowledge of God. For unless we repent, we will not so conceive God in such a way that he can show up in the world, can show up, that is, to our consciousness and knowledge

---

see Robert M. Grant, *Gods and the One God* (Philadelphia: The Westminster Press, 1986). Chapter Six canvasses more philosophical opinion.

as the God who is the first principle and last end of all things. Unless the idea of God comes together with the idea of the repentance we owe before him, he cannot show up either as the God whom Paul preaches or the God as known according to the dictum of *Dei Filius*.

There are of course conditions of the possibility of our repentance. We won't repent if we think it is useless to repent, and it is useless to repent if there is no possibility of re-establishing good relations with the God who made us, and there is no possibility of that without satisfaction for sin—just another way of speaking of repentance—and there is no satisfaction for sin without the Passion and death of the God-man. There is a sort of concave-convex relation between the possibility of repentance and the Passion of Christ. Moreover, this connects the second thing Paul speaks of—repentance—to the third thing he announces, the *Resurrection* of Christ. Without the Resurrection of Christ, we cannot recognize his satisfaction for sin and the possibility of reconciliation with God.

Our immediate task here, however, is to relate the possibility of repentance to the knowledge that God is the first principle and last end of all things. To begin with, we don't repent unless we think we should repent, and we cannot think that on certain views of the world and human agency. For instance, we won't repent if we think that we have never voluntarily and knowingly done wrong. And according to Plato, as we know, the evil we do is sufficiently explained by the evil we suffer. We would never knowingly do wrong.[19] Accordingly, Plato does not live in a world whose first principle is a personal principle. He rather lives in a world where the One-Good presides over all the descending participations of goodness that proceed from it automatically and necessarily, but are unfortunately necessarily impeded and frustrated betimes by the refractoriness of matter or the receptacle of the forms. In this construction of things, the universe has no need of the forgiveness of sins and so no need of the God of Abraham, Isaac, and Jacob. He can't show up to Plato.[20]

Nor can God show up to the ordinary run of Athenians, religious as they are, for whom the gods are to be served by hands as needing this service (Acts 17:25a), and whom the Athenians house, at least in their representations in gold and silver, in shrines and temples (vv. 24, 29). Paul's

---

[19] *Timaeus*, 86D–E.

[20] According to Reinhard Hütter, apart from the sanation of natural reason by revelation, reason arrives either at a depersonalized divinity, as with Plato and Hindu mysticism, or at a multi-personal polytheism mired in myth. See his "Happiness and Religion: Why the Virtue of Religion is Indispensable for Attaining the Final End," *Nova et Vetera* 14 (2016): 15–60, at 25n25.

God, on the other hand, rather gives *us* good things, life and breath (v. 25b), and houses *us* in that we live and move and have our being in him (v. 28). Paul reverses the relation between divinity and humanity as conceived by the Greeks. In this way, the ordinary religious sense of pagan Athens is of course important as a foil against which the true God is made to appear.[21] St. Paul is not speaking into a void or trying to write on a religious *tabula rasa*. But the God of Jesus Christ shows up only by way of a great reversal within this prior religious sensibility.

It is instructive to take up the Epicureans and Stoics St. Luke reports as frequenting the marketplaces of Athens (17:18). Evidently God cannot show up to professional atheists like the Epicureans. But why are the Stoics impeded from attaining to his eternal power and deity? Paul presents us with a free God who is not identical with the world but makes it, and whose inhabitants are free human beings who can therefore be called by the command of God to Christian repentance and conversion, and for whom there is a remedy for the misuse of their freedom by way of the satisfaction achieved by their judge, the One raised from the dead. All of this is announced together. It is announced over against the Stoic sense of the divine, according to which the world is not distinct from god, and within which world all is determined, including human choice, and whose history is not history but the endless cycle of *ekpýrôsis* and *palingenesis*, world-destroying fire and world-regeneration. There is a Stoic religious sense indeed, but it can serve only as a foil for what Paul announces.

Repentance is evidently bound up with the idea that God is our end, the God whom we should seek, according to Paul in Acts. It is not just *any* end, however, because it is not just *any* repentance. It is not a change of mind or even regret and remorse over past deeds, such as *metánoia* denoted for pagan Greeks.[22] The repentance commanded is a change of heart and a radical re-direction of life according to the moral law in the hope that the past no longer controls me before God for eternity. Therefore it is not just any divine end that is in question. It is not the term of neo-Platonic *reditus*. That end is reached automatically. That end requires no action of the God who is the *finis* directed to me, re-writing his law on my heart, even plucking out

---

21 See Robert Sokolowski, *Eucharistic Presence: A Study in the Theology of Disclosure* (Washington, DC: The Catholic University of America Press, 1994), 161–62.

22 J. Behm, "Metanoéô, metánoia," *Theological Dictionary of the New Testament*, vol. IV, ed. Gerhard Kittel (Grand Rapids, MI: Eerdmans, 1967), 976–79, who says: "For the Greeks metánoia never suggests an alteration in the total moral attitude, a profound change in life's direction, a conversion which affects the whole of conduct" (979), and again: "Whether linguistically or materially, one searches the Greek world in vain for the origin of the NT understanding of metanoéô and metánoia" (980).

the heart of stone and replacing it with a heart of flesh. Nor is it the end that is the non-end of Stoic eternal recurrence. Christian repentance indicates a God who changes hearts and forgives sin because he creates the heart and so can re-create it. In other words, if the God who makes heaven and earth is our end, then repentance follows. If repentance does not follow, because it is either unthinkable or simply refused, then we won't be thinking of God as our end, won't know that God is our end. It will be hidden from us, perhaps by our own hiding, but hidden nonetheless. It is St. Paul's preaching that un-hides it, or as we say, re-veals it and so perhaps gives us a chance to end our ignorance.

Without repentance, there will therefore be no acknowledgment of the God who is my end. Catholic theology easily recognizes that grace is a necessary condition of coming to know God by the natural light.[23] This is so because repentance is needed in order to free up and re-orient the capacity to know God. But also, the very *idea* of a God who can give such grace cannot originally show up without repentance—God cannot appear to one for whom Christian repentance is unknown or unthinkable. The ideas of God as Creator and of repentance before him arrive in the world only together, not one without the other. But the idea of Christian repentance— big surprise—arrives in the world only with Christ, with the Incarnation.

That Christian repentance is bound up with the idea of the omnipotence of the Creator, and so with the idea of the Creator, is fairly easy to discern in Scripture. So in Proverbs 21:1 we learn that the heart of the king is in the hand of God, and God turns it whithersoever he will. Queen Esther prays that God change the heart of King Ahasuerus from anger to gentleness, and so he does (Greek Esther 15:7–8). This unique capacity of God to govern the hearts of men is also asserted in the New Testament. Paul tells the Philippians to work out their salvation in fear and trembling, because God is at work in them "both to will and to work" (Phil 2:13). God's knowledge of our heart and his capacity to rule it follows from the fact that he knits us together in our mother's womb (Ps 139:13). The proposal of the law and precepts of the Lord to the psalmist is not only exterior but also interior (Ps 119:125). And God writes on hearts in both the Old and New Testaments (Jer 31:33; 2 Cor 3:2).

The idea of God as Creator arrives in Athens with the idea of Christian repentance. Without the idea of God as Creator antecedent to any argument, however, there will be no demonstration of his existence mounted in virtue of the natural light. Augustine, Anselm, Aquinas—they all have the idea of

---

[23] Lonergan, "Natural Knowledge of God," 133.

God before ever they make an argument for him. They know the conclusion before they light on any premises. There is no argument for God that apart from that pre-possession of the conclusion just happens, by some chance, to touch on him. Metaphysics is not, in this respect, an experimental science. It won't make a chance discovery of God. We don't stumble into the conclusion of an argument for the existence of God. The knowledge of God is first of all and necessarily a gift of revelation before it is a product of reason. The Acts of the Apostles show us this relative to the Athenians as an obvious fact of history.

PAUL'S THIRD STATEMENT: THE JUDGE OF THE WORLD IS ONE RISEN FROM THE DEAD

We come to the last of the three truths Paul proclaims on the Areopagus. As has been intimated, if there is no resurrection of the body, then Christ did not rise (1 Cor 15:13), and our faith in Christ is vain (v. 17a), for then there is no sacrifice of reconciliation, and we are still in our sins (v. 17b), as St. Paul points out to the Corinthians. This returns us to the consideration of repentance.

But also, there is another argument that bears on the issue of this essay, that bears on the resurrection of the dead in general. Unless there is resurrection of the body, there is no argument to the existence of God from the things that have been made.

The argument here is simple. Without resurrection from the dead, repentance cannot be thought to be real. Repentance that is real restores friendship with God, and the original pattern of friendship with God had no place for death in it (Gen 2:17; 3:22). So, repentance that is real leads to that kind of full human life that includes bodily life. Without this restoration, there is no successful repentance—no repentance. Repentance without resurrection (or the hope of it) cannot bespeak a God who really forgives, who gives me a heart of flesh, and who "does not delight in the death of the living" (Wis 1:13), a death that entered the world only by the envy of the devil (2:24). So, no resurrection, no repentance; no repentance, no acknowledgment of the Creator of heaven and earth. No such acknowledgment, no rational argument to what has not been acknowledged, God as the principle and end of all things.

There is also a more technical philosophical consideration to advance here. If we think we know the incorruptibility of the substantial form of man from the immateriality of human intellectual operations,[24] then without the

---

[24] St. Thomas, *Summa theologiae* I, q. 75, aa. 2 and 6.

prospect of the resurrection of the body, the death of human beings implies a sort of everlasting stockpiling of human souls in some celestial lumber room, a laying up of souls who, without the body, are incapable of completing their defining operations of understanding and judging and deciding.[25] This state of affairs is so contrary to nature that we cannot suppose that any God creatively responsible for nature—here, human nature—presides over it.[26] Therefore, such a God does not exist, a God who created such a paradoxically composed human being. Could it be with such a God that incorruptible souls are re-cycled in an everlasting turn and turn again of metempsychotic exchange? Such exchange rather bespeaks an eternal return, and declares the futility of human existence, and once again precludes any conclusion to a good Creator God.

A third possibility will suggest itself: the human soul is not, after all, incorruptible. But this turns the experienced world into a place of manifest injustice, a world that therefore cannot come from a good God. As the Book of Job observes, reward and punishment are not meted out by God in this life. Thus, were there absolutely no other life, the world would be unjustly ordered and impossibly the creation of a God who, if he exists, must be good. The idea that there is no immortality and that, although God exists, there is no divinely administered justice for men is entertained by Ecclesiastes.[27] But it is hard to maintain. The impossibility that the world of purely mortal men who disappear at death and who do not meet justice in the world—the impossibility that such a world be created is the default position today in the post-Christian West. Without the Gospel, without faith in the Gospel, it is hard to maintain a confident intellectual grip on the immortal soul and the existence of God, for faith in the Gospel is faith in the Resurrection of Christ and of all the dead on the last day. And without the Resurrection, as was just argued, it will be hard to maintain a confident grip on immortality, and without a confident grip on immortality, we lose our grip on a God who can be thought to be just.

As was noted above, the Resurrection of Christ played a role in the formation of the doctrine of *creatio ex nihilo* (see notes 13 and 14). That it would

---

[25] The argument that such operations occur imperfectly in separated souls via acquired and infused species can be found in St. Thomas, *Summa theologiae* I, q. 89, a. 1.

[26] St. Thomas, *Super 1 Cor.*, no. 924: "If the resurrection of the body be denied, it is not easy, rather, it will be hard to maintain the immortality of the soul." That the soul be without a body is both *per accidens* and contrary to nature, and such a thing cannot be thought to perdure infinitely.

[27] "Who knows whether the spirit of a man goes upward and the spirit of the beast goes down to the earth?" (3:21). For the pervasive injustice of human affairs: 3:1–3; 5:8; 7:15; 9:11—"The race is not to the swift nor battle to the strong, nor bread to the wise."

play a role is easy to see if we observe how close the Resurrection of Christ and creation are in Scripture. There are several places to consider. In the first place, because of his Resurrection, the Lord is Lord of the living and the dead (Rom 14:9). In Christ we will all be made alive (1 Cor 15:22), and death is subject to Christ (vv. 25–26). Christ is, then, the cause of our own resurrection.[28] This means that death, non-life, cannot in the end constrain the God who is Living and who is Life. And this implies that non-being does not constrain the God Who Is.[29] There is, then, no pre-existing condition that constrains his causality. So also Paul has it that, just as God is in charge of things that are, so also he is charge of things that are not (1:28). This is said in an immediately anthropological context, where the things that are not are foolish and weak men, and the things that *are* are the wise and strong.

Nonetheless, it has metaphysical implications. If God is in charge of things that are not, then what is not, nothing, does not constrain his power.[30] Paul says this in a context, moreover, where the Resurrection of Christ is presupposed, and it is therefore not surprising that Paul gives his teaching here a practically metaphysical formulation. An expressly metaphysical formulation is to be found in Romans 4:17, where he speaks of the God "who gives life to the dead and calls into existence the things that do not exist (*kalountos ta mē onto hōs onta*)."[31] Right. The Resurrection bespeaks the power of the very word by which God calls into being the heavens and the earth in Genesis 1, "God said, 'Let there be . . . ,'" the same power celebrated in the Psalm, "By the word of the LORD the heavens were made, and all their host by the breath of his mouth" (33:6).[32]

* * * * *

The change of heart Christianity demands and the resurrection it promises both call on the omnipotence of God, and omnipotence implies that the world depends on God unconditionally, which is to say he makes it out of nothing. Both imply that God is Creator. And, to the point of this essay,

---

[28] See St. Thomas, *Summa theologiae*, III, q. 56, a. 1.

[29] For the identity of *esse* and *vivere*, see St. Thomas Aquinas, *Commentary on the Book of Causes*, trans. Vincent Gagliardo, OP, *et al.* (Washington, DC: The Catholic University of America Press, 1996), Proposition 12, p. 87. See also Fran O'Rourke, *Pseudo-Dionysius and the Metaphysics of Aquinas* (Notre Dame, IN: University of Notre Dame Press, 2005), 175–80.

[30] See Marion, *Givenness and Revelation*, 69.

[31] Marion, *Givenness and Revelation*, 69: God "repeats in the resurrection what he accomplished in creation."

[32] The Lord raises Lazarus by his word in John 11:43—"Lazarus, come out."

without them God cannot show up to us as the Creator of the world. The three things St. Paul adduces in his sermon at the Areopagus are bound together and condition one another. That is, the affirmation of one conditions the possibility of affirming the others. Thus, if the possibilities of repentance and the resurrection of the body are not affirmed, there is no ascent to the first principle and last end of things, the God of Jesus Christ. Recognizing these possibilities, known by revelation, is one thing with recognizing that God is the Creator and that he could exist in undiminished goodness and glory and infinite splendor whether the world exists or not. Once this distinction is introduced into the world, however, we can marshal reason in its native strength to argue that the distinction is a genuine one— that God exists. But introducing the distinction into the world is the work of Christ.[33]

What does this mean for the shape of apostolic hope, of Christian hope as it was first offered to the world? It is a shape that offers a comprehensive solution to evil, both evil done and evil suffered. As to evil done, the solution is repentance. As to evil suffered, the answer is the resurrection of the dead. Both answers are guaranteed by the work of Christ, a Christ who is Son of the Most High and who with him creates the world. The shape of apostolic hope is a complex shape because our despair is complex. This complex shape—all three of the truths Paul announces on the Areopagus—must be maintained in the Church's presentation of the Gospel and all the more so in an age whose studied secularity strives to match the pagan world in the ignorance of God and moral weakness. The three legs of the stool are all needed to support a hope for "an eternal weight of glory beyond all comparison" (2 Cor 4:17) and that certainly transcends our misery.[34]

The complex shape of apostolic hope that matches the complex shape of despair is also Trinitarian in outline. The grace of the Holy Spirit presides over our repentance and makes our moral power less fragile. The incarnate Son gives hope for a resurrection that undoes the evil we suffer, and since his

---

[33] I have argued for some of these connections among the God who creates, repentance, and resurrection in an earlier essay, "Apologetics, Evil, and the New Testament," *Logos* 4 (2001): 152–68.

[34] I have been speaking of Christian hope. But the supports for Christian hope are of course prepared for in the Old Testament. See the solution to the problem of evil suffered and evil done in Job. God appears especially as Creator in his speech in the last chapters, and this is bound up with the truth that the solution to the problem of evil done is the reward and punishment God measures out in the next life. Knowing this provokes repentance, and indeed, Job offers expiatory sacrifice for his friends. Not only is Job's innocence vindicated (which then is tied to repentance now) but Job's faith in the resurrection (Job 19:25–27) is confirmed.

death is for our sake, we are confident that his judgment, though just, will also be merciful. Last, the Father to whom we can appropriate the work of creation makes us no longer orphans but his sons and daughters, giving us an identity that surpasses any identity that a this-worldly naming of persons can achieve.

Messianic Banquet and the Christian Proclamation:
How the Jewish Backdrop of the Christian Story Addresses the *Human* Question

ANDREW D. SWAFFORD
Benedictine College, KS

EARLY IN THE TWENTIETH CENTURY, Henri de Lubac pushed for an apologetic approach that could tap into the human condition, an approach that would illumine the way in which the Christian story fulfills the human story.[1] This paper will explore how the Jewish tradition of the messianic banquet motif, particularly as background for the Last Supper and the centrality of the Eucharist, does just this.

In the following, we will highlight significant messianic banquet passages from which this tradition emerges in the Old Testament and explore how it is picked up in the New, noting its links to liturgy and kingdom restoration. Along the way, we will emphasize how this procedure fits with de Lubac's aforementioned apologetic ethos; and finally, we will discuss the significance of the messianic banquet motif for the specifically Catholic proclamation, particularly with reference to the sacramental life of the Church.

---

[1] See Henri de Lubac, "Apologétique et théologie" *Nouvelle Revue Théologique* 57 (1930): 361–78. In English, in de Lubac, *Theological Fragments* (San Francisco: Ignatius, 1989). See my *Nature and Grace: A New Approach to Thomistic Ressourcement* (Eugene, OR: Pickwick, 2014), 68.

MESSIANIC BANQUET

The most concentrated expression of this hope is found in the "Isaiah apocalypse" (chapters 24–27). As Isaiah's oracles against the nations draw to a close (chapters 13–23), the book slides into a more universal and apocalyptic coda, as a summation of this literary unit. For example, Isaiah 24:1 opens with: "Behold [הִנֵּה], the LORD will lay waste the earth and make it desolate." Judgment and salvific oracles oscillate back and forth, with promises that the Lord will reign on Mt. Zion and unveil his "glory" (Isa 24:23).

While in popular expression the Jewish messianic hope is often caricatured as if it never concerned anything beyond mere political restoration, we have here in Isaiah something far richer. After speaking of the Lord's enthronement on Zion, Isaiah goes on to describe explicitly and powerfully the hope of the messianic banquet.

In this context, Isaiah 25:6 describes a "feast" of "oil and wine" [מִשְׁתֵּה שְׁמָנִים מִשְׁתֵּה שְׁמָרִים] (LXX πίονται οἶνον, χρίσονται μύρον).[2] Intriguingly, ancient near eastern parallels suggest that this divine banquet is an *enthronement*,[3] which here in Isaiah seems to have liturgical echoes, particularly with

---

[2]   Paul Kang-Kul Cho and Janling Fu write of this phrase: "Not only are the food and drink items themselves rich and distinctive, so too is the prosody employed to express their richness. The poetic quality of the verse draws attention to itself and, in turn, points to the splendor of the host of the feast." Cho and Janling, "Death and Feasting in the Isaiah Apocalypse (Isaiah 25:6–8)," in *Formation and Intertextuality in Isaiah 24–27*, ed. J. Todd Hibbard and Hyun Chul Paul Kim (Atlanta, GA: Society of Biblical Literature, 2013), 136.

[3]   See Beth Steiner, "Food of the Gods: Canaanite Myths of Divine Banquets and Gardens in Connection with Isaiah 25:6," in *Formation and Intertextuality in Isaiah 24–27*, 99–115, here 108–10. Steiner points to examples from Marduk and Ba'al, particularly the latter's feast on Mt. Zaphon (108). She writes: "Not only was victory—enthronement—feast a common pattern in the ancient Near East, but it is apparent that it was applicable to various eras: in *Enuma* Elish, it was set in primordial time; in the Ugaritic texts it is ambiguous and possibly cyclical; and here in Isaiah we have an eschatological setting. The finality of the Israelite passage is emphasized by Yahweh's swallowing death in verse 8, and John Day points out that the fact that Baal's kingship was associated with his victory over Mot and followed his feast on Zaphon shows that this verse is appropriately positioned after verse 6" (108–9). Steiner notes the connection between this passage and other enthronement psalms, such as Pss 47, 93, 96–99 (110). Philip J. Long likewise sees the meal in Isa 25 as the enthronement of the Lord on Zion: "Isaiah 24:23 indicates location of the enthronement (Zion) as well as the presence of the elders of Jerusalem. . . . [T]here are significant hints that Isaiah has a re-enactment of the covenant of Exod 24 in mind. The small unit of 25:6–8 is a description of the victory banquet on Mount Zion at the enthronement of the Lord." Long, *Jesus the Bridegroom: The Origin of the Eschatological Feast as a Wedding Banquet in the Synoptic Gospels* (Eugene, OR: Pickwick, 2013), 56. See also p. 66. See also Christopher Hays, *The Origins of Isaiah 24–27: Josiah's Festival Scroll for the Fall of Assyria* (Cambridge: Cambridge University Press, 2019), 54–61.

reference to the "oil" and "wine."[4] In addition, the phrase "this mountain," as Paul Kang-Kul Cho and Janling Fu write, "no doubt refers to Mount Zion, the royal mountain of God,"[5] which corroborates the liturgical sense of this passage, as Mt. Zion is of course linked to the Temple and even to Eden as the primordial sanctuary.[6]

Isaiah 25:7–8 employ the verb "to swallow" [וּבִלַּע], ultimately with reference to death—and it does so in universal terms: "And he will swallow up on this mountain the covering that is cast over *all peoples*. . . . He will swallow up death forever" (ESV). In the words of Stephen Cook, "In Isa 25:6–8, death meets its match in God."[7]

The reference to "all peoples" [כָּל־הָעַמִּים] (LXX πᾶσι τοῖς ἔθνεσιν) was first emphasized in v. 6: "On this mountain the LORD of hosts will make for *all peoples* [כָּל־הָעַמִּים] a feast."[8] Thus, this passage envisions a transnational gathering on Mt. Zion, much like the depiction of eschatological Zion in Isaiah 2:2–3, with the nations streaming to Zion and the word of Lord pouring forth from Zion.[9]

---

4   The Targum of Isaiah here describes this banquet meal as a "feast and a festival." See K. Cathcart, M. Maher, and M. McNamara, eds., *The Aramaic Bible: The Isaiah Targum*, vol. 11, Isa 25:6, trans. B. D. Chilton (Collegeville, MN: The Liturgical Press).

5   Cho and Fu, "Death and Feasting," 134. See also Jon D. Levenson, *Sinai and Zion: An Entry into the Jewish Bible* (New York: HarperCollins, 1985), 122; Hans Wildberger, *Isaiah 13–27: A Continental Commentary*, trans. Thomas H. Trapp (Minneapolis, MN: Fortress, 1997), 454.

6   See also Steiner, "Food of the Gods," 101–6, as well as Long, *Jesus the Bridegroom*, 60.

7   Stephen L. Cook, "Deliverance as Fertility and Resurrection: Echoes of Second Isaiah in Isaiah 26" in *Intertextuality and Formation of Isaiah 24–27*, 177. Cook continues: "God accomplishes a literal eradication of death on earth. Premodern Jewish commentators rightly point to this passage as a warrant for the rabbinic doctrine of life after death" (177). Similarly, Cho and Fu write: "The climactic event of this extravagant feast YHWH prepares for all peoples is YHWH feasting on death, God swallowing the swallower" (ibid., 118). Hays, *Origins of Isaiah 24–27*, 74–83, demurs, however, arguing that such "resurrection" language of overcoming death should be seen in political terms: "The thematic associations between Isa 25:7–8 and the Baal Myth are widely recognized. . . . In the Baal Myth, Death's swallowing likely calls for a seasonal interpretation . . . with Baal's descent into Mot's gullet symbolizing the passing of the rains and the dying off of vegetation. By contrast, the myth was adapted to convey a political meaning for the author of Isa 25:7–8. An analysis of all the items that YHWH removes in Isa 25:7–8—not only Death—brings the historical significance of the passage into focus. . . . Each [of the select terms here] alludes to one or more of the powers that remained to surround and harass Judah after the fall of Assyria: Egypt, Moab, and Ammon" (on 83; see also 85).

8   Isa 25:7 uses כָּל־הָעַמִּים in parallel with כָּל־הַגּוֹיִם as shown here: "And he will destroy on this mountain the covering that is cast over all peoples [כָּל־הָעַמִּים], the veil that is spread over all nations [כָּל־הַגּוֹיִם]" (RSV2CE). The LXX simply uses *ethnos* ("nations") throughout.

9   Long notes that מִשְׁתֶּה often extends boundaries, often in a covenantal context. See Long,

Finally, Isaiah 25:8 speaks of God removing the "reproach" of his people [וְחֶרְפַּת עַמּוֹ יָסִיר], a word commonly associated with sin and shame.[10]

In sum, as Isaiah outlines here, this future messianic banquet consists in:

- a gathering of *all peoples*;

- a *liturgical* feast of rich wine on Mt. Zion;

- which overcomes *sin* and *death*.

Clearly, this hope is heavenly and looks far beyond mere political liberation; it looks for God's definitive victory over death and points to a sacred banquet that liturgically ushers in the new age.

Intriguingly, the Isaiah apocalypse goes on to reference the hope of resurrection: "Your *dead shall live*, their *bodies shall rise*. O dwellers in the dust, awake and sing for joy!" (Isa 26:19), a passage similar to other Old Testament resurrection passages, such as Daniel 12:2.[11] In fact, as Annemarieke van der Woude suggests: here "death stands in opposition to feast"—that is, in and through this liturgical feast, the tyranny of death is overcome.[12]

Finally, the last chapter of this section in Isaiah turns to the defeat of "Leviathan," the fleeing "serpent" [נָחָשׁ] (Isa 27:1).[13] Hence, the overthrow of sin and death is connected with the defeat of mythic diabolic powers, the dark forces keeping Israel and humanity in bondage.

Later passages in Isaiah also pick up this theme of an eschatological feast—as for example here in Isaiah 55:1–3, which also alludes to Davidic restoration:

Jesus the Bridegroom, 51. He continues: "Isaiah is describing an international pilgrimage to Mount Zion" (51).

[10] See *New International Dictionary of Old Testament Theology & Exegesis*, ed. Willem A. VanGemeren (Grand Rapids, MI: Zondervan, 1997), 2:281–82.

[11] While Hays reads these passages differently than I am suggesting here, he likewise recognizes the links between Isa 26:19 and Dan 12:1–3 (see Hays, *Origins of Isaiah 24–27*, 91–94).

[12] Annemarieke van der Woude, "Resurrection or Transformation? Concepts of Death in Isaiah 24–27" in *Intertextuality and Formation of Isaiah 24–27*, 143–63, here 162.

[13] From Long, *Jesus the Bridegroom*, 64: "Since Isa 27:1 mentions Leviathan, a primordial chaos-monster and a later banquet text refers to Rahab (*2 Bar. 29*), it is likely that Isa 25:8 should be understood as an allusion to Mot. Mot is destroyed in the way he has destroyed all others, he is swallowed up לָנֶצַח 'forever.'" See also p. 93: "In Isa 25:6–8 the Lord summoned both his people and the nations to his mountain for a banquet of fine foods, but the Lord himself consumed the mythological creature Mot or Death. In Isa 51:9 the Lord cuts the mythological creature Rahab to pieces."

Ho, every one who *thirsts*,
    come to the *waters*;
and he who has no money,
    come, buy and eat!
Come, buy *wine* and milk
    without money and without price.
Why do you spend your
    money for that which is not bread,
and your labor for that
    which does not satisfy?
Listen diligently to me,
    and *eat* what is good,
and delight yourselves in *rich food*.
Incline your ear, and come to me;
    hear, that your soul may *live*;
and I will make with you an everlasting covenant,
    my steadfast, merciful love for David.[14]

Isaiah 62:8–9 speaks of eating and drinking in the "courts of my sanctuary," and Isaiah 65:13 speaks of the "servants" of the Lord eating and drinking, culminating in the new creation and new Jerusalem (65:17–18). Summing up the movement of the latter chapters of Isaiah, Philip J. Long writes: "Like Isa 25:6–8, Zion is the location of this joyful meal and like Isa 40–55, this shared meal is described in Eden-like terms."[15]

---

[14] Long notes that both Isa 55:3 and Prov 9:5–6 give the promise of food that leads to life (*Jesus the Bridegroom*, 96). For the parallels between Isa 55:1–5 and Isa 25:6–8, see pp. 95–99. Joshua Jipp also draws these Isaianic texts together. See Joshua W. Jipp, *The Messianic Theology of the New Testament* (Grand Rapids, MI: Eerdmans, 2020), 93. See also Cho and Fu, "Death and Feasting," 138–39.

[15] Long, *Jesus the Bridegroom*, 101. Intriguingly, Long notes that the messianic banquet motif can have a judgment aspect. See Long, *Jesus the Bridegroom*, 51, where he discusses Jer 51:37–39 in this vein. See also Cho and Fu, "Death and Feasting," 117–42, here 119n5 and pp. 132, 141. Perhaps this sentiment lies behind St. Paul's famous line about "eating and drinking judgment upon oneself" in 1 Cor 11:27–29. See Brant Pitre, Michael P. Barber, and John Kincaid, *Paul, a New Covenant Jew* (Grand Rapids, MI: Eerdmans, 2019), 225: "Nowhere in Paul's letters does the apostle ever use the *blood of Christ* as an image for the church—a point that suggests that an offense against the elements of the meal themselves is his primary meaning." See also my review of this book in *Nova et Vetera* 19.1 (2021): 313–20. The Targum of Isaiah here in Isa 25:6–8 points in this direction as well, speaking of this banquet as also a judgment scene against the nations.

KINGDOM RESTORATION AND LITURGICAL BANQUET

The Chronicler also seems to point to the *liturgical* restoration of the king-dom. On two occasions, he recounts Davidic kings hosting a national Passover, with overtones of pan-Israelite restoration. For example, Hezekiah sends messengers to "all Israel" [כָּל־יִשְׂרָאֵל], evoking the theme of the United Kingdom and the restoration of all twelve tribes (2 Chron 30:1).[16] Hezekiah sends out messengers to invite "all Israel, from Be'ershe'ba to Dan," specif-ically inviting *"all Israel and Judah"* (2 Chron 30:5–6). Some recipients of this invitation "laughed them to scorn, and mocked them" (2 Chron 30:10) while others accept the invitation—a dynamic also in the background of Jesus's parable regarding the great wedding feast where some decline the invitation and some accept (see Matt 22:1–14).[17] In a similar vein, Josiah keeps a national Passover (see 2 Chron 35:1–19), a passage which once again brims with eschatological expectation, as *"all Judah and Israel"* are present (2 Chron 35:18).[18] Such passages, particularly when read in light of messi-anic banquet hopes, point toward the *liturgical* restoration of the kingdom.

Zechariah likewise draws together messianic banquet motifs and hopes for Davidic restoration. In Zechariah 9, we find the famous pas-sage behind Jesus's triumphal entry into Jerusalem on a donkey (Zech 9:9), which itself draws from Solomon's coronation—which similarly came about by Solomon's riding on David's "mule" or "donkey" and being "anointed" (1) (וַיִּמְשָׁח Kgs 1:33–38). When Zechariah emphasizes this future messianic figure as an instrument of "peace" (שָׁלוֹם) (Zech 9:10), the figure of Solo-mon is likewise in view (see 1 Chron 22:9: "For his name shall be Solomon [שְׁלֹמֹה], and I will give peace [וְשָׁלוֹם]"). This Solomonic connection is also at play when Zechariah describes this future messianic rule as being "from sea to sea, and from the River to the ends of the earth" (Zech 9:10), directly paralleling Psalm 72:8—a psalm which is both about Solomon and the one to whom Solomon points.

In this context of Davidic expectation, Zechariah refers to the "blood of my covenant" (Zech 9:11) and a day of salvation marked by "grain" and "new wine" (Zech 9:17). As we will see, this language refers back to messianic banquet hopes. Moreover, Zechariah also speaks here of the Lord setting

16 See Scott W. Hahn, *The Kingdom of God as Liturgical Empire: A Theological Commentary on 1–2 Chronicles* (Grand Rapids, MI: Baker Academic, 2012), 176–80.

17 Brant Pitre, "Jesus, the Messianic Wedding Banquet, and the Restoration of Israel," *Letter and Spirit* 8 (2012–2013): 35–54, here 42–47.

18 See Hahn, *The Kingdom of God as Liturgical Empire*, 184. Christopher Hays sees the entirety of Isa 24–27 as having a Josianic backdrop, "celebrating the end of Assyrian power . . . and summoning the north back to Judah in the name of the Lord" (Hays, *Origins of Isaiah 24–27*, 266).

"captives free from the waterless pit" (Zech 9:11), a reference to overcoming death (e.g., see Isa 38:17). Hence, here in Zechariah, we have allusions to Davidic restoration alongside the messianic banquet motif—with the latter once again including hope for an eschatological victory over death.

MESSIANIC BANQUET AND SECOND TEMPLE LITERATURE

This Messianic banquet hope is certainly not absent from the literature of the Second Temple period.[19] Commenting on the Qumran community, Lawrence Schiffman writes: "The Dead Sea sect envisaged an *eschatological meal* at which the priestly 'messiah' would join the messiah of Israel in eating *bread and wine* amidst the congregation of Israel."[20] The document (*Rule of the Congregation*) from which we find the relevant passage begins this way: "This is the rule of all the congregation of Israel *in the final days*" (1QSa 1:1). Shortly thereafter, the text continues:

> At [a ses]sion of the men of renown, [those summoned to] the
> gathering of the community council, *when [God] begets
> the Messiah* with them: [the] chief [priest] of all the congrega-
> tion of Israel shall enter, and all

---

[19] See Brant Pitre, *Jesus and the Last Supper* (Grand Rapids, MI: Eerdmans, 2015), 453–58. According to Lawrence Schiffman, the idea of a messianic banquet was widespread in the Second Temple Judaism and continued into the rabbinic period. See Lawrence H. Schiffman, "Rule of the Congregation" in *Encyclopedia of the Dead Sea* Scrolls, ed. Lawrence H. Schiffman and James Vanderkam (Oxford University Press, 2000), 2:797–99, here 798. In fact, it may be the case that some meals at Qumran served to pre-enact the future messianic banquet. See Long, *Jesus the Bridegroom*, 161 and Lawrence H. Schiffman, *The Eschatological Community of the Dead Sea Scrolls: A Study of the Rule of the Congregation* (Atlanta, GA: Society of Biblical Literature, 1989), 70. See also Brant Pitre, "Jesus, the Messianic Banquet, and the Kingdom of God," in *Letter and Spirit* 5 (2009): 125–54, here 128–32. Similarly, John Bergsma writes: "[T]he 'thanksgiving meal' of the Qumranites was an *anticipation* of the messianic banquet when the 'kingdom of God' would be established." John Bergsma, *Jesus and the Dead Sea Scrolls: Revealing the Jewish Roots of Christianity* (New York: Image, 2019), 90 (emphasis original).

[20] Schiffman, *The Eschatological Community of the Dead Sea Scrolls*, 53 (emphasis added). Schiffman continues, describing how the regular ritual meals of the community mirrored their expectation of the eschatological banquet meal (68): "As a reflection of the deep messianic consciousness of this group, participation in the communal meals was a central eschatological ritual. The messianic banquets to be presided over by the priest and the messiah of Israel were enacted as well in the day-to-day lives of the sectarians at their communal meals. They saw these meals as a *foretaste* of the world to come. Both the messianic meals and those of this world required a quorum of ten, ritual purity of the participants, bread and wine, or either of them" (70, emphasis added).

[his] br[others, the sons] of Aaron, the priests [summoned] to the assembly, the men of renown, and they shall sit

be[fore him, each one] according to his dignity. After, [the Mess]iah of Israel shall [enter] and before him shall sit the heads of the

th[ousands of Israel, each] one according to his dignity, according to [his] po[sition] in their camps and according to their marches. And all

the heads of the cl[ans of the congre]gation with the wise [men . . .] shall sit before them, each one according

to his dignity. And [when] *they gather [at the tab]le of community [or to drink the n]ew wine*, and the table of

the community is prepared [and the] *new wine* [is mixed] for drinking, [no-one should stretch out] his hand to the first-fruit

of the *bread* and of [the new wine] before the priest, for [he is the one who bl]esses the first-fruit of *bread*

and of the *new win[e* and stretches out] his hand towards the *bread* before them. Afterwar[ds,] the *Messiah of Israel* [shall str]etch out his hands

towards the *bread*. [And afterwards, they shall ble]ss all the congregation of the community, each [one according to] his dignity. And in accordance with this precept one shall act

at each me[al, when] at least ten me[n are gat]hered (1QSa 2:11–22).[21]

Similarly, in *1 Enoch*, we find the day of salvation described in terms of eating, alongside resurrection language:

> The righteous and elect ones shall be *saved on that day*; and from thenceforth they shall never see the faces of the sinners and the

---

[21] 1QSa 2:11–22, cited in Florentino García Martínez, and Eibert J. C. Tigchelaar, *The Dead Sea Scrolls Study Edition* (Leiden; New York: Brill, 1997), 103. See James Vanderkam, *The Dead Sea Scrolls Today*, sec. ed. (Grand Rapids, MI: Eerdmans, 2010), 212–14, who comments on this passage as follows: "The meal is messianic in the most literal sense because it is eaten in the presence of the messiah of Israel and his priestly colleague. . . . It is also explicitly eschatological, as the first words of the composition [*Rule of the Congregation*, 1QSa] state: '*This is the Rule for all the congregation of Israel in the last days*'" (213, emphasis original). This last quote is from 1QSa 1:1 and is cited above. Intriguingly, the presence of bread and wine here may call to mind Melchizedek, who is elsewhere in the Scrolls depicted in Messianic—even quasi-divine—ways. See 11Q *Melch*. And the "ten person" requirement may call to mind first-century Passover regulations found in Josephus. For more, see Brant Pitre, *Jesus and the Last Supper*, 454.

oppressors. The Lord of the Spirits will abide over them; *they shall eat and rest and rise with that Son of Man* forever and ever. The *righteous and elect ones shall rise from the earth* and shall cease being of downcast face. They shall wear the *garments of glory.* These garments of yours shall become the *garments of life* from the Lord of the Spirits. Neither shall your garments wear out, nor your glory come to an end before the Lord of the Spirits (*1 En.* 62:13–16).[22]

A passage from *2 Baruch* also draws together messianic banquet motifs, alongside hope for eschatological manna, and seemingly resurrection as well:

And he answered and said to me:
That which will happen at that time bears upon the whole earth. Therefore, all who live will notice it. For at that time I shall only protect those found in this land at that time. And it will happen that when all that which should come to pass in these parts has been accomplished, the *Anointed One will begin to be revealed.* And *Behemoth* will reveal itself from its place, and *Leviathan* will come from the sea, the two great monsters which I created on the fifth day of creation and which I shall have kept until that time. And they will be *nourishment* for all who are left. The *earth will also yield fruits ten thousandfold.* And on one *vine* will be a thousand branches, and one branch will produce a thousand clusters, and one cluster will produce a *thousand grapes*, and one grape will produce a cor of *wine.* And *those who are hungry will enjoy themselves and they will,*

---

[22] J. H. Charlesworth, *The Old Testament Pseudepigrapha*, vol. 1 (New York; London: Yale University Press), 44. See also:

And the elect will be presented with its fruit for life. He will plant it in the direction of the northeast, upon the holy place—in the direction of the house of the Lord, the Eternal King.

Then they shall be glad and rejoice in gladness,
and they shall enter into the holy (place);
its fragrance shall (penetrate) their bones,
long life will they live on earth,
such as your fathers lived in their days. (*1 En.* 25:5–6)

While the text in the body of the paper above is from the section of *1 Enoch* known as the *Similitudes* (*1 Enoch* chs. 37–71), which is not present in the Enochic texts found among the Dead Sea Scrolls (in which case it likely dates later than other Enochic materials), the passage here in the footnotes from *1 Enoch* ch. 25 dates to the late second century BC. See Daniel M. Gurtner, *Introducing the Pseudepigrapha of Second Temple Judaism: Message, Context, and Significance* (Grand Rapids, MI: Baker Academic, 2020), 24, 36.

moreover, see marvels every day. For winds will go out in front of me every morning to bring the fragrance of aromatic fruits and clouds at the end of the day to distill the dew of health. And it will happen at that time that *the treasury of manna will come down again from on high,* and *they will eat of it in those years because these are they who will have arrived at the consummation of time.*

And it will happen after these things when the time of the *appearance of the Anointed One* has been fulfilled and he returns with glory, that then all who sleep in hope of him will *rise.* And it will happen at that time that those treasuries will be opened in which the number of the souls of the righteous were kept, and they will go out and the multitudes of the souls will appear together, in one assemblage, of one mind. And the first ones will enjoy themselves and the last ones will not be sad. For they know that the time has come of which it is said that it is the *end of times.* But the souls of the wicked will the more waste away when they shall see all these things.[23]

Such passages demonstrate the currency of messianic banquet ideas—of feasting, abundance of wine, and defeat of death—in the Second Temple period, marking the fullness of time and often the hope of resurrection. This background lends credence to pursuing how such messianic banquet motifs may inform our reading of select New Testament passages.

But before we turn directly to the New Testament, let us make explicit what seems to be implicit regarding the foundation of the messianic banquet hope—namely, Israel's experience at Sinai.

SINAI AS PROTO-TYPE

As suggested above, Zechariah 9:11 draws a direct link to Sinai with the phrase "blood of the covenant," since this phrase hearkens back to the sacrifice at Sinai that seals the covenant (see Exod 24:8). But importantly, this

---

[23] See Long, *Jesus the Bridegroom,* 104 for the Jewish hope of the return of Manna. Also relevant is *Testament of Levi* 18:10–11:

And he shall open the gates of paradise;
he shall remove the sword that has threatened since Adam,
and he will grant to the saints to eat of the tree of life.
The spirit of holiness shall be upon them.

Both the *Testament of Levi* and *2 Baruch* are cited from Charlesworth, *The Old Testament Pseudepigrapha,* 44, emphasis added to both.

scene at Sinai does not culminate in sacrifice but in a *sacred meal* in the very presence of God: "Then Moses and Aaron, Na'dab, and Abi'hu, and seventy of the elders of Israel went up, and they *saw the God of Israel. . . . they beheld God, and ate and drank*" (Exod 24:9–11). Accordingly, the "top" of Mt. Sinai evokes God's sacred presence. Here, atop Sinai, they share in a sacred banquet meal in the very presence of God. This heavenly meal seems to serve as the prototype from which prophets like Isaiah and Zechariah derive their hope for a future messianic banquet which will inaugurate the eschatological age to come.[24]

In the words of Long: "Exod 24:1–11 is perhaps *the most important text* for understanding the idea of an eschatological banquet."[25]

---

[24] Joseph Blenkinsopp comments on Isaiah 25 as follows: "The sumptuous banquet described here enlarges on the earlier reference to the meal of which the elders partook at Sinai (Exod 24:11), but it is also the conclusion to the ceremony of the accession of Israel's God to the throne on Mount Zion and in Jerusalem (24:23)." Blenkinsopp, *Isaiah 1–39: A New Translation with Introduction and Commentary*, vol. 19 (New Haven; London: Yale University Press, 2008), 358. Hays also recognizes the obvious thematic connection between the two passages (Exod 24:9–11 and Isa 25:6–8); see Hays, *Origins of Isaiah 24–27*, 238, 258.

[25] Long, *Jesus the Bridegroom*, 52 (emphasis added). He continues: "Both texts [Exod 24 and Isa 25] describe a gathering of people on a mountain where they eat in God's presence" (53–54). The movement from creation to this Sinai covenant banquet is the culmination of a certain biblical "age"—in which case, Isaiah's allusion back to this banquet meal looks forward to the culmination of the age to come. Long writes: "The motivation for the allusion to the covenant meal in Exod 24 in the apocalyptic Isa 25 may be to connect the beginning of the coming age and the beginning of the old. . . . At the beginning of God's relationship with Israel, he overcame his enemies in the plagues, triumphing over Egypt and bringing his people out of slavery to Mount Sinai where he establishes his covenant on the mountain. At the beginning of the eschatological age, God will overcome his enemies once again and recall his people to his mountain (Sinai or Zion) and renew his covenant with them. In both cases there is a meal which celebrates the covenant. . . . Th[e] 'universal' element of the meal in Isaiah is not unlike David's distribution of food to all people when he first took possession of Jerusalem and Zion [see 2 Sam 6]. The time of restoration of Israel will be like a New Exodus and will include a New Conquest as well. God will call all people to 'the mountain' (now Zion) and enact a covenant with them. While his people eat the banquet the Lord himself prepares, the Lord will 'swallow up death forever' and 'wipe away all tears forever.' The banquet of Isa 25:6–8 therefore represents the ultimate vindication of the people of Israel" (*Jesus the Bridegroom*, 54). Importantly, Isaiah of course makes abundant use of Exodus themes throughout (see p. 53). For the Sinai meal as backdrop to Isa 25:6–8, see also Otto Kaiser, *Isaiah 13–39: A Commentary* (OTL; Philadelphia: Westminster, 1974), 195, and Pitre, *Last Supper*, 450. Schiffman, *The Eschatological Community of the Dead Sea Scrolls*, 70, similarly describes the Dead Sea Scroll community as fundamentally rooted in the hope of the recapitulation of the Sinai experience in the age to come: "[T]he sect utilized the terminology of the Exodus from Egypt . . . as the prototype of the ultimate redemption, for it represented the closest possible relationship to God, with God's direct intervention in history and His revelation of the law. . . . The coming cataclysm would inaugurate both a return to the past and a new previously unachievable future of observance of

JESUS AND THE MESSIANIC BANQUET

We've already suggested that Jesus's parable of the wedding feast in Matthew 22:1–14 draws on these motifs, both that of the messianic banquet and kingdom restoration.[26] Certainly, passages in Revelation describing the "wedding supper of the lamb" refer back to this hope as well (see Rev 19:7, 9).

This motif also seems to be in the background of Matthew's account of Jesus's healing of the centurion's servant. After he heals the servant and is moved by the centurion's faith, he proclaims:

> Truly, I say to you, not even in Israel have I found such faith. I tell you, many will come from east and west and sit at table with Abraham, Isaac, and Jacob in the kingdom of heaven, while the sons of the kingdom will be thrown into the outer darkness; there men will weep and gnash their teeth. (Matt 8:10–12)

The reference here of "sitting at table" (or "reclining," ἀνακλιθήσονται), likely points to the banquet motif.[27] The fact that Abraham, Isaac, and Jacob are said to be present suggests an eschatological orientation—a point emphasized by the counterpart to this banquet: namely, being cast "into the outer darkness," to "weep and gnash their teeth" (Matt 8:12).[28] Even the language of returning from "east and west" seems to indicate more than mere geography.[29]

---

the law, ritual purity and perfection. . . . The redemption from Egypt and the desert-wandering, crowned by the revelation at Sinai, were for the sectarian a paradigm of that which would be once again repeated in the end of days in which he was soon to share."

[26] It is worth noting that Year A in the liturgical cycle pairs Isa 25 with Matt 22:1–14 (see, for example, the readings from Sunday, Oct. 11, 2020). Jipp, *Messianic Theology of the New Testament*, 93–94: "Jesus's frequent meals are all anticipations of the final messianic banquet (most obviously Luke 9:11–17; 22:14–30; 24:28–35)." For the emeritus pope, the feast celebrating the return of the Prodigal Son is also Eucharistic. See Benedict XVI, *Jesus of Nazareth*, vol. 1 (New York: Crown Publishing Group, 2007), 206.

[27] See Long, *Jesus the Bridegroom*, 227.

[28] See Long, *Jesus the Bridegroom*, 207: "The fate of those not included in the feast in [Matt] 8:11 is identical to the man cast out of the wedding banquet in Matt 22:13 and similar to the virgins who are not admitted to the wedding feast in 25:12." Amy-Jill Levine, *Sermon on the Mount: A Beginner's Guide to the Kingdom of Heaven* (Nashville, TN: Abingdon, 2020), 80–81, also cites Isa 25:6–9 alongside Matt 8:11–12 as describing messianic banquet hopes; in fact, she suggests that the Our Father ("give us this day our daily bread") points in the same direction.

[29] Commenting on this language of gathering "from east and west" in Zech 8:7, George Klein writes: "The Lord's promise to save 'my people' from the east and the west indicates that Zechariah predicted more than the end to the exile when the chosen people would return from Babylon in the east. The combination of east and west speaks not only of geographical

While some have seen in this Matthean passage a polemic against the Jews and evidence of the parting of the ways between Jew and Gentile,[30] one need not necessarily understand this saying in that vein. As we saw earlier, the messianic banquet motif is for "all peoples" (Isa 25:6). In this light, we can understand Jesus here as referring to the eschatological gathering of the combined faithful of Israel and the Gentiles—joining together in the eschatological feast that overcomes their common plight of sin and death (see Isa 2:2–3 and 25:6–8).[31]

At the Last Supper, Jesus refers to the "blood of the covenant" (Matt 26:28; Mark 14:24; see Luke 22:20), which of course alludes back to Moses's words at Sinai (and likely Jeremiah 31's prophecy of a new covenant as well).[32] We can assume that in evoking Exodus 24:8 ("blood of the covenant"), his hearers would also call to mind the sacred communion meal of Exodus 24:9–11—where Moses and the elders "beheld God, and ate and drank" (Exod 24:11). In doing so, Jesus evokes the very foundation of the messianic banquet hope.[33]

Here, not on Mt. Sinai but on Mt. Zion—the latter having clear Temple and Davidic overtones—the Apostles share in a sacred communion meal in the very presence of the (divine) Messiah.[34] In other words, in the Last

---

locales, but also serves as another merism, encompassing Abraham's seed everywhere. These far-flung people God would bring back to Zion. Similar themes occur in Isa 11:1–11; 43:5–6; Jer 31:8." *Zechariah*, vol. 21B (Nashville, TN: B & H Publishing Group, 2008), 238. See also Isa 43:5–9: "Fear not, for I am with you. I will bring your offspring from the east, and from the west I will gather you" (v. 5). Pitre, *Jesus and the Last Supper*, 470, argues similarly: "This re-gathering is not just from all places, but from *all times*—hence, Abraham, Isaac, Jacob." Zech 8:20–23 points to a time when the nations will join Israel in worshiping the God of Israel in Jerusalem: "Many peoples and strong nations shall come to seek the Lord of hosts in Jerusalem, and to entreat the favor of the Lord" (8:22)—which is similar to the picture recounted in Isa 2:2–3 and 25:6–8.

[30] See Pitre, *Jesus and the Last Supper*, 461.

[31] Pitre, *Jesus and the Last Supper*, 469–70.

[32] See Eugene LaVerdiere, *Dining in the Kingdom of God: The Origins of the Eucharist according to Luke* (Chicago, IL: Liturgical Training Publications, 1994), 140.

[33] See Long, *Jesus the Bridegroom*, 203: "The 'blood of the covenant' in Exod 24:8 is followed by a meal on Sinai which Moses, Aaron and the seventy elders eat and drink before God. This meal at the establishment of the first covenant is the foundation on which the meal at the establishment of the new covenant is built in Isa 25:6–8. . . . If the breaking of bread was a messianic self-revelation then it would be strong evidence in favor of the Last Supper as a messianic banquet." See Scot McKnight, *Jesus and His Death: Historiography, the Historical Jesus, and Atonement Theory* (Waco, TX: Baylor University Press, 2005), 291, 331: "Thus, Jesus connects the last supper with the eschatological banquet (cf. Ps 107:1–9; Isa 25:1–10a; 49:10–13; Joel 2:24; 3:18; Amos 9:13; *1 En.* 10:19; 62:14; *2 Bar.* 29:5; 1QSa)" (331). See also LaVerdiere, *Dining in the Kingdom of God*, 128.

[34] See Jipp, *Messianic Theology of the New Testament*, 271–72, for his comments regarding

Supper, that which was anticipated in the banquet meal on Mt. Sinai in the very presence of God—which is then picked up and projected forward by the prophets—finds fulfillment. In the words of Brant Pitre, Jesus here brings about the "eucharistic restoration of all Israel."[35] What Hezekiah and Josiah anticipate in an earthly sense finds fulfillment: in the New Covenant Passover, Jesus *liturgically* brings about Davidic restoration, vanquishing sin and death.[36]

In this way, Jesus's actions bring not only Israel's story to its climax but humanity's as well. After all, Israel's story embodies humanity's larger story. And the ultimate alienation is not just the exile to Babylon (or the scattering of the northern tribes by Assyria), but the curse of death begun in the garden: "You are dust, and to dust you shall return" (Gen 3:19).

Hebrews 12:22: "[T]he author makes the important claim that his audience has now come to 'Mount Zion, the city of the living God, the heavenly Jerusalem.'. . . The mention of Mount Zion evokes the royal Davidic dynasty and kingdom, perhaps most emphatically associated with such texts as 2 Samuel 7, Psalms 2, 89, and 110—all of which appear in some sense in Hebrews 1:5–14 in order to portray the Son's entrance into his heavenly kingdom and reign (respectively: Heb 1:5b, 5a, 6a, and 13b)."

[35] Pitre, *Jesus and the Last Supper*, 512. It's worth noting that St. Cyril of Jerusalem alludes to this passage in Isaiah (25:6–8) with reference to the sacramental economy of the Church: "It was of this anointing that in ancient times the blessed Isaia prophesied saying: 'And the Lord shall make unto all people in this mountain' (elsewhere also he calls the Church a mountain, as when he says: 'And in the last days the mountain of the Lord shall be manifest') '. . . and they shall drink wine, they shall drink gladness, they shall anoint themselves with ointment.' To alert you to the mystical meaning of 'ointment' here, he says: 'All this deliver to the nations: for the counsel of the Lord is upon all the nations'" (*Mystagogical Lectures* III.7). The last line is a direct quotation from LXX Isa 25:7. Eusebius seems also to connect Isa 25:6–8 and the Eucharist. See Eusebius, *Proof of the Gospel* I.10, cited in Jean Danielou, *The Bible and the Liturgy* (Notre Dame, IN: University of Notre Dame Press, 1956), 159.

[36] See Jipp, *Messianic Theology of the New Testament*, 95: "[T]he context of Passover and the scriptural associations between Israel's kings and the celebration of the (eschatological) Passover function to portray Jesus and his messianic community as celebrating God's restoration of the Davidic kingdom (see 2 Chr 30:1–8; 35:16–18; Ezek 45:21–23)." Also on 56, emphasis added: "Jesus' promise to give Peter the 'keys of the kingdom of heaven' likely echoes Isaiah 22:21–22 . . . thereby positioning the *disciples as priests of the Messiah's eschatological temple* who, through their teaching, judging (cf. Matt 19:28), and dispensing of Jesus' forgiveness (i.e., 'binding' and 'loosing'), continue the Messiah's ministry. This authority is explicitly grounded in the Messiah's ongoing presence and authority." And speaking of Mark 10:37–38 (Jesus's association of the "drinking the cup," "baptism," and his impending suffering), Jipp writes on p. 84: "These two images resonate powerfully with the way Christians 'drink the Lord's cup at communion and thus proclaim his death until he comes' (cf. 1 Cor 11:26) and their sharing 'in that death in a deep sacramental sense through baptism' (cf. Rom 6:3)." Jipp is citing Joel Marcus, *Mark 8–16*, Anchor Bible Commentary (New Haven, CN: Yale University Press, 2009), 754.

Christ's victory on the Cross and the gift of himself in the Eucharist overcomes death, as John's bread of life discourse makes clear: "He who eats my flesh and drinks my blood has eternal life, and I will raise him up at the last day" (John 6:54). This is of course picked up by the tradition, as St. Ignatius of Antioch describes the Eucharist as the "medicine of immortality and the antidote against death" (Letter to the Ephesians, ch. 20).[37]

A NUPTIAL BANQUET

In a Catholic context, Jesus's direct allusion to Exodus 24:8 at the Last Supper is incredibly significant. For it is not uncommon for both scholars and laity outside the Church to find it simply incomprehensible that Jesus "founded a Church"—i.e., that Jesus envisioned the sacramental interim before his return. For example, those who see Jesus as a thoroughgoing apocalyptic prophet—expecting the imminent end of all of things—tend not to see much temporal space for Jesus's liturgical command (*"Do this* in memory of me").[38] If Jesus thought the end was imminent, there is no sense in establishing the ongoing sacramental praxis of the Church.

But consider how much time transpired between Moses's day and that of Jesus—well over a thousand years. If Jesus looks back to Moses's primordial sacrifice and meal as the prototype of what he is offering at the Last Supper, the biblical logic would run thus: when Jesus uses the phrase "covenant in my blood" and then commands the Apostles, *"Do* this in remembrance of me" (Luke 22:19–20), he certainly would seem to imply a *significant interim* between this moment and his final return.

The ongoing memorial of this messianic banquet meal is already a pledge and a foretaste of the victory promised by Isaiah—that God would "swallow up death for ever" and remove "the reproach of his people" (Isa 25:8). In and through the Eucharist, the Church becomes the spotless Bride of Christ and enters the new creation (see Rev 21:1–2; Eph 5:26, 31–32; 2 Cor 5:17).

---

[37] G. G. Walsh, *The Letters of St. Ignatius of Antioch*, in F. X. Glimm, J. M.-F. Marique, and G. G. Walsh, trans., *The Apostolic Fathers*, vol. 1 (Washington, DC: The Catholic University of America Press), 95. Similarly, Pitre, Barber, and Kincaid, *Paul, a New Covenant Jew*, 246–47, comment as follows on Paul and the Lord's Supper: *"In the Lord's Supper . . . participants have a foretaste of the resurrected body and the life of the world to come. . . .* While Paul does not (of course) use the language of 'real presence' or 'transubstantiation,' to insist that 'spiritual' is merely a metaphor resists the *eschatological and Christological realism* of Paul's language" (emphasis original).

[38] Pitre, *Last Supper*, 22–23; see Bart D. Erhman, *How Jesus Became God: The Exaltation of Jewish Preacher from Galilee* (New York: HaperOne, 2014), 103–6 and *Jesus: Apocalyptic Prophet of the New Millenium* (Oxford University Press, 1999), 125–39, 231–34.

Further, it seems that Sinai is also the origin of the nuptial metaphor between Israel and her divine spouse. After the golden calf, Moses declares to Aaron: "What did this people do to you that you have brought a *great sin* upon them?" (Exod 32:21, כִּי־הֵבֵאתָ עָלָיו חֲטָאָה גְדֹלָה), which closely parallels Abimelech's words to Abraham—when Abraham almost caused Abimelech to commit *adultery*: "What have you done to us? And how have I sinned against you, that you have brought on me and my kingdom a *great sin*?" (Gen 20:9, כִּי־הֵבֵאתָ עָלַי וְעַל־מַמְלַכְתִּי חֲטָאָה גְדֹלָה).

In other words, the golden calf was Israel's primordial act of adultery—precisely because Sinai first represents her nuptial marriage to the Lord.

Seeing the covenant at Sinai as the beginning of this nuptial bond between Israel and the Lord makes sense of the combination of *banquet* and *wedding* motifs (as in the *marriage supper* of the lamb, see Rev 19:7, 9).[39] Herein, the Eucharist becomes the messianic banquet meal which overcomes sin and death *and* that which simultaneously consummates the nuptial marriage between God and his people. The Sinai experience is here transfigured, as the pilgrim Church already participates in the heavenly Zion.[40]

In conclusion, the power of the messianic banquet motif lay in its ability to showcase the relevance of Israel and Jesus to the human condition. Precisely in this Jewish backdrop of the Gospel, we find its anthropological and even cosmic significance. This is an apologetic that matters; in a Lubacian vein, it helps make the very *Jewish* Gospel relevant to modern man.

---

[39] For Long, it precisely Matthew's Jesus that combines the marriage metaphor with eschatological banquet motifs. See Long, *Jesus the Bridegroom*, 223; in other words, what is implicit in the Old is made explicit in the New.

[40] In the words of Brant Pitre, *Jesus and the Last Supper*, 511: "[I]n the new exodus of Jesus, Jerusalem is the point of departure and the kingdom of God is the ultimate destination." Also, if we see the unity of the movement from the Passover in Exodus 12 to the solemn consummation of the Sinai covenant in chapter 24 (particularly, with the banquet meal in the presence of God in 24:11)—and all of this as Israel's nuptial marriage to her divine spouse—then we can see in Jesus's words at the Last Supper the evocation (and consummation) of this entire movement. In other words, with the words "blood of the covenant" in the context of the Passover, Jesus evokes the marriage bond between Israel and the Lord—a bond initiated in the Passover and consummated in the Sinai banquet meal. Jesus renews and recapitulates this bond in fulfillment of the Messianic Banquet in and through the Eucharist. In the words of Claude Chavasse: "In the Last Supper, [Jesus] was as much enacting a Marriage Feast as keeping the Passover. Essentially, the Passover itself was nuptial. The foundation of the Marriage between Yahweh and his People was the Covenant between them. . . . It is therefore no playing with words, but the sober truth, to say that Jesus, if not enacting *a* marriage at the Last Supper, was solemnizing *the* Marriage between himself and his Church in this, the New Covenant." Claude Chavasse, *The Bride of Christ: An Enquiry into the Nuptial Element in Early Christianity* (London: Religious Book Club, 1939), 60–61. Cited in Brant Pitre, *Jesus the Bridegroom: The Greatest Love Story Ever Told* (New York: Image, 2014), 51.

Evolution and Eschatology:
Jesus Christ, the Alpha and Omega of All Creation in the Thought of Joseph Ratzinger

Benedictine College, KS

INTRODUCTION

What, if anything, does the beginning of life on this planet have to do with man's last end of eternal life in heaven? The task of this essay is to reflect on this connection in light of Joseph Ratzinger's oft-repeated use of evolutionary language as a springboard for glimpsing the nature of Christian hope. Specifically, I aim to probe the meaning of the emeritus pontiff's frequent teaching that the end of human life and of the cosmos as a whole—the "new heaven and new earth"—may be described in terms of an "evolutionary leap" and a "transubstantiation" into Christological fullness that offers a powerful motive for Christian hope.

Over the course of these reflections, I will be referring to Ratzinger's language of evolutionary transformation as an anagogy for the definitive transformation that all created reality will undergo on the Last Day. As understood in the Catholic tradition, the anagogical sense is that which "leads upwards" by reasoning from things visible to invisible, raising the minds of believers from the things of earth to the life of heaven.[1] In the

---

[1] For a thorough overview of the anagogical sense, see Henri de Lubac. *Medieval Exegesis*, vol. 2, *The Four Senses of Scripture* (Grand Rapids: Eerdmans, 1998), 179–226. As de Lubac

following anagogy, we will contemplate the emeritus pontiff's teaching that the dynamic of evolutionary history on earth (a long story of life and death by which God brought about new and ever greater forms of life, preparing for the advent of man and culminating in the Incarnation of the God-man) has a profound connection to the definitive heavenly transfiguration of the cosmos at the end of time (where, passing through death, all life will be transfigured and conformed to the image of Jesus Christ).

As a final word of introduction, it may be helpful to consider that what Ratzinger is endeavoring to achieve with his evolutionary anagogy is comparable to what Jesus seeks to achieve with his words about the grain of wheat that bears no fruit unless it "dies" (John 12:24) and St. Paul's teaching that a body "sown" into the ground perishable will one day be raised imperishable (1 Cor 15:42–54). As Jesus and Paul found deep intimations of resurrected life within nature, so, too, does Ratzinger find a profound glimpse of this same reality in the long history of life in our universe. With these biblical reference points in place and recognizing that every anagogy has its limits, we may now proceed to explore this connection as developed in Ratzinger's thought across his career—a theme he returned to time and again as a scholar, as pope, and even into retirement.[2]

JESUS CHRIST AS THE ALPHA AND OMEGA OF CREATION AND THE CALL TO SHARE IN HIS "EVOLUTIONARY LEAP"

The close relationship between the beginning and end of creation is abundantly clear in the New Testament, and this link is none other than the person of Jesus Christ. He is the Word who was "in the beginning" (John 1:1) and the "first-born of all creation" *through whom* all things were created (Col 1:15–16). At the same time, he is "the first-born from the dead" (v. 18), *for whom* all things were created (v. 16). Nowhere is this captured more powerfully than in the Bible's climactic chapter: "I am the Alpha and the Omega, the first and the last, the beginning and the end" (Rev 22:13; cf. 1:8; 21:6). Reflecting on this truth, Pope Benedict writes:

explains, anagogy fosters hope as allegory builds up faith and tropology facilitates charity. On this sense, see also *Catechism of the Catholic Church*, §115–18.

[2] This essay at times refers to the one man Ratzinger/Benedict by his surname and at other times by his papal name in the effort to distinguish writings composed during his pontificate from those preceding it. When not referring specifically to a text, the name Benedict or "emeritus pontiff" is employed since this essay was written during the period of his retirement.

Christ is the *protòtypos,* the first-born of creation, the idea for
which the universe was conceived. He welcomes all. We enter in
the movement of the universe by uniting with Christ. . . . We reach
the roots of being by reaching the mystery of Christ, his living
word that is the aim of all creation.[3]

One of the remarkable points in the above text is how Benedict draws
out the cosmic implications of Christ's incarnation and salvific death. By
teaching that our union with Christ causes us to "enter in the movement
of the universe," the then-pontiff suggests that not just man but indeed the
whole universe is in some way moving toward Christ as its *telos.*

This thought is profound enough in its own right, but what makes it
especially timely in light of modern scientific discoveries is that Ratzinger
has consistently described this movement as an "evolution." For instance, in
his classic *Introduction to Christianity,* he writes that Christification—the
transformation of all in Christ—is "the real drift [*die eigentliche Drift*] of
evolution . . . the real goal of the ascending process of growth or becoming."[4]
Inspired by the language of Pierre Teilhard de Chardin, the pioneering
priest-paleontologist whose thought he frequently draws upon while refin-
ing, Ratzinger expands in more detail:

Faith sees in Jesus the man in whom—on the biological plane—the
next evolutionary leap [*der nächste Evolutionssprung*], as it were, has
been accomplished; the man in whom the breakthrough [*Durch-
bruch*] out of the limited scope of humanity, out of its monadic
enclosure, has occurred.[5]

---

[3] Benedict XVI, Address, October 6, 2008, https://www.vatican.va/content/benedict-xvi/
en/speeches/2008/october/documents/hf_ben-xvi_spe_20081006_sinodo.html. For other
discussions of this connection, see Benedict XVI, Homily at Easter Vigil, April 23, 2011,
https://www.vatican.va/content/benedict-xvi/en/homilies/2011/documents/hf_ben-xvi_
hom_20110423_veglia-pasquale.html.
[4] Ratzinger, *Introduction to Christianity* (San Francisco: Ignatius Press, 1990), 236–37; *Einführung in das Christentum* (München: Kösel, 1968), 223.
[5] Ratzinger, *Introduction to Christianity,* 238–39; *Einführung in das Christentum,* 225. Especially apropos to our present topic, Ratzinger adds here that Teilhard de Chardin, though
not without his flaws, provided an "important service" to theology by rethinking this notion
within modernity's broader evolutionary understanding of the cosmos. Ratzinger's overall
assessment of Chardin's thought is grasped from this statement: "It must be regarded as an
important service of Teilhard de Chardin's that he rethought these ideas from the angle
of the modern view of the world and, in spite of a not entirely unobjectionable tendency
toward the biological approach, nevertheless on the whole grasped them correctly and in
any case made them accessible once again" (236). Elsewhere, Ratzinger seeks to purify a

The connection between the nature of Christ and the vocation of man is so tight that, for Ratzinger, Christology *is* anthropology.[6] Moreover, what concerns Christ—the "definitive evolutionary leap" he brought about—in turn applies to the ultimate vocation of *all* human beings. Like Christ, the person who dies having been totally transformed by love transcends the limits of space and time and all the suffering that is part and parcel of existence here below. In the eschaton, all facets of our natural life (*bios*) will be "encompassed by and incorporated in the power of love," which itself is not bound to the material world but lives on perpetually. Accordingly, after departing the present temporal "realm of biological evolutions and mutations," Ratzinger describes the blessed man as undergoing a "last stage of evolution," a "leap" (*Sprung*).[7]

Expanding on how precisely a person goes about making this definitive "leap" with Christ, Ratzinger teaches that this movement of *theosis* (being "God-ized", i.e., divinization) only occurs when we make a free and total offering of ourselves in love and even then will only be complete in heaven:

> Only where someone values love more highly than life, that is, only where someone is ready to put life second to love, for the sake of love, can love be stronger and more than death. If it is to be more than death, it must first be more than mere life. But if it could be this, not just in intention but in reality, then that would mean at the same time that the power of love had risen superior to the power of the merely biological and taken it into its service. . . .

certain "tendency" in Chardin's thought (as well as in *Gaudium et Spes*) by emphasizing that the authentic process of christification that he has in mind is not that of a "technological utopia" that can be achieved in this world. See Ratzinger, *Theological Highlights of Vatican II* (New York: Paulist Press, 1966), 226–29 and Benedict XVI, *Spe Salvi* (Nov. 30, 2007), §§16–23.

    For more on Ratzinger's appropriation of Chardin's language of life in Christ as mankind's definitive "evolutionary leap" in which the body will no longer be subject to decay (1 Cor 15:44), see Ramage, *The Experiment of Faith: Pope Benedict XVI on Living the Theological Virtues in a Secular Age* (Washington, DC: Catholic University of America Press, 2020), 106–8, 123, 147n28, 269–70. For his knowledge of Chardin, Ratzinger is at least partially in debt to Henri de Lubac's nuanced treatments of the former's thought. See Henri de Lubac, *The Religion of Teilhard de Chardin* (New York: Desclee Co., 1967) and Lubac, *Teilhard de Chardin: The Man and His Meaning* (New York: Hawthorn Books, 1965).

[6] For a discussion of this point in Ratzinger's commentary on *Gaudium et Spes*, see Ratzinger, "Dignity of the Human Person," in vol. 5 of *Commentary on the Documents of Vatican II*, ed. Herbert Vorgrimler (New York: Herder and Herder, 1969), 118–19 and remarks on the text in Emery de Gaál, *The Theology of Pope Benedict XVI: The Christocentric Shift* (New York: Palgrave Macmillan, 2010), 107–8.

[7] Ratzinger, *Introduction to Christianity*, 304.

Such a final stage of "mutation" and "evolution" would itself no longer be a biological stage. . . . The last stage of evolution needed by the world to reach its goal would then no longer be achieved within the realm of biology but by the spirit, by freedom, by love. It would no longer be evolution but decision and gift in one.[8]

In sum, Ratzinger agrees with Paul in that, if we do not have love, then we have nothing. For at that point, we would have achieved no higher calling than any other species on this planet. On the other hand, in having love, we have everything since "love is the foundation of immortality, and immortality proceeds from love alone."[9] Speaking first of Christ but, in turn, of all of us called to share in his nature through grace, Ratzinger goes so far as to make the bold claim that "he who has love for all has established immortality for all."[10]

MAKING ALL THINGS NEW: THE BIBLICAL VISION OF CREATION'S ESCHATOLOGICAL TRANSFIGURATION

A remarkable feature of Ratzinger's Christological perspective on evolution is that it is not just about the salvation of individual human beings but the glorious transformation *of all creation*.[11] Ratzinger's lofty claim about the destiny of the created world—a hope echoed in the teachings of the Second Vatican Council—finds its basis in multiple New Testament texts. With their exalted expectations for the future of the created universe, these letters clearly share the profound conviction that the evolving world we inhabit is "very good" (Gen 1:31) and therefore destined in some way—however inscrutable it is to us here below—to share with us in eternal glory.[12]

---

8   Ratzinger, *Introduction to Christianity*, 304.

9   Ratzinger, *Introduction to Christianity*, 306.

10   Ratzinger, *Introduction to Christianity*, 306.

11   This section on cosmic transubstantiation has been adapted from Ramage, *The Experiment of Faith*, 106–9. For another discussion of this dynamism in light of the New Testament witness regarding the effect of Christ's redemptive work upon all orders of creation, see Telford Work, *Jesus—The End and the Beginning* (Grand Rapids, MI: Baker Academic, 2019), 67.

12   See Second Vatican Council, Light of Nations *Lumen Gentium* (November 21, 1964), §48: At the time of the "restoration of all things," the council writes, "the human race as well as the entire world, which is intimately related to man and attains to its end through him, will be perfectly reestablished in Christ." Similarly, Pope Paul VI, Church in the Modern World *Gaudium et Spes* (Dec. 7, 1965), §39, teaches that, while the form of this world will pass away (1 Cor 7:31), "all that creation which God made on man's account will be unchained from the bondage of vanity." On this topic, see also CCC §§1042–60.

Perhaps most famously, St. John envisions "a new heaven and a new earth" to be revealed in the fullness of time (Rev 21:1; cf. Isa 11:6–9; 25:7–9; 65:17–25; 66:22) and sees the Lord declaring, "Behold, I make *all things* new" (Rev 21:5, emphasis added). In the same vein, 2 Peter 3:8–14 informs us that when the day of the Lord arrives like a thief, "then the heavens will pass away with a loud noise, and the elements will be dissolved with fire"—not in order to abolish creation but rather to *renew* it as a "new heavens and a new earth in which righteousness dwells."[13] Expanding on this eschatological vision in his own turn, Paul depicts the whole creation "groaning [*systenazei*] with labor pains" as it waits to be "set free from its bondage to decay and obtain the glorious liberty of the children of God" (Rom 8:21–22).[14]

It is noteworthy that Paul sees the redemption of believers as a prerequisite for the liberation of the cosmos: "For the creation waits with eager longing for the revealing of the sons of God" (Rom 8:19).[15] As Scott Hahn puts it, "The relationship between man and the world is so close that the fate of the one is tied up with the fate of the other."[16] That is to say, while

---

[13] For the Old Testament background of Peter's text and that it is describing the renewal rather than abolition of creation, see Richard Bauckham, *2 Peter, Jude* (Dallas: Word, Incorporated, 1983), 325–26: "The cosmic dissolution described in vv. 10, 12, was a return to the primeval chaos, as in the Flood (3:6), so that a new creation may emerge (cf. 4 Ezra 7:30–31). Such passages emphasize the radical discontinuity between the old and the new, but it is nevertheless clear that they intend to describe a renewal, not an abolition, of creation (cf. *1 Enoch* 54:4–5; Rom 8:21),"

[14] For more on the theme of "groaning" in Paul and in his writings' Old Testament background, see Moisés Silva, ed., *New International Dictionary of New Testament Theology and Exegesis* (Grand Rapids, MI: Zondervan, 2014), 365–67. In the background of Paul's eschatological vision lies the Septuagint of Gen 3:16, which portrays God saying, "I will greatly multiply your pain in childbearing; in pain you shall bring forth children." Noting the verbal connection between Romans and the LXX of Genesis, Scott Hahn comments, "Creation, like Adam and Eve, and because of them, is under divine judgment," adding that "Paul also appears to be indebted to the prophets [Isa 26:16–18; Jer 4:31; Hos 13:13; Mic 4:9–10], who used the 'pangs of childbirth' motif to describe the Lord's people in distress." Hahn, *Romans* (Grand Rapids, MI: Baker Academic, 2017), 139. Indeed, in Paul's day many Jews expected that a period of intense suffering would come just before the end of the age, sometimes referred to as the "birth pangs of the Messiah." Craig Keener and John Walton, eds., *NIV Cultural Backgrounds Study Bible: Bringing to Life the Ancient World of Scripture* (Grand Rapids, MI: Zondervan, 2016), 1962.

[15] Brant Pitre, Michael Barber, and John Kincaid, *Paul, a New Covenant Jew: Rethinking Pauline Theology* (Grand Rapids, MI: Eerdmans, 2019), 219.

[16] Hahn, *Romans*, 139. The universal character of God's plan appears already in Gen 9:12, where God tells Noah that he is setting his "bow in the cloud" as a sign of his "covenant which I make between me and you and *every living creature* that is with you, for all future generations" (emphasis added). For a survey and analysis of the biblical view that creation will not be a mere spectator to man's liberation and glorification but rather a participant in it, see Joseph Fitzmyer, *Romans* (New York: Doubleday, 1993), 505–11.

Christ has willed "to reconcile to himself *all things*, whether on earth or in heaven" (Col 1:20, emphasis added; cf. Eph 1:10), Paul insists that believers have a pivotal role to play in this eschatological drama as they "complete what is lacking in Christ's afflictions" (Col 1:24), a marvel described well by Constantine Campbell when he writes, "The sweep of Paul's eschatology includes the entirety of creation. . . . [C]reation is the arena *and object* of God's restorative work. All things in heaven and on earth will be transformed through renewal and unification around Christ."[17]

The above notion underlies the Apostle's personification of creation as a woman crying out in labor pains and as a slave yearning for freedom.[18] By dramatically depicting creation as awaiting the redemption of man, Paul reveals that creation's own "exodus" from death and decay is contingent upon the faithful first attaining this freedom in their own lives.[19] Just as the Jewish world of Paul's day held that all of creation had been tragically drawn into Adam/Israel's ruin, so, too, Paul reveals that the New Adam's glorious redemption is no less cosmic in scope. Indeed, the Apostle envisions creation as the transfigured arena that the coheirs with Christ will inhabit with their resurrected bodies. As Campbell says, "It seems that resurrected human beings will require a new creation in which to live. . . . [T]heir renewed creaturely status will be matched by the renewed creation."[20] Accordingly,

---

[17] Constantine Campbell, *Paul and the Hope of Glory* (Grand Rapids, MI: Zondervan Academic, 2021), 241.

[18] The Old Testament image evoked by Paul in this context is Exod 2:23, where the children of Israel "groaned in their slavery." As N. T. Wright observes, this imagery is part of Paul's larger retelling of the Exodus story in which the Apostle sees both human beings and God's good creation alike as subject to the "slavery" of futility and decay and therefore equally in need of finding freedom through an "exodus." N. T. Wright, *The Resurrection of the Son of God* (Minneapolis: Fortress Press, 2003), 258. For more on the groaning motif in Romans, see also James Dunn, *Romans 1–8*, vol. 38A, *Word Biblical Commentary* (Dallas: Word, Incorporated, 1988), 472–73.

[19] James Dunn suggests an anagogy to explain this vision: "The thought [of creation awaiting the *apokalypsis* or heavenly 'unveiling' of the faithful] may be paralleled to that of a play in which the final curtain is drawn back to reveal the various actors transformed (back) into their real characters—creation being, as it were, the audience eagerly watching the human actors play their parts on the world stage." Dunn, *Romans 1–8*, 470.

[20] Campbell, *Paul and the Hope of Glory*, 235; cf. p. 217. Whether this renewed creation is, strictly speaking, *required* for man's beatitude may be a matter of debate, yet one may at least confidently say that it is supremely fitting that man with his risen body will inhabit a world with other transfigured physical things. For a valuable article that explores Aquinas's teaching that non-human creation is not necessary for man's final beatitude and yet will provide the saints with enjoyment as its transfigured existence leads them to contemplate the glory of God, see Aquinas, *Compendium of Theology* (St. Louis, MO: B. Herder Book Co., 1947), I, 170 and Bryan Kromholtz, O.P., "The Consummation of the World: St. Thomas Aquinas

the created universe is not merely a means by which we humans reach our end in heaven but rather a gift that will accompany us on our journey toward beatitude and truly share in the final perfection of heavenly glory.[21]

CHRIST AND COSMIC TRANSUBSTANTIATION

With the above biblical data in place, we may now consider the theology that Benedict unfolds in its light. In the first installment of his *Jesus* trilogy, Pope Benedict described the Bible's grand eschatological vision as having a "great Christological—indeed, cosmic—dynamism."[22] Meanwhile, in the second volume of the same series, he would write even more boldly:

> If there really is a God, is he not able to create a new dimension of human existence, a new dimension of reality altogether? Is not creation actually waiting for this last and highest "evolutionary leap," for the union of the finite with the infinite, for the union of man and God, for the conquest of death?[23]

In his first Easter homily as pope, Benedict preached along the same lines, using biological terms like "evolution" and "mutation," to describe

---

on the Risen Saints' Beatitude and the Corporeal Universe," which originally appeared in *Nova et Vetera* 19.4 (2021), 1271–87, but is also included in this volume.

[21] Bryan Kromholtz captures a powerful implication of the above teaching when he writes, "It may even be possible that the very quality of *not* being necessary for human beatitude can make the promised eschatological renewal of creatures act as a salutary reminder that there is a higher purpose to the ontological universe than serving us—for God himself is that purpose. . . . Thomas's sharp insistence that human happiness cannot be achieved through material creation points us rightly toward the One on whom our attention should be fixed even in this life." Kromholtz, "The Consummation of the World" (see chapter in this volume). To my mind, this eloquent point regarding the transfigured presence of creatures in heaven further bespeaks the gratuity of God's love. For while man cannot be fulfilled through anything less than God himself, and, strictly speaking, God alone is necessary for our beatitude, the Lord nevertheless allows creatures to contribute in a variety of ways to one another's happiness even now. And in heaven, Aquinas says, nature is not done away with but rather perfected. Aquinas, *ST* II-II, q. 26, a. 13, sc.; Aquinas, *In IV Sent.* d. 49, q. 2, a. 3, ad 8. In light of this, Kromholtz suggests, "The 'joy' that such sensible perception of God's creatures might afford, coexisting with the beatific vision but distinct from it, would likely fall under the category of those delights that follow human reason but do not arise from nature." Kromholtz, "The Consummation of the World"; cf. Aquinas, *ST* I-II, q. 31, a. 3.

[22] Benedict XVI, *Jesus of Nazareth: From the Baptism in the Jordan to the Transfiguration* (New York: Doubleday, 2007), 270.

[23] Benedict XVI, *Jesus of Nazareth: Holy Week: From the Entrance into Jerusalem to the Resurrection* (San Francisco: Ignatius Press, 2011), 246–47.

heavenly life anagogically (as one must always speak when dealing with Last Things):

> If we may borrow the language of the theory of evolution, [Christ's Resurrection] is the greatest "mutation," absolutely the most crucial leap into a totally new dimension that there has ever been in the long history of life and its development: a leap into a completely new order that does concern us, and concerns the whole of history. . . . It is a qualitative leap in the history of "evolution" and of life in general towards a new future life, towards a new world which, starting from Christ, already continuously permeates this world of ours, transforms it and draws it to itself.[24]

As an indication of just how close this theme was to his heart, it is telling that the emeritus pontiff wished to expand upon it in his rare writings penned in retirement. For instance, in one he writes, "If we really wanted to summarize very briefly the content of the Faith as laid down in the Bible, we might do so by saying that the Lord has initiated a narrative of love with us and wants to *subsume all creation* in it. The counterforce against evil, which threatens us and the whole world, can ultimately only consist in our entering into this love."[25] In his landmark volume *Eschatology*, Ratzinger spoke of this state that encompasses all of creation as a "pan-cosmic existence" that leads to "universal exchange and openness, and so to the overcoming of all alienation." Making his own the words of St. Paul, he expounds, "Only where creation achieves such unity can it be true that God is 'all in all' [Eph 1:23] . . . where each thing becomes completely itself precisely by being completely in the other."[26]

In another, even more stunning text—this time a brief post-retirement address given on the sixty-fifth anniversary of his priestly ordination—Benedict went so far as to speak of this transformative dynamic as one of *cosmic transubstantiation*:

> The cross, suffering, all that is wrong with the world: he transformed all this into "thanks" and therefore into a "blessing." Hence

---

24 Benedict XVI, Homily (April 15, 2006).

25 Benedict XVI, "The Church and the Scandal of Sexual Abuse," April 10, 2019 (emphasis added), https://www.ncregister.com/news/pope-benedict-essay-the-church-and-the-scandal-of-sexual-abuse.

26 Ratzinger, *Eschatology: Death and Eternal Life*, trans. Michael Waldstein (Washington, DC: The Catholic University of America Press, 1988), 192; Eph 1:23; Col 1:20.

he fundamentally transubstantiated life and the world [*fondamen-talmente ha transustanziato la vita e il mondo*]. . . . Finally, we wish to insert ourselves into the "thanks" of the Lord, and thus truly receive the newness of life and contribute to the "transubstantiation" of the world [*transustanziazione del mondo*] so that it might not be a place of death, but of life: a world in which love has conquered death.[27]

In this short paragraph, the emeritus pontiff emphasizes that the "transubstantiation of the world" is a reality that has at once already begun and yet which will continue to unfold to the extent that we disciples insert ourselves into Christ's saving work as his co-redeemers.[28]

What, exactly, will it look like in the new heaven and new earth when the entire cosmos is transformed in Christ? The truth is that Scripture reveals to us *that* this is the vocation of all creation, but comprehending *what it means* is another thing. For instance, the above biblical data strongly suggest that whatever good is present in the Ramage family cat and in our backyard orchard will be present in the hereafter in an even more perfect way than it is now ("set free from its bondage to decay" and having obtained "the glorious liberty of the children of God"). Or we might consider the countless bacteria that inhabit our digestive tracts and which we now know to play an indispensable role in keeping us healthy. Seeing as they are so important to our lives here below—as are trees, pets, and innumerable other

---

[27] Benedict XVI, Address at the Commemoration of the 65th Anniversary of the Priestly Ordination of Pope Emeritus Benedict XVI (June 28, 2016), https://w2.vatican.va/content/francesco/en/speeches/2016/june/documents/papa-francesco_20160628_65-ordinazione-sacerdotale-benedetto-xvi.html. Benedict is not the first pontiff to draw out the role of the Eucharist for the transformation of the cosmos. See for example St. John Paul II, *Ecclesia de Eucharistia* (April 17, 2003), §8: "[The celebration of the Eucharist has a] cosmic character. . . . Yes, cosmic! Because even when it is celebrated on the humble altar of a country church, the Eucharist is always in some way celebrated on the altar of the world. It unites heaven and earth. It embraces and permeates all creation. The Son of God became man in order to restore all creation, in one supreme act of praise, to the One who made it from nothing."

[28] For an example of a Pauline text in which this theme appears, see 2 Cor 5:17 ("Therefore, if any one is in Christ, he is a new creation; the old has passed away, behold, the new has come") and Phil 3:20, where Paul says that the true "citizenship" of the believer lies in the heavenly realm even now. For an excellent treatment of the reality that the new creation envisioned by Paul is both already present and still awaiting its completion, see Pitre, Barber, and Kincaid, *Paul, a New Covenant Jew*, 71–73: "Paul affirms that, in some sense, the end of this world and the beginning of the new creation have already taken place. . . . Through the passion, death, resurrection, and exaltation of Christ, the old world was put to death and the new world began. Because of this, believers who are 'in Christ' live in a kind of 'in-between' realm, where the old and new creations 'intermingle' with one another."

creatures—does this give us reason to think that bacteria will exist somehow in heaven?

When pondering these sorts of questions, it is important to remember the words of St. Paul: no eye has seen, no ear heard, and no heart conceived what God has prepared for those who love him (1 Cor 2:9, citing Isa 64:4). Accordingly, Andrew Davison thus speaks of three contrasting ways one may understand the eschatological vision that we are reflecting upon here: the universal resurrection of every living thing, that of certain creatures whose lives became interwoven with particular human stories, and the traditional view that heaven will exclude the presence of all non-human physical beings. In the end, though, none of these seems to precisely coincide with Benedict's position, and at any rate, Davison wisely concludes, "We may do well to leave the discussion at that: speculative eschatological physiology is best avoided."[29] Summing up this matter, Ratzinger likewise says:

> In conclusion: the new world cannot be imagined. Nothing concrete or imaginable can be said about the relation of man to matter in the new world, or about the "risen body." Yet we have the certainty that the dynamism of the cosmos leads towards a goal, a situation in which matter and spirit will belong to each other in a new and definitive fashion. This certainty remains the concrete content of the confession of the resurrection of the flesh even today.[30]

In sum, it is beyond our ken as finite human beings to know whether and how this or that creature might exist on the other side of this vale of tears. Yet what believers do know is that, while our origin is natural, our end is divine—and what awaits us on the other side of death is not less but infinitely more glorious than we could ever imagine.

THE EUCHARIST AS ANTICIPATION AND CAUSE OF CREATION'S MOVEMENT TOWARD DIVINIZATION

Given the overt sacramental language with which Benedict describes the transformation of our world into Christological fullness (transubstantiation, thanksgiving, blessings), we might expect the emeritus pontiff to explicitly discuss the Eucharist somehow in this connection. Indeed, this is precisely

---

[29] Andrew Davison, "Christian Doctrine and Biological Mutualism: Some Explorations in Systematic and Philosophical Theology," *Theology and Science* 18.2 (2020): 258–78 at 270–71.

[30] Ratzinger, *Eschatology*, 194.

what Benedict does on multiple occasions. For instance, he has connected man's divinization to that of the cosmos and suggests that the bridge between the two lies in Eucharistic communion: "I myself become part of the new bread that he is creating by *the resubstantiation of the whole of earthly reality*."[31] To this, he adds that "the very goal of worship *and of creation as a whole* are one and the same—divinization."[32]

Again invoking evolutionary language in an anagogical manner, Benedict writes that God has drawn his creation ever closer to himself through a series of ontological or "evolutionary leaps" in which the transubstantiated host becomes "the anticipation of the transformation and divinization of matter in the Christological fullness" and in turn "provides the movement of the cosmos with its direction; it anticipates its goal and at the same time urges it on."[33] As a final illustration of this point, consider this homily that Benedict gave on the feast of Corpus Christi:

> This little piece of white Host, this bread of the poor, appears to us as a synthesis of creation. In this way, we begin to understand why the Lord chooses this piece of bread to represent him. Creation, with all of its gifts, aspires above and beyond itself to something even greater. Over and above the synthesis of its own forces, above and beyond the synthesis also of nature and of spirit that, *in some way, we detect in the piece of bread, creation is projected towards divinization*, toward the holy wedding feast, toward unification with the Creator himself.[34]

---

[31] Joseph Ratzinger, *Pilgrim Fellowship of Faith* (San Francisco: Ignatius Press, 2005), 78, 118. Emphasis in original.

[32] Ratzinger, *Spirit of the Liturgy* (San Francisco: Ignatius Press, 2000), 28. Emphasis added.

[33] Ratzinger, *Spirit of the Liturgy*. 29. The full paragraph reads: "Against the background of the modern evolutionary world view, Teilhard de Chardin depicted the cosmos as a process of ascent, a series of unions. From very simple beginnings the path leads to ever greater and more complex unities, in which multiplicity is not abolished but merged into a growing synthesis, leading to the 'Noosphere,' in which spirit and its understanding embrace the whole and are blended into a kind of living organism. Invoking the epistles to the Ephesians and Colossians, Teilhard looks on Christ as the energy that strives toward the Noosphere and finally incorporates everything in its 'fullness.' From here Teilhard went on to give a new meaning to Christian worship: the transubstantiated Host is the anticipation of the transformation and divinization of matter in the christological 'fullness.' In his view, the Eucharist provides the movement of the cosmos with its direction; it anticipates its goal and at the same time urges it on."

[34] Benedict XVI, Homily for the Mass of Corpus Christi (June 15, 2006), emphasis added. For some other examples of the pontiff's appropriation of Teilhard de Chardin's cosmic liturgy wherein the whole of creation becomes a living host, see Benedict XVI, Homily (July 24, 2009); Benedict XVI, Homily (April 15, 2006); Ratzinger, *Introduction to Christianity*,

Beyond hinting that the Eucharist plays a central role in the movement of all creation toward divinization, Benedict once again does not say much about what the process might look like concretely. Nor does he suggest how precisely to reconcile a possible eschatological existence of the created world with the likelihood that entropy will eventually cause the physical universe to fizzle out—not with a bang but with a whimper. Indeed, the reason Benedict does not address these topics is because, as we saw above, he simply does not consider it possible to speak much more about what precisely will happen at the end of time. Rather, the only thing we may be able to cogently do is to profess *that* a great cosmic transformation will happen. Nevertheless, I think that we can piece together some of the details by drawing on resources across the broader tradition.

There is an abundance of biblical, patristic, and liturgical backing for Ratzinger's theology of divinization or *theosis*. The writings of the Fathers are one of these resources, where we find this classic formula that runs in many variations throughout the Christian tradition: The Son of God became man so that the sons of men might become God.[35] In this line, we find both the great Christian hope of *divinization* (man's becoming God) along with the reason it is possible: the *hominization* of God—that is, because the eternal Word of God became man. Or, as St. Maximus the Confessor puts it, "By this blessed inversion, man is made God by divinization, and God is made man by hominization."[36] Like so many other Patristic teachings, this majestic teaching is nothing other than an exegesis of biblical texts like 2 Peter 1:3–4 (we are called to "become partakers of the divine nature"), 1 John 3:1–3 ("when he appears we shall be like him, for we shall see him as he is"), Ephesians 3:19 (a prayer that we will "be filled with all the fulness of God"), and 1 Corinthians 15:28 (in the end, God will be "all in all"),[37] which reveal that man's last end is to be totally conformed to God and share in his very life.

234–45; and Ratzinger, *Eschatology*, 93. Notably, Pope Francis cites this very text as part of his ecological vision in his encyclical *Laudato Si'* (June 18, 2015), §236.

[35] For instance, see Athanasius, *On the Incarnation of the Word* (Crestwood, NY: St. Vladimir's Seminary Press, 1993), 93. As I mentioned above, the theme of *theosis* runs throughout the Christian tradition from authors as diverse as St. Peter, Augustine, Pseudo-Dionysius, John of Damascus, Maximus the Confessor, Thomas Aquinas, Thomas à Kempis, Francis de Sales, Benedict XVI, and countless others in between. For a work that surveys St. Augustine's theology of divinization, see David Meconi, S.J., *The One Christ: St. Augustine's Theology of Deification* (Washington, DC: The Catholic University of America Press, 2013).

[36] St. Maximus the Confessor, *On the Cosmic Mystery of Jesus Christ* (Crestwood, NY: St. Vladimir's Seminary Press, 2003), 45–75.

[37] NRSVCE translation.

In addition to Scripture and the Fathers, the liturgy offers an unrivaled treasury of insight into divinization. Among the many liturgical prayers that speak and pray for our divinization that one might recall, consider the words of the offertory rite, uttered *sotto voce* while the priest pours water into the chalice: "By the mystery of this water and wine may we come to share in the divinity of Christ who humbled himself to share in our humanity." In this text, the Church enacts ritually what St. Maximus above described verbally, a dynamic so profound that Benedict describes it as the "mutual compenetration between Christ and the Christian" in which we reside in Christ and Christ in us.[38] Or, to draw from another liturgical prayer, it enacts a change so astounding that we are "transformed into what we consume" and become by grace what Christ is by nature.[39]

As we see here, the text of the liturgy reveals the same dynamic that Benedict describes in his writings: in the act of consecration, ordinary bread miraculously becomes Christ, which in turn becomes the vehicle to gradually transform into Christ those who receive it. Yet, what of the emeritus pontiff's point that in some way *all of creation* is to be divinized? I would suggest that insight into this mystery might be found in the words of the Second Vatican Council and its teaching that the faithful are called to unite themselves with Christ in a liturgical existence and so "consecrate the world itself to God."[40] In other words, our reception of the Eucharist endows us with the power to extend the transforming love of God to the whole world so that it achieves its end. In this way, suggests Benedict, we the faithful contribute to the "transubstantiation" or "resubstantiation" of the cosmos.

THE INEVITABLE LIMITATIONS OF THIS ANAGOGY

Of course, all analogies and anagogies fall short of reality at some point, and the ones developed here are no exception. To understand their grandeur, we must therefore reiterate that the eschatological transformation of creation or "evolutionary leap" that we are discussing is such by way of an anagogy to that of biological evolution in this world. A number of observations bear this out. For instance, biological evolution transpires across immensely long intervals whereas creation's definitive leap will only occur at the end of time.

---

[38] Benedict XVI, "St. Paul's New Outlook," General Audience (November 8, 2006); Rom 8:1–2,10, 39; 12:5; 16:3, 7, 10; 1 Cor 1:2–3; 2 Cor 13:5; Gal 2:20. See also Bl. Columba Marmion, *Christ in His Mysteries* (St. Louis, MO: Herder, 1924), 54–55: "All Christian life, all holiness, is being by grace what Jesus is by nature: the Son of God."

[39] Roman Missal, Prayer after Communion for the 27th Sunday of Ordinary Time.

[40] Second Vatican Council, *Lumen Gentium*, §§34, 11; cf. 1 Pet 2:5.

What is more, whereas in biological evolution the biological life of individuals comes to an end through death, in the graced transfiguration of man and the cosmos, creatures do not pass away but rather attain definitive life and become more truly themselves precisely by being united with God—man remaining completely united to and yet distinct from the rest of creation as its crown and steward.[41] Finally, in contrast with earlier stages of evolution, it must be emphasized that this definitive "leap" will not occur naturally or within the present physical universe. It involves, as Ratzinger says, movement to a quite different plane of existence altogether: that of "definitive" life [*zoe*] where the blessed have "left behind the rule of death."[42] This transformation is therefore neither the kind of thing that will simply happen if we leave nature to itself nor something that we can achieve through technological progress on this side of eternity.

While we are on the subject of this anagogy's limitations, it may also be helpful to recall an emphasis of Benedict that helps to avoid a misunderstanding of creation's "divinization." For, as he and other recent pontiffs have taught, to speak of the divinization of creation is not to say that creation itself should be worshipped. While extolling the beauty and dignity of creation, Benedict rather emphasizes that creation ought not to be made into an idol that man cannot "subdue" (Gen 1:28) and "keep" (Gen 2:15) as its lawful steward. Indeed, the emeritus pontiff insists that it is part of our vocation as humans to "collaborate in God's work, in the evolution that

---

[41] Without digressing into a deep Thomistic discussion of this topic, it is worth observing that the Angelic Doctor has resources that are helpful in the endeavor to clarify the uniqueness of man in relation to the rest of creation even in its "divinized" state. For instance, Thomas deploys the notion of obediential potency as a way to explain the miraculous glorification of the cosmos and its distinction from the elevation of the rational creature man at the end of time. See for example Aquinas, *In 4 Sent.*, d. 48, q. 2, a. 1, ad 3 and ad 4, in Aquinas, *Commentary on the Sentences, Book IV, Distinctions 43–50*, trans. Beth Mortensen and Dylan Schrader (Lander, WY: Aquinas Institute for the Study of Sacred Doctrine, 2018). Explaining the difference between the transformation of man and that of other creatures at the end of time, Lawrence Feingold explains, "Non-spiritual natures cannot receive spiritual perfections without losing their irrational nature and receiving a new spiritual nature. Spiritual creatures, on the contrary, can receive new spiritual perfections above their nature without losing their nature! This is the most sublime dignity of man. Thus spiritual creatures have transcendent obediential potencies that are unique to them." Feingold, *The Natural Desire to See God According to St. Thomas and His Interpreters* (Ave Maria, FL: Sapientia Press, 2004), 112. I am grateful to Aaron Henderson for putting me on to these last pair of texts and for fruitful conversation on the topic. For a penetrating treatment of Aquinas's thought concerning the resurrection and restoration of the cosmos, see also Bryan Kromholtz, O.P., *On the Last Day: The Time of the Resurrection of the Dead, according to Thomas Aquinas* (Fribourg: Academic Press Fribourg, 2010).

[42] Ratzinger, *Introduction to Christianity*, 304 (*Einführung in das Christentum*, 286).

he ordered in the world [*all'opera di Dio, all'evoluzione che Egli ha posto nel mondo*]"—a role we fulfill by protecting creation, developing its gifts, and leading it towards its fulfillment in Christ on the Last Day.[43]

CONCLUSION: RATZINGER'S ANAGOGY AS AN ENCOURAGEMENT FOR CHRISTIAN HOPE

Despite these misunderstandings to avoid and distinctions that must be made, I have found Ratzinger's evolutionary anagogy to bear immense value for fostering Christian hope in a world so often bereft of it. For instance, it reminds us that eternal life will be a truly incarnate communion between man and God—one that takes place not in the vacuum of space but rather in a real world where our resurrected bodies interact with other transfigured creatures. Further, to develop a line from C. S. Lewis, pondering the sublime destiny of all creation has a very "practical" implication: just as pondering our neighbor's divine calling should lead us to recognize his dignity all the more even now, so, too, should contemplating the dignity of creation impel us to appreciate and care more deeply for the marvelous world in which we live—a theme dear to our recent pontiffs and reflected in the teachings of the Second Vatican Council.[44]

Another tangible consequence of the present reflection is that it offers a powerful motive for Christian hope by helping believers to grapple with the mystery of suffering and death in their daily lives—much of which is integral to the evolutionary dynamic. For whereas naturalistic accounts of evolution posit that its processes terminate in the death of individuals with no hope of future restoration, Benedict's thoroughly Christian alternative invites us to ponder how glorious our expectation truly is. Like Jesus's image of the grain of wheat that bears no fruit unless it "dies" (John 12:24) and St. Paul's teaching that a body sown into the ground perishable is raised imperishable (1 Cor 15:42–54), Benedict's anagogy of creation's final "evolutionary leap" should lift our gaze to the things of heaven, pondering the reality that God

---

[43] Benedict XVI, Meeting with the Clergy of the Dioceses of Bolzano-Bressanone (August 6, 2008); cf. Benedict XVI, *Caritas in Veritate* (July 7, 2009), §48, and Ramage, *The Experiment of Faith*, 185–89.

[44] C. S. Lewis discusses the "practical use" of speculating on the eternal destiny of man in *The Weight of Glory, and Other Addresses* (New York: Macmillan, 1980), 45. As the Second Vatican Council teaches, "[T]he expectation of a new earth must not weaken but rather stimulate our concern for cultivating this one." *Gaudium et Spes*, §39. For more on recent papal teaching on the importance of care for creation and a discussion of Pope Francis's designation of it as a corporal and spiritual work of mercy, see Ramage, *The Experiment of Faith*, ch. 9.

has been at work guiding our evolving universe for billions of years with the goal of eventually leading all of his creatures to a state that transcends our existence in this world with all of the suffering and death that it entails—a transformation or "transubstantiation" made possible not *despite* but *precisely by* undergoing these trials in union with Jesus Christ and the rest of creation.

On a personal note, I have found this imagery of cosmic transubstantiation so fruitful for navigating all the sufferings of my life over the past two decades that I have been meditating on it. For, as with the bread and wine offered at Mass, the fact that we are being "transubstantiated" into Christ does not cause our daily existence to lose its apparently mundane character. No matter how much we might offer up a hectic day at work, disappointment at school, strife within our family, or struggle with an illness, the "accidents" of our suffering do not simply go away. Yet, as I have learned, especially through having to deal with myriad sources of pain every day since coming down with lupus half my life ago, the act of offering up such things—bearing the cross joyfully—does change the inner character of the experience from one of rebellion to one of sanctification.[45]

So it was with the passion of Jesus Christ, "the pioneer and perfecter of our faith" (Heb 12:2) who "in every respect has been tempted as we are, yet without sinning" (Heb 4:15). The victory of our Lord on the Cross did not immediately destroy suffering, but rather what it did was to endow it with redemptive power. In his life, death, and Resurrection, Christ began the work of transubstantiation. Having changed bread and wine into his Body and Blood, he now wishes to transform us into his nature through grace. And we, in turn, now have the joyful duty of bringing his work to completion by consecrating the world—our joys, our sorrows, our work, our families, our entire being—to God.

---

[45] While not engaged in the same overall project as I am here in this essay, I find that this dynamic is captured well by David Fagerberg when he speaks of the liturgy having the transformative power to "anchor the substance of our lives" and of the possibility of reaching a point where "the substance of the liturgy becomes the substance of the soul." See Fagerberg, *Liturgical Mysticism* (Steubenville, OH: Emmaus Academic, 2019).

"Hear What the Spirit Says to the Churches":

On Reading the Apocalypse Apocalyptically

WILLIAM M. WRIGHT IV
Duquesne University, PA

FOR A WRITING largely comprised of symbolic, heavenly visions, the Book of Revelation begins firmly on earth. John the Visionary explicitly reports being on the Greek island of Patmos when he receives his visions (Rev 1:9). He also relates that he was commissioned by the glorified Jesus to compose his book and circulate it among seven churches in west Roman Asia (1:11). Before the heavenly visions begin in 4:1, there are seven messages from the glorified Jesus, one for each of these seven churches. As has been explored, these letters to the seven churches in Revelation 2–3 contain numerous allusions to the local traditions and situations of each city.[1]

The seven letters explicitly invite their audiences to hear the Lord Jesus speaking to them in each of the compositions. Each letter introduces Jesus's words with the oracular formula "thus says," (Greek: τάδε λέγει), a phrase which is a frequent LXX rendering of the introductory formula of a prophetic oracle: "Thus says the Lord" (LXX: τάδε λέγει κύριος; Heb: כה אמר יהוה). Each letter ends with the exhortation "He who has an ear, let him hear what the Spirit says to the churches" (Rev 2:7). In this essay, I wish to

---

[1] See Colin J. Hemer, *The Letters to the Seven Churches of Asia in Their Local Setting* (Sheffield: JSOT Press, 1986; repr. Grand Rapids and Livonia: Eerdmans and Dove Booksellers, 2001).

examine the letters to the seven churches and identify cues in the text by which Revelation invites its audience to receive it so as to hear "what the Spirit says to the churches." More specifically, I will highlight ways in which the seven letters open up the Book of Revelation and lead the audience to understand this composition and their own particular situations in figural ways that can be justifiably labeled as apocalyptic.

I. READING "APOCALYPTICALLY"

A basic tenet in Christian biblical interpretation is that the biblical texts and the realities they mediate have dimensions of meaning beyond the obvious and the original. Theologically, recognition of this point flows primarily from the Resurrection of Jesus. The New Testament writings variously associate Jesus's resurrection with a new way of interpreting Scripture. Many examples of this can be cited with perhaps the most memorable being the Resurrection appearances in Luke 24. Here the risen Jesus enables the disciples traveling to Emmaus, as well as those disciples to whom he appears on Easter Sunday evening, to understand the Scriptures with reference to himself (Luke 24:27, 32, 45).

The resurrection of the dead was a staple belief in sectors of Jewish eschatology and apocalypticism in particular.[2] The Resurrection of Jesus can be identified as an apocalyptic event in several respects. In terms of temporal eschatology, the Resurrection is an end-time event which attends the passing away of the "present evil age" and the permanent in-breaking into the world of the "future age to come" (or the kingdom of God or the new creation). Thus, soon after speaking of Christ who "was raised," Paul writes, "if any one is in Christ, he is a new creation; the old has passed away, behold, the new has come" (2 Cor 5:15, 17).

While apocalypticism deals in temporal eschatology, it is important, as Christopher Rowland reminds us, to regard apocalypticism primarily in the terms which its etymology suggests: that is, the revelation of heavenly mysteries. Rowland writes, "The key to the whole movement is that God reveals his mysteries directly to man and thereby gives them knowledge of the true nature of reality so that they may organize their lives accordingly."[3] Thus when Paul talks about his encounter with the risen Jesus in Galatians

---

[2]   For discussion, see Jon D. Levenson, *Resurrection and the Restoration of Israel: The Ultimate Victory of the God of Life* (New Haven: Yale University Press, 2006); N. T. Wright, *The Resurrection of the Son of God* (Minneapolis: Fortress Press, 2003).

[3]   Christopher Rowland, *The Open Heaven: A Study of Apocalyptic in Judaism and Early Christianity* (New York: Crossroad, 1982), 11.

1:15–16, he speaks of it as an apocalyptic revelation of Jesus's divine Sonship: "He who had set me apart before I was born, and had called me through his grace, was pleased to reveal [ἀποκαλύψαι] his Son to me." The Paschal Mystery, in this sense, is an apocalyptic event which reveals aspects of Jesus's identity and accomplishments which are accessible neither before his Resurrection or apart from its illumination.

When we recognize the revelational aspects of Jesus's Resurrection as an apocalyptic event, we can also see that the new way of interpreting Scripture in light of his Resurrection is likewise apocalyptic. In other words, post-Resurrection Christian biblical hermeneutics are apocalyptic hermeneutics. Orthodox theologian John Behr has made this point as regards early Christian exegesis, which he labels as "apocalyptic."[4] He sums up the apocalyptic dimensions ingredient to this interpretive mode: "Both Jesus of Nazareth, whom we thought we knew, and the meaning of Scriptures, which we thought we understood, turn out to be other than what we had thought, when the veil is lifted and the glory of Christ shines in Scripture through the cross, so revealing his true and eternal identity."[5] According to Behr, recognition of the fundamentally apocalyptic nature of Christian exegesis serves to remind us to place the revelation of the crucified and risen Jesus at the front and center of our interpretation. He writes, "What is important is not to define the right method or strategy for reading these texts, but that they are read *as Scripture*, that is within an apocalyptic framework pivoted upon the cross."[6]

With these considerations in mind, I will turn to the letters to the seven churches in Revelation 2–3 and examine how the Book of Revelation, in these passages, leads its audience to understand itself, their own situations, and indeed the whole of reality apocalyptically—that is, in light of the risen Jesus—and in so doing, "hear what the Spirit says to the churches."

II. LETTERS TO THE SEVEN CHURCHES

There are three elements in the seven letters that I wish to highlight as factoring into an apocalyptic mode of understanding: first, the opening appearance of the glorified Jesus and its framing of the seven letters; second, the circular character of the seven letters; third, the revelatory aspects of the letters which invite figural reading.

---

[4] John Behr, *John the Theologian and His Paschal Gospel* (New York and Oxford: Oxford University Press, 2019), 130.

[5] Behr, *John the Theologian*, 130.

[6] Behr, *John the Theologian*, 130.

A. The Authority of the Son of Man in Glory

John tells us in Revelation 1 that while he was on Patmos, the Holy Spirit took him up into ecstatic rapture, and in this rapture, John had a vision of the exalted Jesus, the Son of Man in glory (1:12–20).[7] John's description of the glorified Son of Man combines an array of images from Scripture and Greco-Roman culture which coalesce together in dizzying effect. At a basic level, this opening vision of the glorified Jesus is a revelation, an ἀποκάλυψις.

This vision of the glorified Jesus granted to John is also a theophany. Several elements in the vision identify Jesus as divine and as possessing divine authority. For instance, the descriptor "his head and his hair were white as white wool, white as snow" (Rev 1:14) identifies the glorified Son of Man with the enthroned Ancient of Days in Daniel 7:9 (thus combining in himself two figures from Dan 7). The appearance's theophanic character is underscored by John's response upon seeing Jesus ("I fell at his feet as though dead"), and Jesus then speaking the customary words of reassurance: "Fear not" (1:17).[8] Jesus's self-identification, "I am the first and the last" (v. 17) squares with the self-identification of the Lord God (i.e., the Father) in 1:8, "I am the Alpha and the Omega."

This manifestation of Jesus's deity reveals his complete and total authority over all, and it connects Jesus's authority to his death, Resurrection, and exaltation. When Jesus speaks to John, he says of himself: I am "the living one; I died, and behold I am alive for evermore, and I have the keys of Death and Hades" (1:18). The pattern here—"I died" then "I am alive for evermore" then "I have the keys"—maps the sequence of his death, Resurrection, and exaltation. This same pattern was established in 1:5 where Jesus was introduced as "the faithful witness [i.e., his death], the first-born of the dead [i.e., his Resurrection], and the ruler of the kings on earth [i.e., his exaltation]." The Son of Man also has "in his right hand . . . seven stars" (1:16). This image likely refers to iconography associated with the Roman emperor, for

---

[7] On the label of John's experience as "rapture" and comparative analysis with similar charismatic experiences in the biblical tradition, see Richard Bauckham, *The Climax of Prophecy: Studies on the Book of Revelation* (Edinburgh: T & T Clark, 1993), 150–59.

[8] The command "not to fear" in the heavenly revelations or theophanies, for instance, to Abraham (Gen 15:1); Isaac (26:24); Jacob (46:3). Moreover, in the theophanies to the patriarchs, the command not to fear is followed by a statement wherein God identifies himself with an "I am" statement—a further point of connection with Rev 1:17–18 where Jesus declares, "Fear not, I am the first and the last, and the living one." See William M. Wright IV, *The Bible and Catholic Ressourcement: Essays on Scripture and Theology* (Steubenville, OH: Emmaus Academic, 2019), 169–71.

numismatic evidence from Domitian's reign depict the emperor's son surrounded by seven stars.[9]

The opening of Revelation gives us to see that the crucified and risen Jesus has total authority over his enemies, spiritual and material. The pair "Death and Hades" (of which Jesus has the keys; see 1:18) later appear in Revelation 20:13–14 where they are forced to give up the dead at the general resurrection and are themselves then condemned to "the lake of fire." The designation of the crucified and risen Jesus as "the ruler of kings on earth" (1:5) establishes him as having sovereignty over all worldly powers. The "kings on earth" appear elsewhere in Revelation as those with power in the world who ally themselves with the Beasts and the Harlot.[10] Revelation further displays contrasting fates of the kings of the earth: they are slain by Jesus's word in 19:21, but later appear in 21:24 as bringing tribute to the new Jerusalem.[11]

The appearance of the glorified Jesus leads into and connects with the seven letters in a variety of ways. First, the opening vision presents Jesus as standing among seven golden lampstands, which are later interpreted to signify "the seven churches" (1:20). The risen Jesus is present to his churches, and he knows their situations in detail. Second, the glorified Jesus commands John to "write" the contents of this revelation to these seven churches. This command is given explicitly in 1:11, 19 and then at the start of each letter (see 2:1, 8, 12, 18; 3:1, 7, 14). Third, the seven letters themselves often refer back to this opening vision. Most prominently, each of the seven letters identifies Jesus as the speaker in the letter and does so by referencing some details in the opening vision. Thus, the first letter (to the church at Ephesus) begins, "The words of him who holds the seven stars in his right hand, who walks among the seven golden lampstands" (2:1). And if the Ephesian church does not repent, Jesus threatens to "remove your lampstand from its place" (2:5).

The literary form of the letters similarly connects back to the opening vision and befits its display of the risen Jesus's supreme authority. The letters

---

[9] For discussion and visuals of pertinent numismatic evidence, see Craig R. Koester, *Revelation*, Anchor Yale Bible Commentary 38A (New Haven and London: Yale University Press, 2014), 253; David L. Barr, *Tales of the End: A Narrative Commentary on the Book of Revelation*, 2nd ed. (Salem, OR: Polebridge Press, 2012), 74–75.

[10] See Rev. 6:15; 17:2; 18:3, 9; 19:19; 21:24. Koester, *Revelation*, 227: "The kings of the earth are not inherently evil, but they are deceived by the agents of evil." See also Bauckham, *Climax of Prophecy*, 313–16.

[11] Koester comments on these two fates of the kings of the earth in *Revelation*, 227: "These contrasting visions are not predictions of the kings' destruction or redemption . . . rather, they show the outcomes of differing responses to Christ."

all exhibit the same structural format. But this format is unlike any of the other epistolary literature in the New Testament. As David Aune has argued, the seven letters blend two known ancient literary forms.[12] Structurally, these letters resemble, Aune argues, the format of "ancient royal or imperial edict."[13] This aspect of the letters' literary form contributes to the presentation of Jesus's sovereignty by appropriating the format of authoritative decrees issued by royal authorities in antiquity. When Jesus addresses the seven churches, he addresses them as the divine King and Judge. His identity as divine King and Judge dovetails with a second literary form exhibited in the letters, a form which Aune calls "paranetic salvation-judgment oracles."[14] The letters are prophetic messages of exhortation in which Jesus commends Christians for their good behavior and reprimands them for their sins and failures. He summons Christians to repent of their sins and to remain faithful and, in this way, "conquer" or "be victorious." To the conquering victors, Jesus promises eschatological rewards, heavenly blessings which he has the authority to bestow.

And so, the revelation of the Son of Man in glory is a theophanic revelation which displays the total and complete authority of Jesus over all. The vision provides many of the essential components for understanding the letters, and the letters continually refer back to this vision. These letters which Jesus instructs John to write are royal statements, issued by the Lord Jesus, who is present to the churches and speaks to them through John. The opening vision of the exalted Jesus in glory provides the horizon or context within which the seven letters are to be received and interpreted. The opening vision is a revelation, an ἀποκάλυψις, and the letters are to be received in its light. In other words, the letters are to be interpreted apocalyptically.

B. Circularity

The circular character of the seven letters also contributes to an apocalyptic mode of interpretation. This is because the circularity implies a hermeneutical principle which is ingredient to the Book of Revelation itself.

At a macro level, the Book of Revelation is formatted as a circular letter. It contains an epistolary greeting in 1:4–5 which identifies the sender and recipients and also includes a trinitarian greeting: "John to the seven

---

12   David E. Aune, "The Form and Function of the Proclamations to the Seven Churches (Revelation 2–3)," *NTS* 36 (1990): 182–204; repr. in David E. Aune, *Apocalypticism, Prophecy, and Magic in Early Christianity: Collected Essays* (Grand Rapids: Baker Academic, 2008), 212–32. Page references are to the reprinted text in the 2008 Baker Academic volume.

13   Aune, "Form and Function," 213; italics removed.

14   Aune, "Form and Function," 226; italics removed.

churches that are in Asia: Grace to you and peace from him who is and who was and who is to come, and from the seven spirits who are before his throne, and from Jesus Christ."[15] Revelation similarly ends with an epistolary closing in 22:21: "The grace of the Lord Jesus be with all the saints. Amen."

This epistolary framing indicates that Revelation was meant to be shared among multiple readerships. The New Testament gives ample evidence that early Christian churches circulated writings among themselves.[16] This exchange of writings between churches led to the writings being read aloud in each other's liturgical assemblies (see Col 4:16)—and Revelation is especially conscious of liturgy as the setting in which it is to be read (see Rev 1:3). The exchange of writings between churches also led to the formation of collections of writings (see 2 Pet 3:16). As Luke Johnson has argued, the circulation and collection of texts by different churches evidence a hermeneutical principle: "By collecting and copying texts originally composed for others, and by reading these in its own assembly, a community asserts the relevance for itself of that which was written for others: the particular bears the possibility of becoming general."[17] That is to say, a writing which was originally destined for one audience comes to be interpreted as meaningful to other audiences in different times and places.

This same principle holds for the seven letters in particular. The seven letters exhibit concern for both specificity and generality. On the one hand, as mentioned earlier, each of these letters is addressed to a specific church in Roman Asia. In each letter, the glorified Jesus speaks to that church's present situation, often with allusions to its city's local traditions and circumstances. At the same time, each letter is also embedded within a larger circular composition, which is read by many. As a result, a letter written to an individual church will also be read by all the other churches who receive the book.

Moreover, each letter invites all audiences to hear the voice of the Spirit speaking to them in it. Repeated verbatim at the end of each letter is the exhortation: "He who has an ear, let him hear what the Spirit says to the churches" (2:7). The exhortation declares that, in a letter addressed to one particular church, the Spirit is speaking in the present moment [Greek: λέγει] to all the church-*es* (ἐκκλησίας). Thus, in a letter primarily intended

---

[15] Same pair "grace and peace" enjoyed wide use in New Testament epistolography. The phrase appears in all the Pauline letters, both Petrine letters, and 2 John 3.

[16] As to the circulation and collection of writings, as well as the hermeneutical principles which this process involves, I am indebted here to Luke Timothy Johnson, *The Writings of the New Testament*, 3rd ed. (Minneapolis: Fortress Press, 2010), 526–33, esp. 527–29.

[17] Johnson, *Writings*, 528.

for one church in one specific city, the Spirit speaks to all "the churches" (plural), that is, to audiences in times and places other than the primarily intended one. In this way, the seven letters speak to an original audience and also transcend it to speak to a broader range of audiences in other circumstances.

Indeed, the situations of these seven churches are different. Craig Koester has helpfully shown that these problems of the churches in these seven letters can be grouped into three typical categories: problems of "assimilation," "persecution," and "complacency."[18] The problem which besets the churches in Ephesus, Sardis, and Laodicea is that some Christians there are becoming cold and lax in living their faith on account of their socio-economic prosperity. The churches of Pergamum and Thyatira are dealing with the problem of illicit accommodation to pagan culture that false prophets are promoting in the churches there. It is only with the churches at Smyrna and Philadelphia that the problem of external persecutions appears, and in both cases, it stems from local Jewish groups who, while the details are not clear, are arguably denouncing Christians to Roman authorities.[19] Yet despite these differences, the Spirit speaks to all the churches in each of the letters.

And so, the circular character of the seven letters exemplifies the larger rhetorical strategy whereby the Book of Revelation opens itself up to be received and interpreted by audiences in different places, times, and settings. Through the seven letters, the Spirit speaks to a specific, primarily intended audience and also to audiences who live in other, likely different, situations. In this way, the Book of Revelation opens itself up to be received and interpreted by Christian audiences beyond the original. The contents of this book are intentionally presented as pertinent and meaningful to Christians in general—and not limited to a single church community at a specific moment in time. Rather, the Book of Revelation is meant to be shared and received by a variety of Christian audiences, all of whom are invited to hear in a writing, even if primarily intended for someone else, the Spirit speaking to them in their present moment as well.

Much can be said about the ways in which Revelation presents the Spirit speaking to the churches.[20] One way in which the seven letters inscribe this

[18] Craig R. Koester, *Revelation and the End of All Things* (Grand Rapids: Eerdmans, 2001), 57, 63, 66; formatting adjusted. For further discussion, see Koester, *Revelation*, 96–103.

[19] For discussion of these conflicts with local Jewish groups and the possibility of their serving as *delatores* against Christians in the Roman legal system, see Hemer, *Letters to the Seven Churches*, 9–10, 66–68. David E. Aune, *Revelation 1–5*, Word Biblical Commentary 52A (Dallas: Word Books, 1997), 162–63; Adela Yarbro Collins, *Crisis & Catharsis: The Power of the Apocalypse* (Philadelphia: The Westminster Press, 1984), 85–87.

[20] On the Holy Spirit in Revelation, see Bauckham, *Climax of Prophecy*, 150–73, and *Theology*

invitation to hear the Spirit speaking to them is by Jesus revealing to the churches the spiritual dimensions (and thus the reality) of their situations. These revelations invite the audience to interpret their situations figurally in light of both episodes in Scripture (i.e., reading backward) and the visions and images to come later in the book (i.e., reading forward). It is to the reve-latory components of the letters and their invitation to read figurally that I now turn.

C. Revelatory Character Leading to Figural Reading

As we have seen, the opening vision of the Son of Man in glory (1:12–20) is a revelation, an ἀποκάλυψις, of the risen Jesus and his total authority, and this vision provides hermeneutical framing for the seven letters. These letters are apocalyptic not only in that they follow upon and continue the display of the exalted Jesus, but they are also, in a sense, revelations to the churches them-selves. The exalted Jesus speaks to these churches and lays bare the hidden, spiritual dimensions of their situations and struggles. One might say that in these letters, the risen Jesus reveals the churches to themselves.[21]

Much of what Jesus reveals to the churches concerns their present situa-tions. The most dramatic revelations are those cases where what Jesus reveals to be the reality of the churches' state before God stands in marked contrast to how they seem to be doing in the world. This appears most vividly in the contrasts between the churches which are undergoing persecutions yet remain faithful and the churches which are socio-economically prosperous but are spiritually cold and complacent.

The churches at Smyrna and Philadelphia are the ones experiencing local persecutions. Moreover, the church at Smyrna is said to be econom-ically poor (2:9), and the church at Philadelphia has "little power" (3:8). And yet, despite their poor socio-economic conditions and sufferings, the spiritual situation of these churches is quite the opposite. Jesus tells the Smyrnean Christians that they are, in fact, "rich" (2:9), arguably because they are suffering on account of their relationship with Jesus and their endur-ing faithfulness to him. Moreover, Jesus promises the powerless yet faithful Philadelphian church two things: first, he will humble their persecutors

---

of the Book of Revelation (Cambridge: Cambridge University Press, 1993), 109–25.

[21] I think of the following text of Second Vatican Council, Pastoral Constitution on the Church in the Modern World *Gaudium et Spes* (Dec. 7, 1965), §22: "The truth is that only in the mys-tery of the incarnate Word does the mystery of man take on light. For Adam, the first man, was a figure of Him Who was to come, namely Christ the Lord. Christ, the final Adam, by the revelation of the mystery of the Father and His love, fully reveals man to man him-self and makes his supreme calling clear," https://www.vatican.va/archive/hist_councils/ ii_vatican_council/documents/vat-ii_const_19651207_gaudium-et-spes_en.html.

before them: "I will make them come and bow down before your feet" (3:9); second, Jesus will hold fast this church in the time of eschatological testing because they have held fast to Jesus's word in time of suffering (3:10). So while these two churches are poor, powerless, and persecuted, Jesus reveals that they are in fact spiritually rich, powerful, and held fast by him—all this because they are vibrantly faithful to Jesus and enduring persecutions on account of him.

By contrast, the letters to the churches at Laodicea and Sardis speak to communities that enjoy socio-economic prosperity and acceptance in their cities. However, on account of their comfortable circumstances, these communities have grown complacent and lax and are on the point of death. To the successful church at Laodicea, Jesus delivers the strongest reprimand and the most striking revelation: "For you say, I am rich, I have prospered, and I need nothing; not knowing that you are wretched, pitiable, poor, blind, and naked" (3:17). Despite their wealth and prosperity, this church is "lukewarm" (3:16) and in desperate need of what Jesus offers them. Similarly, the church at Sardis has the reputation of being a lively community, but because of its complacency, it is on the verge of spiritual death: "You have the name of being alive, and you are dead. Awake, and strengthen what remains and is on the point of death" (3:1–2). Jesus summons them to deeper conversion and obedience to the faith which they received (3:3).

Ingredient to these revelations to the churches is a mode of understanding that comes by way of figural interpretation. These revelations from Jesus invite the churches to interpret and so understand their situations by way of a figural reading of both Scripture and the visions to come later in the book (i.e., reading backward and reading forward).[22]

On the one hand, the seven letters lead the churches to understand their present with an eye to the past by interpreting their situations through a figural reading of the Old Testament. This appears, for instance, with the two false prophets, who are given the symbolic names "Balaam" (2:14) and "Jez'ebel" (2:20) in the letters to Pergamum and Thyatira respectively. Both figures, it seems, are early Christian prophets who are permitting or advocating Christians to eat meat from animals sacrificed to pagan deities. By giving these symbolic names to the two prophetic figures, the letters discern

---

[22] See also David E. Aune, "Charismatic Exegesis in Early Judaism and Early Christianity," in *The Pseudepigrapha and Early Biblical Interpretation*, eds. J. H. Charlesworth and C. A. Evans (Sheffield: Sheffield University Press, 1993); repr. in David E. Aune, *Apocalypticism, Prophecy, and Magic in Early Christianity: Collected Essays* (Grand Rapids, MI: Baker Academic, 2008), 280–99.

a connection between situations in the churches' present time with individuals from the biblical past.

In the letter to Pergamum, Jesus reprimands some Christians there "who hold the teaching of Balaam, who taught Balak to put a stumbling block before the sons of Israel, that they might eat food sacrificed to idols and practice immorality" (2:14).[23] Appearing in Numbers 22–24, Balaam, the son of Beor, is a famous Mesopotamian prophet and diviner, whom King Balak of Moab enlists to put a curse on the Israelites encamped near him. While given four opportunities to curse the Israelites, Balaam instead pronounces four oracular blessings on them at the behest of the LORD—and much to the dismay of King Balak. Immediately following this episode in the narrative of Numbers is the account of some Israelites' participation in the ritual worship of Ba'al through their sexual relationships with Moabite women: these women "invited the people to the sacrifices of their gods, and the people ate, and bowed down to their gods. So Israel yoked himself to Ba'al of Peor" (Num 25:2–3). While Balaam does not appear in Numbers 25, he is mentioned in Numbers 31:16 as being the instigator of this apostasy: "These [Moabite women] caused the sons of Israel, by the counsel of Balaam, to act treacherously against the LORD in the matter of Peor."

A similar indictment is leveled in the letter to Thyatria. Here, the church is reprimanded by Jesus for tolerating a false prophet given the name "Jez'ebel," whose teachings some Christians have started to follow. Similar to "Balaam," the prophet "Jez'ebel," Jesus says, "is teaching and beguiling [πλανᾷ] my servants to practice immorality and to eat food sacrificed to idols" (Rev 2:20).[24] The association of Jez'ebel in Thyatira with "immorality [πορνεῦσαι]" (2:20) most likely picks up 2 Kings 9:22 where Jehu speaks of "the "harlotries [LXX: αἱ πορνεῖαι] and the sorceries" of Jez'ebel, which "are so many." In this way, the text calls attention to the actions of Queen Jez'ebel to promote the worship of Ba'al in Israel. Unlike "Balaam," Jesus has more to say about "Jez'ebel": he gives her the opportunity to repent, but she is refusing to do so; thus, he threatens to strike down Jez'ebel and those who follow her teachings (Rev 2:20–22).

Through these links, the letters invite their audiences to interpret figurally the Old Testament and their present moments in light of each other. The figural connections between John's contemporaries and the Old Testament personages reveal that the same spiritual realities, which were manifest with

---

[23] It is not clear whether "immorality" or "fornication" [Greek: πορνεύω] (2:14) in the seven letters means idolatry, sexual sin, or perhaps both. See Aune, *Revelation 1–5*, 188.

[24] The Greek verb πλανάω appears in LXX Deut 13:6 to designate the activity of a false prophet.

Balaam and Jez'ebel in the Old Testament, are again being instantiated in these first-century false prophets. Balaam and Jez'ebel, whether in ancient Israel or in John's day, come to light as agents of apostasy. John's audience occupies the same position as the Israelites in the biblical narrative, who are confronted by these agents and must respond. Within the divine economy, there are (to employ the phrase of Lewis Ayres and Stephen Fowl) "persistent patterns of figuration," and John's first-century audience participates in the same economy of salvation as the ancient Israelites.[25] Through these figural associations, the audience of Revelation is invited to see themselves within the horizon of the biblical narrative and interpret it figurally in light of the revelation of Jesus.

This same strategy for "reading backward" has a correlate strategy in Revelation for "reading forward." As the seven letters invite the churches to understand themselves in terms of the biblical narrative, so also do the letters position the churches to understand themselves in light of the images to come later in Revelation.

An important way in which the seven letters do this is by introducing details, images, and motifs which are later developed and displayed in the heavenly visions (Rev 4:1–22:5). Examples of this technique appear in the promise of a heavenly reward to the victor or conqueror which ends each of the seven letters. Revelation regularly uses the conventionally Johannine term "to conquer" (Greek: νικάω), a term which connotes victory in both military and athletic contests.[26] Jesus himself is said to "conquer" in both the seven letters and the heavenly visions. In the letter to Laodicea, Jesus says, "I myself conquered and sat down with my Father on his throne" (3:21). This statement connects with the vision of heaven in Revelation 5 and its identification of the messianic "Lion of the tribe of Judah [who] . . . has conquered" with the Lamb who was slain (5:5–6). The conquering language also sets up the victory that Jesus wins at the Parousia by putting down his enemies simply by his word (17:14; 19:21).

What was announced in the opening vision and the seven letters is, therefore, displayed in the visions that follow: Jesus conquers through his faithfulness unto death and his Resurrection and the authority of his word. These connections not only display for the churches what it is for them to conquer—that is, to be faithful and obedient unto death—but it also

---

[25] Lewis Ayres, "On the Practice and Teaching of Christian Doctrine," *Gregorianum* 80 (1999): 33–94; here, Ayres (71n85) attributes this expression to Stephen Fowl. I am using this phrase in a somewhat different sense than Ayres does in this article.

[26] On "conquering" in Revelation, see Bauckham, *The Theology of the Book of Revelation*, 73–76, 88–94.

positions the churches to emulate those figures in the narrative who similarly "conquer" like the Lamb, especially the martyrs (12:11; 14:1–6; 15:2).

The closing of each of the seven letters features a promise of heavenly reward from Jesus to those who conquer by their faithfulness. Nearly all heavenly rewards promised in the seven letters pick up a detail or element in the visions of heaven or of the new Jerusalem. To the church at Philadelphia, the Lord Jesus says that if one conquers, he "will write on him the name of my God, and the name of the city of my God, the new Jerusalem which comes down from my God out of heaven" (3:12). Not only does this anticipate the marking of the one hundred forty-four thousand (a mark of ownership in 7:3–8) but also the vision of the new Jerusalem descending from heaven (21:2).[27] In the letter to the Ephesian church, Jesus promises "to him who conquers I will grant to eat of the tree of life, which is in the paradise of God" (2:7). When John is given to see the inside of the new Jerusalem, there appears "the tree of life" (22:2). In the final visions of the book, the One upon the Throne (i.e., the Father) declares programmatically, "He who conquers shall have this heritage, and I will be his God and he shall be my son" (21:7).

The seven letters thus act as a kind of lens. The revelations from the exalted Jesus given in the seven letters lay bare spiritual dimensions of the churches' present situations. By revealing the hidden dimensions of their situations, the Lord Jesus invites these churches to see themselves in a new light even though the spiritual reality of their situations runs contrary to surface appearances or seems counterintuitive. The kind of "spiritual understanding" given in the seven letters entails that audiences read Scripture figurally in both backward and forward manners.[28] That is, the churches are to understand themselves within the same economy of salvation given in the Scriptures and so interpret them figurally. The churches are also positioned to see themselves in light of the images and contents that are given later in the book. The seven letters act as texts by which the churches can (to use the

---

[27] Rev 7 uses the term σφραγίς for the "seal" put on the one hundred forty-four thousand (7:2; 9:4) as a kind of "branding" (Aune's term) to be juxtaposed to the "mark" (χάραγμα) of the beast from the sea (Rev 13:16–17; 14:9, 11; 16:2; 19:20; 20:4). According to Aune, both signal a kind of branding which denotes ownership. See David E. Aune, *Revelation 6–16*, Word Biblical Commentary 52B (Nashville: Thomas Nelson, 1998), 452–59, 766–68.

[28] Henri de Lubac employs the phrase "spiritual understanding" to designate the apprehension of the Christological mystery in the realities given by the biblical text, a mode of apprehension which is enabled by the Holy Spirit. See Henri de Lubac, SJ, *Scripture in the Tradition*, trans. Luke O'Neill (New York: Herder & Herder, 2000 [1968]), 1–84, esp. 11–24.

phrase of David Grummet) "read the world."[29] Such reading and interpretation takes place in light of the revelation of the crucified, risen, and exalted Jesus, revealed in Revelation 1:12–20. It is to interpret apocalyptically.

III. CONCLUSION

The letters to the seven churches in Revelation 2–3 are apocalyptic compositions in several respects. They proceed from the revelation of the Son of Man in glory given in Revelation 1:12–20. As circular compositions to be read in liturgical assemblies, the seven letters (and the Book of Revelation as a whole) address both particular situations of original addresses and also transcend those original settings to speak to Christian audiences in other times and places. Through these letters, the glorified Jesus reveals the hidden, spiritual dimensions of the churches' situations and encourages their fidelity. Ingredient to these disclosures is the figural interpretation of Scripture in light of Christ's revelation as well as the reception of the heavenly visions in the book as a kind of lens for interpreting their life in the present world and into eternity.

Through these and other ways, the letters to the seven churches encourage Christian audiences to understand themselves, the Scriptures, and the whole of reality in light of the revelation of the Son of Man in glory. This, as John Behr reminds us, must be our indispensable starting point if we are going to "hear what the Spirit says to the churches" today through the Scriptures. To do so is what it means to read the Apocalypse apocalyptically.

---

[29] David Grumett, "Henri de Lubac: Looking for Books to Read the World," in *Ressourcement: A Movement for Renewal in Twentieth-Century Catholic Theology*, eds. Gabriel Flynn and Paul D. Murray with Patricia Kelly (Oxford: Oxford University Press, 2012), 236–49, here 236; typeset adjusted.

Hope & Suffering

PART TWO

Technology, Medical Cures, and Eschatological Healing:
Reflections on Anointing of the Sick and Christian Dying

ROGER W. NUTT
Ave Maria University, FL

IN INSPIRED AUTOBIOGRAPHICAL words offered to the Christian community at Philippi in light of the truth of Christ's resurrection, St. Paul declares, "For me to live is Christ, and to die is gain" (Phil 1:21). "Death" and "gain" have not been words frequently associated with each other for quite some time. At least in Western societies today, it has become as uncouth to speak about death as religion and politics. In our economically comfortable and morally indifferent post-Christian societies, Joseph Ratzinger observes, "Death is placed under a taboo. It is unseemly. So far as possible, it must be hidden away, the thought of it repressed in waking consciousness."[1]

In his famed futuristic dystopian novel, *Brave New World*, set in the year 2540, Aldous Huxley describes how hospitals in the godless "new world" are set up to distract people from death and void it of any personal significance. One of the main characters, Linda, ends up in a hospital structured according to the ideas of the new world:

---

[1] Joseph Ratzinger, *Eschatology: Death and Eternal Life*, trans. Michael Waldstein (Washington, DC: The Catholic University of America Press, 1988), 69.

Linda was dying in company—in company with all modern conve-
niences. The air was continuously alive with gay synthetic melodies.
At the foot of every bed, confronting its moribund occupant, was a
television box. Television was left on, a running tap, from morning
till night. Every quarter of an hour, the prevailing perfume of the
room was automatically changed.[2]

Linda passes away suddenly in this hospital in the presence of her son
John. John is grief-stricken at his mother's passing and seeks a nurse. The
nurse, however, is not concerned about the deceased patient but about
John's uncouth reaction to his mother's death. She wonders how to handle
the situation:

> Should she speak to him? try to bring him back to a sense of
> decency? remind him of where he was? of what fatal mischief he
> might do to these poor innocents? Undoing all their wholesome
> death-conditioning with this disgusting outcry—as though death
> were something terrible, as though any one mattered as much as all
> that! It might give them the most disastrous ideas about the subject,
> might upset them into reacting in the entirely wrong, the utterly
> anti-social way.[3]

So, Huxley's new world of the future seeks to distract people from death,
from ever thinking or reflecting on the possibility that their lives might
actually matter. The dystopian world conditions people to avoid thinking
about life's meaning and to live and die as if nothing and no one had a purpose beyond this world.

A certain superficial view of scientific progress has promised to solve all
of humanity's problems. "By becoming a product," Joseph Ratzinger observes,

> death is supposed to vanish as a question mark about the nature
> of being human, a more-than-technological enquiry. The issue of
> euthanasia is becoming increasingly important because people wish
> to avoid death as something which happens *to me*, and replace it

---

[2] Aldous Huxley, *Brave New World* (New York: Harper and Row, 1989), 203. Cited by
Matthew Levering, introduction to *On Christian Dying*, ed. Matthew Levering (Lanham,
MD: Rowman and Littlefield Publishers, Inc., 2004), xii.

[3] Huxley, *Brave New World*, 211–12, xiii.

with a technical cessation of function which I do not need to carry out myself.[4]

Medical doctor L. S. Dugdale pinpoints a shift away from the Christian "art of dying" attitude toward life and death to the post-modern flight from death: "Whereas the *ars moriendi* taught that a person cultivated good life habits with a view to dying well, the early twentieth century came to focus solely on living well—death and dying be damned."[5] The cultural drift away from the foundations of the faith coupled with the great advances in medical science have altered peoples' understanding, Christians included, of healing—spiritual, sacramental, or otherwise. The Christian doctrine of healing, which is realized most fully in eternal beatitude and bodily resurrection, is not to be conflated with a scientific-medicinal understanding of healing.[6] This narrow view of healing as a cure for an ailment has grave consequences in the life of the Church when the Sacrament of Anointing of the Sick is re-cast in these terms.

The late abbot of the Greek Orthodox monastery of Simonos Petras on Mt. Athos, Aimilianos, made the following subtle observation: "The basic feature which is new, however, in modern technology, is that it has turned everything on its head. While in former times people attempted to use science to improve their dominion over nature, it has now infiltrated into the very innermost laws of nature with results likely to prove positive but also with terrible and limitless opportunities for intervention in these laws themselves."[7] Indeed, when it comes to a proper attitude toward death, there is no question that technology has turned our expectation "on its head."

Following the work of Fr. Christopher Saliga, Fr. Paul Keller points out that when explaining the purpose of holy anointing to the faithful, we must distinguish between "healing" in the theological sense of being saved by God and "cure" in a medical sense. Presenting Saliga's insights, Keller explains,

He writes about the misunderstanding regarding the anointing of the sick when it is thought to be the only alternative left,

---

[4] Ratzinger, *Eschatology*, 71.

[5] L. S. Dugdale, *The Lost Art of Dying: Reviving Forgotten Wisdom* (New York: Harper Collins Publishers, 2020), 42–43.

[6] I am indebted to the work of John C. Kasza for the distinction between full, eschatological healing and medicinal healing. See John C. Kasza, *Understanding Sacramental Healing: Anointing and Viaticum* (Chicago: Hillenbrand Books, 2007), esp. 21.

[7] Archimandrite Aimilianos, "Orthodox Spirituality and the Technological Revolution," in *Spiritual Instruction and Discourses*, vol. 1, *The Authentic Seal*, trans. (Ormylia, Greece: Ormylia Publishing, 1999), 345–46.

a sacramental last-ditch effort or placebo-type palliative intervention. A cure, he says, "refers to a patient's scientifically measurable positive response to a therapeutic intervention or a combination of such interventions." Someone with a severe infection may be said to be cured when medical treatment has been successful. "Healing" within the Catholic sphere, however, is something that transcends temporality: It "may or may not involve cure even when cure is fairly holistically defined. This is the case because healing is understood relative to the ultimate reason for which we exist, the face-to-face beatific union with God for all eternity."[8]

Modern medicine can cure many significant bodily ailments, but God's healing brings salvation, eternal happiness, and bodily resurrection. The cure mentality towards sacramental healing forgets that Christ did not redeem us from having to die. Rather, he redeemed us from the eternal loss that results from sin.

The Sacrament of Anointing of the Sick reveals many aspects of the faith of the Church and the true nature of the full salvific healing accomplished by Christ. It does so by clarifying the effects of the fall, the nature of sin, and the role of the sacraments and sacramental healing in Christ's redemptive plan. Western culture is currently in a crisis about the meaning of life, suffering, and death. We live at a time in which the doctrinal message of the sacrament of the sick and the graces that it confers are needed—more than ever.

In the remaining portions of this chapter, I sketch in three overlapping sections how the nature of sin and its effects, especially the so-called "remnants of sin," and the primary effects that the Church ascribes to Holy Anointing, correspond to the spiritual needs that every human being has during the dying process. When understood within its proper division of labor in the Christian life, Anointing of the Sick can be fully appreciated as a gift to be cherished, not as a technological cure for the sake of clinging to this life but for the sake of dying in union with God so as to be with him for eternity.

THE LASTING EFFECT OF SIN

As a result of the fall from grace by our first parents, the tendency to sin is especially strong in relation to those things that bring bodily comfort and

---

[8]   Paul Jerome Keller, OP, *101 Questions and Answers on The Sacraments of Healing: Penance and Anointing of the Sick* (New York/Mahwah: Paulist Press, 2010), 106–7.

pleasure. St. Paul personifies and personalizes this tendency to sin within each human being in a powerful description of his own struggles: "So I find it be a law that when I want to do right, evil lies close at hand. For I delight in the law of God, in my inmost self, but I see in my members another law at war with the law of my mind and making me captive to the law of sin which dwells in my members" (Rom 7:21–23). Thomas Aquinas explains how this tension within each human being plays out:

> Now man is placed between the things of this world, and spiritual goods wherein eternal happiness consists: so that the more he cleaves to the one, the more he withdraws from the other, and conversely. Wherefore he that cleaves wholly to the things of this world, so as to make them his end, and to look upon them as the reason and rule of all he does, falls away altogether from spiritual goods.[9]

This struggle is something that every human being, including followers of Christ, experience within themselves. It is easy to think of each particular sin as a transient action that has no abiding impact on the moral, spiritual, or bodily life of those who commit them. However, as St. Paul reminds the Romans, while God's free gift of grace leads to "eternal life in Christ Jesus our Lord," the life of sin also pays out negative rewards: "The wages of sin is death" (6:23).

Sin is thus not just an ailment of the soul; it also impacts bodily life. The gift of grace heals the soul and brings forgiveness, but the lasting impact of sin remains, leaving every person vulnerable to recurring inclinations to sinful behavior or weakness. In the early Church, the doctrine of "deadly sins" was developed to underscore that sinful actions can become vicious habits that remain within us.[10]

---

[9] Thomas Aquinas, *Summa theologiae*, I-II, q. 108, a. 4. Taken from Thomas Aquinas, *Summa theologiae*, vol. 16, eds. John Mortensen and Enrique Alarcón, trans. Laurence Shapcote, OP (Lander, WY: The Aquinas Institute for the Study of Sacred Doctrine, 2012), 434–35.

[10] As Robert Fastiggi explains, "Sins engaged in freely and repetitively inevitably result in 'perverse inclinations, which cloud conscience and corrupt the concrete judgment of good and evil' CCC 1865). These perverse inclinations to sin can also be called vices, which are habits that 'have arisen through the repetition of acts.' Following St. John Cassian (c. 360–433) and St. Gregory the Great (c. 540–604), Church tradition has emphasized seven capital sins or vices; they are called 'capital' because they engender other sins, other vices (CCC 1866). These seven sins or vices are pride, avarice, envy, wrath, lust, gluttony, and sloth (or *acedia*)." Robert Fastiggi, *The Sacrament of Reconciliation: An Anthropological and Scriptural Understanding* (Chicago/Mundelein: Hillenbrand Books, 2017), 5.

Contrasting Adam's condition before and after the Fall in relation to the benefit of Anointing of the Sick, Fr. Romanus Cessario explains:

> Adam, with his preternatural human perfection lacked the beatific vision of God. Sinful Adam and his heirs find themselves further disadvantaged by reason of their attachment to sinful disorders and the "remains"—the *reliquiae*—that even forgiven sins leave on the soul and in the body. According to the ordinations of divine wisdom, each sacrament distinctly readies a believer for heavenly bliss by restoring and perfecting his or her Godly image.[11]

When we are especially vulnerable to weakness during the dying process, these "remains" of sin more readily assault us. In his short work *The Death of Ivan Ilyich*, Russian novelist Leo Tolstoy powerfully explores how fear, regret, and despair—the remnants of a sinful life—play out in the soul of someone ill-prepared to face his own death. Finding himself alone but unable to sleep, the dying Ivan Ilyich

> cried like a baby. He cried about his helplessness, about his terrible loneliness, about the cruelty of people, about the cruelty of God, about the absence of God.
>
> "Why hast Thou done all this? Why hast Thou brought me to this? What dost Thou torture me so? For what?"
>
> He did not expect an answer, and he cried because there was no answer and there could be none. The pain started up again, but he did not stir, did not call out. He said to himself, "Go on then! Hit me again! But what for? What for? What have I done to Thee?". . .
>
> "What do you want?" was the first thought sufficiently intelligible to be expressed in words. "What do you want? What do you want?" he repeated inwardly. "What? Not to suffer. To live," he replied. . . .
>
> His marriage—a mere accident—and his disillusionment with it, and his wife's bad breath, and the sensuality, and the pretense! And that deadly service, and those worries about money; and so it had gone for a year, two years, ten years, twenty years—on and on in the same way. And the longer it lasted, the more deadly it became. "It's as though I had been going steadily downhill while I

---

[11] Romanus Cessario, OP, "Anointing of the Sick: The Sanctification of Human Suffering," *Nova et Vetera* 17 (2019), 300.

imagined I was going up. That's exactly what happened. In public opinion I was moving uphill, but to the same extent life was slipping away from me. And now it's gone and all I can do is die!

"What does it all mean? Why has it happened? It's inconceivable, inconceivable that life was so senseless and disgusting. And if it really was so disgusting and senseless, why should I have to die, and die in agony? Something must be wrong. Perhaps I did not live as I should have," it suddenly occurred to him. "But how could that be when I did everything one is supposed to?" he replied and immediately dismissed the one solution to the whole enigma of life and death, considering it utterly impossible. . . .

"Now comes the judgment! But I'm not guilty!" he cried out indignantly. "What is this for?" And he stopped crying and, turning his face to the wall, began to dwell on one and the same question: "Why all this horror? What is it for?"

But think as he might, he could find no answer. And when it occurred to him, as it often did, that he had not lived as he should have, he immediately recalled how correct his whole life had been and dismissed this bizarre idea.[12]

Tolstoy's arresting account of Ivan Ilyich's deathbed confusion probes in fiction the experience of one ill-prepared for the end of his pilgrim journey on earth. Anointing of the Sick is Christ's spiritual antidote to the bodily remnants of sin that remain in each human being. If the remnants of sin in the body weigh down or tie the soul to earthly attachments, fears, or regrets, the soul can be impeded from surrendering to the will of God at the end of one's life. "Because the soul is preparing for its immanent departure," John Boyle explains,

it most especially needs to attend to those remains of sin that have served to weaken it and render it less than fit for glory. And so it is that this sacrament is not given against those defects by which the spiritual life is simply removed, namely original and mortal sin, but against those defects by which a man is spiritually weakened such that he has not the perfect vigor requisite for the acts of a life of grace and glory.[13]

---

[12] Leo Tolstoy, *The Death of Ivan Ilyich*, trans. Lynn Solotaroff (New York: Bantam Books, 1981), 118–20 (chapter nine).

[13] John Boyle, "Saint Thomas Aquinas on the Anointing of the Sick," in *Rediscovering Aquinas*

Articulating the relationship between soul and body in terms that help people understand the unity of the human person is challenging. Some Christian thinkers use the metaphor of the impact that weather has on a body of water. A windy, raucous climate disturbs the water. So, too, the acts of the body can disturb the soul, and disordered movements of the soul can disturb the body. Father of the Church St. Gregory of Nyssa (d. 395) uses the example of a mirror in his work *The Life of Moses*:

> If, then, one should withdraw from those who seduce him to evil and by the use of his reason turn to the better, putting evil behind him, it is as if he places his own soul, like a mirror, face-to-face with the hope of good things, with the result that the images and impressions of virtue, as it is shown to him by God, are imprinted on the purity of his soul.[14]

In our earthly journey, it is difficult to eradicate the reflections of the unholy things and actions to which we have subjected the soul. These sinful reflections weigh upon us, attach us to the world, and leave us vulnerable— especially during the physical and emotional pain and fatigue that burden those departing this life. As the despairing, regretful, doubt-filled thoughts of the dying Ivan Ilyich illumine, it should not be forgotten that, in the words of Thomas Aquinas, "fear of dangers of death has the greatest power to make man recede from the good of reason."[15]

THE REMNANTS OF SIN AND WHO IS TO RECEIVE HOLY ANOINTING

A simple question or two will help us to appreciate how the remnants of sin relate to sacramental healing and the theology of Anointing of the Sick. If the Fall was a fall from grace—a spiritual death leading to bodily corruption—and if the grace given in Baptism cleanses original sin and personal

---

and the Sacraments, ed. Michael Dauphinais and Matthew Levering (Chicago: Hillenbrand Books, 2009), 79.

[14] Gregory of Nyssa, *The Life of Moses*, trans. Abraham J. Malherbe (New York: Harper San Francisco, 2006), 44.

[15] *ST* II-II, q. 123, a. 12: "Fortitude holds the first place, because fear of dangers of death has the greatest power to make man recede from the good of reason: and after fortitude comes temperance, since also pleasures of touch excel all others in hindering the good of reason." Taken from Thomas Aquinas, *Summa theologiae*, vol. 18, eds. John Mortensen and Enrique Alarcon, trans. Laurence Shapcote, OP (Lander, Wyoming: The Aquinas Institute for the Study of Sacred Doctrine, 2012), 256. I am grateful to my colleague Michael Dauphinais for bringing this passage to my attention.

sin from the soul, then why do the baptized struggle, suffer temptations, and die? Or, again, if the Holy Spirit is alive and active in the souls of believers by grace, elevating them to union with God, then why do they still suffer bodily weakness and death? In short, why is post-baptismal life shrouded with the same challenges as pre-baptismal life? In fact, given how challenging post-baptismal life can be, it could be tempting to think that Baptism and the other sacraments are perhaps empty and devoid of the power that the Church attributes to them.

The differences between the condition in which Adam and Eve received grace prior to the Fall and the condition in which their descendants receive the grace of the New Law provides an answer to this difficulty. The grace and intimacy with God that Adam and Eve enjoyed prior to the Fall was bestowed upon human natures that had not been touched by sin. After the Fall, when anyone receives the graces of Baptism, they are receiving grace into human natures that have been touched by sin and its consequent disorders.

In this fallen world in need of redemption, the healing received from the sacraments is progressive and ongoing. It is not fully realized until the resurrection of the body and the restoration of all things under Christ. The break of a bone can heal, and the function of the wounded area can return, but remnants and vulnerabilities of the old injury remain. "Certain temporal consequences of sin remain in the baptized," the *Catechism* explains,

> such as suffering, illness, death, and such frailties inherent in life as weaknesses of character, and so on, as well as an inclination to sin that Tradition calls concupiscence, or metaphorically, "the tinder for sin" (*fomes peccati*); since concupiscence "is left for us to wrestle with, it cannot harm those who do not consent but manfully resist it by the grace of Jesus Christ."[16]

Christ redeemed us from the eternal loss caused by sin by dying on the cross, but we must complete the temporal journey of this life in union with him in order to enjoy the fruits of his risen life in the next life. The effect of the grace of Christ, Charles Journet observes, "is not, like that given to Adam, to eliminate but, since derived from Christ, to illuminate suffering and death. Jesus did not eliminate suffering and death for himself,

---

[16] CCC §1264.

but illuminated them; and the grace of Redemption causes us to follow his footsteps."[17]

Before treating the theology of the effects of Anointing of the Sick, it is important to clarify for whom Christ instituted this sacrament—a point about which there has been some confusion since Vatican II. Christ instituted each sacrament of the Church for a specific spiritual purpose. Like each of the sacraments, there are necessary conditions for the reception of Anointing of the Sick. This sacrament, in particular, has been subject to abuse in regards to its administration. This abuse has contributed to a false perception of the healing that Christ intends to accomplish in each recipient of this sacrament.

For example, I was once at a parish that celebrated Anointing of the Sick on a fixed day each month after a Sunday Mass. At the end of the Mass, the priest announced that this was the Sunday for the celebration of Anointing of the Sick. He invited "anyone who is not feeling quite right" to stay after Mass and receive the sacrament.[18] This type of administration of the sacrament, decoupled from dying or grave illness, however, is not only theologically and liturgically problematic; it is also incredibly misleading and confusing for the faithful.[19]

This sacrament is to be given to the faithful at the time when the remnants of sin are especially difficult to overcome. Bodily infirmity, Thomas Aquinas observes, "at times . . . tends to hinder spiritual health: so far as bodily infirmity hinders the virtues. Therefore, it was suitable to employ some spiritual medicine against sin, in accord with the fact that bodily infirmity flows out of sin. . . . And for this a sacrament was established—extreme unction."[20]

The sacrament of Anointing of the Sick is not intended for those who are ill in the sense of being a bit off, having a cold or flu, and it is certainly not intended for those who are feeling off emotionally. As Romanus Cessario points out, Christ's intention in instituting Anointing of the Sick

---

[17] Charles Journet, *The Meaning of Grace*, trans. A. V. Littledale (Princeton: Scepter Publishers, 1996), 119.

[18] For a well-reasoned theological response to this misguided practice, see Matthew Levering, *Dying and the Virtues* (Grand Rapids: William B. Eerdmans Publishing Company, 2018), 135–47.

[19] The Church teaches that: "The practice of indiscriminately anointing numbers of people . . . simply because they are ill or have reach an advanced age is to be avoided." From *Pastoral Care of the Sick: Rites of Anointing and Viaticum*, (Collegeville, MN: The Liturgical Press, 1983), 108.

[20] Thomas Aquinas, *Summa contra gentiles*, Book 4: *Salvation*, trans. Charles O'Neil (Notre Dame, IN: University of Notre Dame Press, 1957), 282–83.

was not as "the appropriate Catholic setting to offer a Christian-tinged form of psychological grief counseling."[21]

Abuse in the administration of Anointing of the Sick is often justified in the name of the teaching of the Second Vatican Council on the false premise that the Council detached the dispensation of the sacrament from serious illness and end-of-life situations. Prior to Vatican II, of course, Anointing of the Sick was spoken of as "extreme unction" (still a valid title for this sacrament). It is "extreme" because it is the last anointing received by a Christian. "Final anointing," in fact, is a very accurate translation of the Latin words for extreme unction. Thomas Aquinas, moreover, refers to Anointing of the Sick as "the sacrament of those departing."[22]

Vatican II does caution against the practice of waiting to administer the sacrament until the recipient's very last moments. As a result, the Council speaks of "Anointing of the Sick" instead of "extreme" anointing. However, the nuanced language and the administration of the sacrament earlier in the dying process in no way decouples the sacrament from sinful vulnerabilities that arise when facing grave illness: "'Final anointing,' which can also and better be called 'anointing of the sick,' is not a sacrament exclusively for those who are involved in the final crisis of life and death. There can therefore be no doubt that *the point when a Christian begins to be in danger of death*, either through illness or old age, is already a suitable time to receive it."[23] The perception that Vatican II taught that the sacrament is not for those who are facing death due to sickness or old age is simply an urban legend that needs correction in light of the clear teaching and practice of the Church. [24]

The Church now offers the sacrament to the sick earlier in the dying process so that the ailing may benefit from its graces throughout their ordeal. This adjustment in the timing of the administration of the sacrament was not intended to modify the basic tenet of faith that Christ

---

[21] Cessario, "Anointing of the Sick," 298.

[22] Thomas Aquinas, *Commentary on the Sentences,* book IV, distinction 23, from *Commentary on the Sentences,* vol. 8, book IV, distinctions 14–25, trans. Beth Mortensen (Green Bay, WI: Aquinas Institute, Inc., 2017), 549.

[23] Second Vatican Council, *Sacrosanctum Concilium* (Dec. 4, 1963), §73. Italics added.

[24] The Fourteenth Session of the Council of Trent in 1551 clarified for whom Christ instituted the sacrament of the sick in terms of their health condition vis-à-vis death: "This anointing is to be used for the sick, in particular those who are so dangerously ill that they seem about to depart from life; and consequently it is also called the sacrament of the departing." Council of Trent, "Fourteenth Session," in *Decrees of the Ecumenical Councils,* vol. 2, Trent–Vatican II, ed. Norman P. Tanner, SJ (Washington, DC: Georgetown University Press, 1990), 711.

instituted the sacrament for those who are gravely ill and facing death.[25] So, the Church does teach that the sacrament need not be administered merely "at the point of death." However, the Church also offers two conditions that the eligible recipient must meet: (1) They must have at least begun to be in danger of death, and (2) the danger of death must be due to sickness or old age.

The point here should not be lost. Christians face many challenges and crises throughout their lives. "One of the principal crises which the Christian has to contend with is ill-health," Colman O'Neill explains, "When it is serious it needs more than the attention of a doctor; it is a crisis of the whole person, affecting his entire outlook."[26] Christ instituted this sacrament precisely for the sake of aiding dying Christians in this last crisis. The Church offers other resources to the faithful to aid them in other crises. The Council of Trent, in fact, recognizes the vulnerabilities that can accompany facing death as the reason why the Lord instituted this sacrament:

> For though our adversary seeks and seizes opportunities through the whole of life of finding ways to devour our souls, yet there is no time at which he draws more strongly on every shred of skill to destroy us utterly, and to deprive us, if he can, of our confidence in the divine mercy, than when he sees that our departure from life is at hand.[27]

The fact that some "temporal consequences" of sin remain a part of the life of each follower of Christ even after Baptism helps explain why Christ instituted two sacraments ordered to post-baptismal healing. The sacraments

---

[25] For a careful theological critique of positions that assume Vatican II's change in language from "extreme unction" to "final anointing" or "Anointing of the Sick" implies that the Church now views the sacrament to be for healing more broadly construed and not, specifically, for the type of sacramental-eschatological healing that is needed to die well, see Levering, *Dying and the Virtues*, especially the notes on 277–80. The position of the Church on this matter is clear as this passage from the *Catechism*, quoting Pope Paul VI following Vatican II, indicates: "The Anointing of the Sick 'is not a sacrament for those only who are at the point of death. Hence, *as soon as anyone of the faithful begins to be in danger of death from sickness or old age, the fitting time for him to receive this sacrament has certainly already arrived.'"* CCC §1514 (emphasis added). Note: By use of the term "faithful," this teaching presupposes that the recipient is a baptized Catholic, as do all sacraments received after baptism.

[26] Colman O'Neill, *Meeting Christ in the Sacraments* (Staten Island, NY: Alba House Publishers, 1991), 281.

[27] Council of Trent, in *Decrees of the Ecumenical Councils*, 711.

of Penance and Anointing of the Sick form a family of sacraments associated with healing in the Christian life.[28]

Sin wounds the bonds of union between the soul and God and the bonds of charity that join believers to each other in Christ's body. Mortal sin vitiates the union of charity uniting a soul to God *and* the Church. The grace of the sacrament of Penance heals and restores these lost bonds of unity between the sinner and God and the sinner and the members of Christ's body.[29] As a result, the healing that is received in the sacrament of Penance restores and revivifies the bonds of grace, especially charity, between God and neighbor that are wounded by our sins.[30]

Why, then, is there need for another sacrament of healing besides Penance? Being forgiven by God through the graces of the sacrament of Penance does not eliminate the remnants of sin in the life of the believer. As already noted, the struggle against sin and the tendency to sin remain after the forgiveness of Baptism and, subsequently, after Penance. Speaking of the distinction between the healing offered in Penance and Anointing of the Sick, Thomas Aquinas observes:

> Spiritual infirmities . . . are to be cured by penance, in that the works of virtue which the penitent performs when he makes satisfaction withdraw him from evils and incline him to good. But, since man, whether due to negligence, or to the changing occupations of life, or even to the shortness of time, or to something else of the sort, does not perfectly heal within himself the weaknesses

---

[28] CCC §1421: "The Lord Jesus Christ, physician of our souls and bodies, who forgave the sins of the paralytic and restored him to bodily health, has willed that his Church continue, in the power of the Holy Spirit, his work of healing and salvation, even among her own members. This is the purpose of the two sacraments of healing: the sacrament of Penance and the sacrament of Anointing of the Sick."

[29] CCC §1468: "'The whole power of the sacrament of Penance consists in restoring us to God's grace and joining us with him in an intimate friendship,'" the *Catechism* teaches, quoting *Roman Catechism*, II.5.18. "Reconciliation with God is thus the purpose and effect of this sacrament. For those who receive the sacrament of Penance with contrite heart and religious disposition, reconciliation 'is usually followed by peace and serenity of conscience with strong spiritual consolation' [Trent: DS 1674]. Indeed the sacrament of Reconciliation with God brings about a true 'spiritual resurrection' [Luke 15:32] restoration of the dignity and blessings of the life of the children of God, of which the most precious is friendship with God."

[30] For a theological development of this point, see Giles Emery, OP, "Reconciliation with the Church and Interior Penance: The Contribution of Thomas Aquinas on the Question of the *Res et Sacramentum* of Penance," *Nova et Vetera*, English Edition, 1, no. 2 (2003): 283–302.

mentioned, a healthful provision for him is made by this sacrament: it completes the healing aforesaid, and it delivers him from the guilt of temporal punishment; as a result, nothing remains in him when the soul leaves the body which can obstruct the soul in perception of glory.[31]

Drawing on the wisdom of St. Thomas Aquinas's theology, Fr. Romanus Cessario offers the following explanation about the multifaceted nature of sin:

> We call the *"malum culpae"* the stain of sin because it chiefly refers to the culpable alienation from God implied in the Christian notion of sin. Sin sullies the Christian soul. In addition, the metaphor of stain also points to the permanent character of sin or debt of punishment (*"reatus poenae"*) which describes the abiding condition present in the sinner.[32]

The important theological distinction between the "stain" of sin and the corresponding "abiding condition present in the sinner" is important for understanding the distinction between Penance and Anointing of the Sick. The Sacrament of Penance remits both mortal and venial sin. However, as the distinction above clarifies, being forgiven of sins in Baptism or Penance cleanses the soul from the mark or stain but does not undue the remaining condition—weaknesses—caused by the fault. Because of the relationship between the soul and body, these remnants afflict our bodily existence.

Simply because we have obtained forgiveness for our sins in Baptism or later in Penance and other sacraments does not mean that the consequences of those sins will not continue to plague us in the body throughout our temporal journey. Following the teaching of Thomas Aquinas, who uses the analogy of the diverse medicines that are needed in relation to various conditions of bodily health, Romanus Cessario observes,

> One may be without illness but still not in good shape. Penance is ordered to spiritual health inasmuch as this sacrament brings healing from the illness of sin, whereas Holy Anointing restores

---

[31] Aquinas, *Summa contra gentiles*, 283 (ch. 73).

[32] Romanus Cessario, OP, *The Godly Image: Christian Satisfaction in Aquinas* (Washington, DC: The Catholic University of America Press, 2020), 112–13. For a sacramental development of this point, see my *General Principles of Sacramental Theology* (Washington, DC: The Catholic University of America Press, 2017), 28–35.

robustness to a fatigued spiritual life. Its medicinal effects attend to the various remains of sin that weaken or limited a healthy but not vigorous spiritual life.[33]

Quitting a vice and receiving forgiveness for it does not mean that the effects of that vice will not linger and cause future vulnerabilities and temptations. The future effects of sinful actions are often underappreciated. The short-term pleasures gained by sins in the present often scourge people disproportionately in the future. In his redemptive plan, God does not stop simply with forgiveness while leaving unaddressed the disorders caused by sin.

SACRAMENTAL GRACE AND THE GRACES OF ANOINTING OF THE SICK

What makes the sacrament of Anointing of the Sick such a profound gift to the Church is that the graces it confers help us overcome the vulnerabilities corresponding to the remnants of sin so that dying can be accepted in a spiritually fruitful manner and made into an offering to God. This sacrament is ordered precisely to aiding Christians in overcoming the vulnerabilities and anxieties that they suffer as a result of bodily weakness and fatigue when they are dying. Thomas Aquinas identifies five effects of grace in the Christian life: "The first is, to heal the soul; the second, to desire good; the third, to carry into effect the good proposed; the fourth, to persevere in good; the fifth, to reach glory."[34] The sacraments are Christ's privileged way of sanctifying each Christian from the first healing given in Baptism to the ultimate attainment of glory in heaven. Moreover, the grace caused by each of the sacraments is not merely generic in nature. In addition to the healing, sanctification, and elevation that are associated with the gift of grace and the infused virtues and gifts, each sacrament also provides graces that are necessary to supporting Christians in the various stages of life and moments of need. Thomas Aquinas explains the purpose of the sacraments vis-à-vis the unique graces that they cause for the sake of assisting Christians in various vocations and circumstances:

> Now the sacraments are ordained unto certain special effects which are necessary in the Christian life. . . . Consequently just as the virtues and gifts confer, in addition to grace commonly so called, a certain special perfection ordained to the powers' [of the soul]

---

[33] Cessario, "Anointing of the Sick," 303.

[34] *ST* I-II, q. 111, a. 3.

proper actions, *so does sacramental grace confer, over and above grace commonly so called, and in addition to the virtues and gifts, a certain Divine assistance in obtaining the end of the sacrament.*[35]

This important point is often misunderstood or hidden from non-Catholic Christians, especially those denominations that descend from the Reformation. The Seven Sacraments are not seven redundant instances of grace generically understood. The sacramental system of the Church provides needed graces to move and support the Christian from initial sanctification unto eternal life.[36] As Paul Keller explains, "The ultimate aim of the sacrament [of Anointing of the Sick] is to usher us into the presence of God, preparing us for the beatific vision."[37] Like each of the sacraments that Christ instituted, Anointing of the Sick gives special graces that cluster around the strengthening, support, and forgiveness that are needed to assist the Christian in dying well so as to enter eternal glory. These graces join the Christian's weaknesses and act of dying to Christ's own suffering, making it spiritually efficacious.

The remnants of sin that remain can make the dying person more susceptible to doubt, anger, fear, loneliness, despair, envy, and other vices that are harder to resist in a condition of physical weakness, exhaustion, and emotional fatigue. As a result, the *Catechism* teaches that the first grace of this sacrament is

> a particular gift of the Holy Spirit . . . one of strengthening, peace and courage to overcome the difficulties that go with the condition of serious illness or the frailty of old age. This grace is a gift of the Holy Spirit, who renews trust and faith in God and strengthens against the temptations of the evil one, the temptation to discouragement and anguish in the face of death.[38]

It is important to note, contrary to the expectations of many Catholics, which are fueled by the modern aversion to death, the cure-based medicinal understanding of healing, and the unfortunate practice of bestowing this

---

[35] *ST* III, q. 62, a. 2. Taken from Thomas Aquinas, *Summa theologiae*, vol. 20, eds. John Mortensen and Enrique Alarcon, trans. Laurence Shapcote, OP (Lander, Wyoming: The Aquinas Institute for the Study of Sacred Doctrine, 2012), 24. Emphasis added.

[36] For a helpful presentation of Thomas Aquinas's doctrine of deification, see Daria Spezzano, *The Glory of God's Grace: Deification According to St. Thomas Aquinas* (Ave Maria, FL: Sapientia Press of Ave Maria University, 2015).

[37] Keller, *The Sacraments of Healing*, 102.

[38] CCC §1520.

sacrament on those who are not in danger of death, that the "first grace" of Anointing of the Sick is not physical healing. The object of this sacrament is not the evasion of death. This is one of the reasons why it was previously administered in closer conjunction to the moment of the death of the recipient. The *Catechism* reminds that "illness can lead to anguish, self-absorption, sometimes even despair and revolt against God."[39] These negative effects are the remnants of past sins. The Church explains the gift of the Holy Spirit given in this sacrament in terms of strengthening in the face of "difficulties" that accompany facing death. This grace of strengthening is ordered to assisting the recipient in trusting God and resisting temptations, such as discouragement, that can result from facing death in a weakened state.

It is natural, on one level, for Catholics to desire a miraculous healing for themselves or their loved ones. However, we know that while death is the end of our earthly journey, it is not the end of human life itself. In fact, from the perspective of faith, we know that life with God in heaven is not only better than this life; it is our true purpose. If a miraculous healing is granted by God through this sacrament, which is very rare but certainly possible, the miracle is not given to save the person who is healed from having to die at some point in the future. Even Lazarus whom Jesus raised from the dead had to suffer death a second time to join Jesus in heaven.

The sacramental symbolism of the priestly anointing of the sick with oil further clarifies the intended effects of the sacrament. By anointing them with oil while they are in the danger of death, the Church consecrates the sick so that they can make of their weakness, suffering, and death an offering to God. The anointing that Christ commissioned the Church to bestow upon the sick joins their suffering with his. Just because Christ has ascended into heaven does not mean that he is no longer present in the lives of believers from birth to death. Thomas Aquinas famously developed a theory of the seven sacraments that sees them corresponding on a spiritual plane to the way that biological life unfolds on the natural plane from birth to death.[40] Whether or not Thomas's analogy between spiritual and biological life works perfectly is not the central point. The point is that he recognized that the sacramental system makes Christ's assistance available to his followers in every major phase of life and moment of need, from birth to death.

The anointings of Baptism and Confirmation symbolize the spiritual consecration of the lives of each and every believer to participate in the Church's life of worship and to the public witness to the faith. The anointing

---

[39] CCC §1501.
[40] *ST* III, q. 65, a. 1, p. 60 (emphasis added).

of orders consecrates the ordained to a life of special ministry and service within the Church. Likewise, the Anointing of the Sick consecrates the recipient in their very condition of weakness to Christ's own suffering and Passion.[41] Even if one is already in the state of grace, the grace of each of the sacraments brings the presence of God to the believer in a newer and fuller way. The grace of Anointing of the Sick both gives to the recipient added strength to persevere against temptations resulting from bodily weakness and joins the sick person to Christ's own suffering and weakness. This sacrament thus mediates the close proximity that Christ has to the sick and dying in a unique and richly merciful fashion.

Christ's incarnation turned the tragedy of the Fall and the power of the "Prince of this world" on its head. In light of Christ's life and teaching, suffering and death have taken on a new meaning and significance. In his encyclical on the "saving" meaning of suffering, St. John Paul II notes a certain joy that can accompany suffering as a result of embracing it in union with Christ:

> Saint Paul speaks of such joy in the Letter to the Colossians: "I rejoice in my sufferings for your sake." A source of joy is found in the *overcoming of the sense of the uselessness of suffering,* a feeling that is sometimes very strongly rooted in human suffering. This feeling not only consumes the person interiorly, but seems to make him a burden to others. The person feels condemned to receive help and assistance from others, and at the same time seems useless to himself. The discovery of the salvific meaning of suffering in union with Christ *transforms* this depressing *feeling.*[42]

Those who are united to Christ can join their sufferings to his, thus giving their trial a spiritual dimension. While in a certain sense Christ has solidarity with all who suffer, Anointing of the Sick confers a special conformity in grace to the recipient of the sacrament to Christ:

> By the grace of this sacrament the sick person receives the strength and the gift of uniting himself more closely to Christ's Passion: in a certain way he is consecrated to bear fruit by configuration to

---

[41] For a helpful explanation of how the priestly ministry in the sacrament of anointing of the sick "seals" the dying person in his illness and last moments to Christ, see J. Augustine DiNoia, OP, and Joseph Fox, OP, "Priestly Dimensions of the Sacrament of the Anointing of the Sick," *The Priest* 62 (2006): 10–13.

[42] St. John Paul II, *Salvifici Doloris* (February 11, 1984), §27.

the Savior's redemptive Passion. Suffering, a consequence of original sin, acquires a new meaning; it becomes a participation in the saving work of Jesus.[43]

Because Anointing of the Sick joins those approaching death to Christ's Passion through the particular effect of the sacrament, their suffering takes on an added dimension that makes it an instrument of Christ's work of redemption. When accepted under the light of the Christian faith, the union with Christ caused by the sacrament of Anointing of the Sick makes the sick person's very weakness and proximity to death a source of prayer, spiritual offering, and service. Far from being pointless and without meaning, when joined to Christ sacramentally, the very acceptance of suffering and the act of dying itself can be offered to God as extensions of Christ's own redemptive work.[44] Their acceptance of suffering in union with Christ is a "service" that the sick and dying can offer to God for the benefit of themselves and others.

In fact, there is a reciprocal relationship between the sick person's reliance on the Church for the graces of the sacrament and the Church's reliance on the sick person for her growth in holiness. "The sick who receive this sacrament," the *Catechism* teaches,

> "by freely uniting themselves to the passion and death of Christ," "contribute to the good of the People of God." By celebrating this sacrament the Church, in the communion of saints, intercedes for the benefit of the sick person, and he, for his part, though the grace of this sacrament, contributes to the sanctification of the Church

---

[43] CCC §1521.

[44] "Faith in sharing in the suffering of Christ," St. John Paul II explains, "brings with it the interior certainty that the suffering person 'completes what is lacking in Christ's afflictions'; the certainty that in the spiritual dimension of the work of Redemption *he is serving*, like Christ, *the salvation of his brothers and sisters*. Therefore he is carrying out an irreplaceable service. In the Body of Christ, which is ceaselessly born of the Cross of the Redeemer, it is precisely suffering permeated by the spirit of Christ's sacrifice that *is the irreplaceable mediator and author of the good things* which are indispensable for the world's salvation. It is suffering, more than anything else, which clears the way for the grace which transforms human souls. Suffering, more than anything else, makes present in the history of humanity the powers of the Redemption. In that 'cosmic' struggle between the spiritual powers of good and evil . . . human sufferings, united to the redemptive suffering of Christ, *constitute a special support for the powers of good,* and open the way to the victory of these salvific powers." John Paul II, *Salvifici Doloris*, §27.

and to the good of all men for whom the Church suffers and offers
herself through Christ to God the Father.[45]

Even though the person who is approaching death because of sickness
or old age is, from a physical standpoint, quite powerless, it is most certainly not the case that he or she has nothing to offer the Church or God.
In the same way, therefore, that we speak of a "baptismal," "eucharistic," or
"priestly" spirituality, Anointing of the Sick opens the way for a spirituality
of suffering and dying. "The anointed Christian," Colman O'Neill explains,
"offering himself as a victim, accepting his own suffering and death in conformity with Christ, can find in them a new baptism from which he will rise
up, as Christ did, to glory."[46]

In fact, Fr. Jean-Philippe Revel points out that the acceptance of suffering by the dying and their conformity to Christ is a work of the common
baptismal priesthood. By being conformed to Christ's own suffering, those
who receive Anointing of Sick assume an important role and office within
the Christian community.[47] Those who reject suffering as pointless and seek
to euthanize or assist the sick in taking their own lives are cheating them of
one of the richest and most fruitful phases of the human journey.[48] Suffering
and weakness might be useless to those who worship brute force and physical productivity, but as the life of Christ teaches, the condition of weakness
and vulnerability is God's chosen vessel for manifesting his true power.

Anointing of the Sick thus provides the healing that those who are sick
and suffering need to make their ordeal fruitful. "While bodily illness may

---

[45] CCC §1522.

[46] O'Neill, *Meeting Christ in the Sacraments*, 292. O'Neill, on p. 289, adds to this point: "Here,
then, is the function of anointing as a sacrament of the sick. It enables the Christian to
incorporate ill-health into the life of the Church. For not only does it make suffering meaningful and profitable for the individual; through his acceptance of pain, the Church takes
on more vividly the characteristics of Christ and is made more perfect as his sacrament in
the world."

[47] Jean-Philippe Revel, *Traité des sacrements*, vol. 6, L'onction des maladies: Rédemption de la
chair par la chair (Paris: Éditions du Cerf, 2009), 189.

[48] As St. John Paul II teaches in his encyclical letter, *The Gospel of Life*, "What might seem
logical and humane, when looked at more closely is seen to be senseless and inhumane.
Here we are faced with one of the more alarming symptoms of the 'culture of death,' which
is advancing above all in prosperous societies, marked by an attitude of excessive preoccu-
pation with efficiency and which sees the growing number of elderly and disabled people
as intolerable and too burdensome. These people are very often isolated by their families
and by society, which are organized almost exclusively on the basis of criteria of productive
efficiency, according to which a hopelessly impaired life no longer has any value." St. John
Paul II, *Evangelium Vitae* (March 25, 1995), §64.3.

be an occasion of spiritual good," John Boyle explains, "as a form of satisfaction for sins . . . such illness may also impede spiritual health as when the weakness of the body impedes the exercise of the virtues. Because therefore the body ought to be properly disposed to the soul, it is only fitting that there be a spiritual medicine directed to corporeal illness as it arises from sin."[49] Anointing of the Sick strengthens the ability to suffer and die virtuously for Christ.[50]

It is difficult for the faithful, especially because of the remnants of sin, to accept suffering and to surrender themselves to God's will. "When, with the help of the sacrament," Matthew Levering explains, "dying persons are freed of all impediments to surrendering themselves to God, they discover, in Andrew Davidson's words, 'what it means to share in Christ'—and thus in his dying—'*right to the end.*'"[51] Far from being without meaning, making of one's death an offering to God through Christ is a most courageous and fruitful end to an earthly pilgrimage.

The supernatural life that is begun with the graces of Baptism and augmented with the other sacraments is brought to completion with this last sacrament: "The Anointing of the Sick completes our conformity to the death and Resurrection of Christ, just as Baptism began it. It completes the holy anointings that mark the whole Christian life: that of Baptism which sealed the new life in us, and that of Confirmation which strengthened us for the combat of this life. This last anointing fortifies the end of our earthly life like a solid rampart for the final struggles before entering the Father's house."[52] The manifold graces of Anointing of the Sick are intended by Christ to bring the whole life of grace to completion and eternal rest.

The connection between Anointing of the Sick and our departure from this life to the next is especially fortified when it can be joined with the reception of the Eucharist. In conjunction with receiving the final anointings of our earthly journey, which especially fortifies the soul and joins the recipient to Christ, the reception of Holy Communion is made uniquely fruitful. "In addition to the Anointing of the Sick," the *Catechism* explains,

---

[49] Boyle, "Saint Thomas Aquinas on the Anointing of the Sick," 80.

[50] In the so-called "supplementum" to the third part of his *Summa theologiae*, which was compiled by Aquinas's students after his death, the "res et sacramentum," or immediate effect of the sacrament, is identified as a "certain interior devotion" (*quaedam interior devotio*). This explanation, while perhaps underdeveloped, does intimate a clear understanding of the spiritual or interior graces to die virtuously—to die devotedly—that Anointing of the Sick causes in the recipient. See, *Summa theologiae, supplementum*, q. 30, a. 3, ad 3.

[51] Levering, *Dying and the Virtues*, 145.

[52] CCC §1523.

the Church offers those who are about to leave this life the Eucharist as viaticum. Communion in the body and blood of Christ, received at this moment of "passing over" to the Father, has a particular significance and importance. It is the seed of eternal life and the power of resurrection, according to the words of the Lord: "He who eats my flesh and drinks my blood has eternal life, and I will raise him up at the last day." The sacrament of Christ once dead and now risen, the Eucharist is here the sacrament of passing over from death to life, from this world to the Father.[53]

As a result, there is a deep spiritual benefit to passing from this life under the assistance of the two sacraments of healing, Penance and Anointing of the Sick, fortified by the Eucharist.

The connection of Anointing of the Sick with Communion given as Viaticum further indicates the relation of this sacrament to death. Indeed, if Anointing of the Sick were not ordered to assisting those facing death, then the practice of coupling it with Viaticum—spiritual food for the journey—for those passing from this life would not make sense. "The Eucharist of course," Matthew Levering explains, "does not bring us immediately into eternal life. The Eucharist is called 'viaticum,' food for the journey, because it 'does not once admit us to glory, but bestows on us the power of coming unto glory.'"[54]

When supported by the full richness of the sacramental life, those who face death are surrounded by the presence of Christ, who is there for them through the ministry of the Church, by the mediation of these three sacraments (Penance, Anointing, and Viaticum). Far from being abandoned or alone in this time of weakness, the sick person is supported in his deepest spiritual needs by Anointing of the Sick and the other sacraments that he is able to receive.

CONCLUSION

In a sobering and realistic assessment of the arduous nature of the journey of each individual Christian life and the unfolding of human history, Vatican II's *Pastoral Constitution on the Church in the Modern World Gaudium et Spes*, teaches:

---

[53] CCC §1524.
[54] Matthew Levering, *Jesus and the Demise of Death* (Waco, TX: Baylor University Press, 2020), 75. The citation in this quotation is from Aquinas's *ST* III, q. 79, a. 2, ad 1.

The whole of man's history has been the story of our combat with the powers of evil, stretching, so our Lord tells us, from the very dawn of history until the last day. Finding himself in the midst of the battlefield man has to struggle to do what is right, and it is at great cost to himself, and aided by God's grace, that he succeeds in achieving his own inner integrity.[55]

Words and phrases like "combat with the powers of evil," "battlefield," "struggle to do what is right . . . at great cost to himself" are not easily embraced as essential components of the life to which Christ calls each of his followers—especially today. Nevertheless, as Matthew Levering rightly observes, citing another line from the same Constitution, that "insofar as dying persons wish to avoid this 'battlefield,' Jesus Christ is not and cannot be 'the fulfillment of all aspirations.'"[56] Indeed, medical science and technology have made many improvements in human life. And yet, the quest to cheat death is most certainly not one of the fruits of scientific progress.

As alien as the description of human life in the language of combat and battle may be for Christians in the post-modern world, the tradition of faith has pressed this point with unambiguous consistency. In particular, the faith reminds believers that the battlefield on which the combat is played out extends to the very last moment of each of our lives.

In one of his famous "sayings" from the desert, the great Egyptian monk of the early Church, Anthony, offers the following advice to a fellow ascetic: "Abba Anthony said to Abba Poemen, 'this is the great work of a man: always to take the blame for his own sins before God and to expect temptation to his last breath.'"[57] Just as the Christian people enter each week into the rest of the Lord's Day, so, too, is the death of every soul claimed by Christ a final Passover into the eternal Sabbath of the risen Lord. St. Paul reminds the Christians in Rome that "none of us lives to himself, and none of us dies to himself. If we live, we live to the Lord, and if we die, we die to the Lord; so then, whether we live or whether we die, we are the Lord's" (14:7–8). To be guided by the reign of the risen Lord, the Christian faithful have to live *and* die for Christ. By turning to the graces of Anointing of the Sick, the faithful end their earthly lives by living the truth of Christ, which carries them unto the rest of eternal glory. In the words of St. Paul in Philippians 1:21, "To die is gain."

---

[55] Second Vatican Council, *Gaudium et Spes* (Dec. 7, 1965), §37.2.

[56] Levering, *Dying and the Virtues*, 62.

[57] *The Sayings of the Desert Fathers*, trans. Benedicta Ward, SLG (Trappist, KY: Cistercian Publications, 1984), 2.

"Courage, Dear Heart":
Recovering Courage amidst Suffering and Death with C. S. Lewis and Thomas Aquinas

MICHAEL A. DAUPHINAIS
Ave Maria University, FL

WE LIVE AMIDST a pandemic of anxiety, depression, and hopelessness. In their 2019 book *The Stressed Years of Their Lives: Helping Your Kid Survive and Thrive during Their College Years*, Janet Hibbs and Anthony Rostain report the following statistics:

- Among college students, 30 percent report being "so depressed it was difficult to function in the past year."

- Compared with their parents' generation, "college students today are 50 percent more likely to say they feel overwhelmed."

- The National Institute of Mental Health reports that one-half of adolescents and adults have been affected by an anxiety disorder.

- The average person typically worries for fifty-five minutes each day; those with generalized anxiety disorder typically worry for five hours each day.[1]

---

[1] B. Janet Hibbs and Anthony Rostain, *The Stressed Years of Their Lives: Helping Your Kid Survive and Thrive during Their College Years* (New York: St. Martin's Press: 2019), 149–50. The first two statistics are taken from the Center for Collegiate Mental Health Annual Report, January 15, 2018.

If this was the situation pre-COVID, pre-increased societal and political tensions, how are we doing now?

A Centers for Disease Control and Prevention study from the summer of 2020 found that "40% of US adults reports struggling with mental health or substance use": 31 percent with anxiety/depression; 26 percent with trauma/stressor-related disorder; 13 percent started or increased substance use; and 11 percent seriously considered suicide. Suicidal ideation is higher in males than in females, but all symptoms are higher in the eighteen to twenty-four age group.[2] A CDC study released in the spring of 2021 reported that 40 percent of adults report "symptoms of an anxiety or a depressive disorder" within the past seven days; that 25 percent are currently on medication or receiving counseling for anxiety or depression; and that "increases were largest among adults aged 18–29 years and those with less than a high school education."[3] Beyond the significant numbers who struggle with diagnosable disorders that impair functioning, many more simply struggle with anxious and depressed moods that impair flourishing. Despite many technological and medical advances, our contemporary culture is not very adept at fostering courage. If we cannot pass on such wisdom to the next generation, who will?

My goal in this present writing is to recover the teachings on courage of C. S. Lewis and St. Thomas Aquinas. Together they elucidate how courage enables us to respond to fears and hardships in light of the Christian faith. I begin by addressing certain initial issues with respect to the understanding of the human person, the role of the emotions, and psychology both in less and more disordered states. Then I consider the way in which Aquinas draws on philosophical as well as theological resources to investigate the phenomena of fears and angers and the courage we need to face them. I next turn to ways in which Lewis complements Aquinas by illustrating courage with his nonfictional reminders and his fictional examples. Finally I offer some suggestions to show how Aquinas's and Lewis's insights lead to practices of courage so that we might learn to face suffering and even death with greater courage and hope.

---

[2] Mark É. Czeisler et al., "Mental Health, Substance Use, and Suicidal Ideation during the COVID-19 Pandemic—United States, June 24–30, 2020," *Morbidity and Mortality Weekly Report* 69.32 (August 14, 2020): 1049–57, https://www.cdc.gov/mmwr/volumes/69/wr/mm6932a1.htm.

[3] Anjel Vahratian, Stephen J. Blumberg, Emily P. Terlizzi, Jeannine S. Schiller, "Symptoms of Anxiety or Depressive Disorder and Use of Mental Health Care among Adults during the COVID-19 Pandemic—United States, August 2020–February 2021," *Morbidity and Mortality Weekly Report* 70.13 (April 2, 2021): 490–94, https://www.cdc.gov/mmwr/volumes/70/wr/mm7013e2.htm.

PRELIMINARY OBSERVATIONS

Before we turn to see what we might learn on courage from Aquinas and Lewis, we should make two preliminary observations. Aquinas and Lewis share a classical view of the human person as having three levels: intellect and will, emotions and passions, and bodily desires. In C. S. Lewis's book *The Abolition of Man*, he memorably names these three as the head (the *logos*), the chest (the *thumos*), and the belly (the *eros*).[4] Lewis summarizes the classical and Christian conception of the integrated moral life in which "the head rules the belly through the chest."[5]

The inclusion of the chest—the *thumos*, the emotions and passions—may surprise modern readers who often think of morality as only about actions. In Aquinas's famous treatment of the moral life in his *Summa theologiae*, he dedicates sixteen questions to human actions compared to twenty-seven on the emotions and passions, and many more on the habits and virtues.[6] Lewis thinks that modern philosophy and education have erred by ignoring and impairing the formation of the chest. By modernity's efforts to make all values subjective and relative, there is no longer any standard by which we might form our emotions. Lewis describes the effect of modern society with the memorable expression "men without chests."[7] He notes, however, that we do not cease to have emotions in a relativistic age. If the chest does not serve the head, the chest will end up serving the belly. Fears and aggression will increase. We will simply lose the skills to learn which passions to encourage or discourage in order to live as passionate beings. Aquinas insists that the full human psychology of the Christian includes not only the theological virtues but also the infused and acquired moral virtues. Courage habituates our emotions to help us endure the trials of this life.

So we observe that human beings have a three-level structure: head, chest, and belly. Any attempt at finding happiness and living well must find a way to integrate all three. The second observation follows from the first. In a chapter from *Mere Christianity* called "Morality and Psychoanalysis," Lewis

---

[4] Aquinas divides the powers of the human soul into the intellective, the sensitive, and the vegetative. In spite of some variations, both authors share an ordered vision of the human person by which the reasoning powers are the highest but exclude neither the role of the emotions or passions nor the more tactile bodily urges or desires.

[5] C. S. Lewis, *The Abolition of Man* (New York, NY: Touchstone Books, 1996), 35.

[6] After treating the end of happiness in *Summa Theologiae* I-II, qq. 1–5, Aquinas devotes qq. 6–21 to human acts, then qq. 22–48 to the passions, and then qq. 49–89 to the virtues and vices. The key takeaway for our present purposes is that Aquinas reduces the moral life neither to reason alone nor to the emotions alone but sees a living integrated harmony of both as necessary for human flourishing.

[7] Lewis, *The Abolition of Man*, 36–37.

distinguishes between different ways the chest or emotions may go wrong.[8] In the case of phobias or extreme anxieties, the emotions overwhelm the person so that the will cannot engage. Such extreme anxieties and fears are not moral disorders but psychological disorders. Just as a broken leg requires physical remedies, so such severe psychological illnesses require psychological remedies. Although bad moral decisions may well cause physical and psychological wounds and hinder recovery from such wounds, moral effort itself is powerless to heal either. We cannot will our leg to heal faster any more than we can will a phobia to stop. What our wills may do is to seek the appropriate help and attempt to follow recommendations for recovery to the best of their ability. The goal of such psychological healing is to bring the person back to the state in which the emotions no longer overwhelm the will. Then the moral struggle to form the emotions may begin. With these distinctions in mind, let us now turn to courage in Aquinas.

AQUINAS ON COURAGE

Aquinas and "the Chest"

Aquinas distinguishes between two kinds of desire (*appetitus*) operating in human nature as a rational animal.[9] The two kinds of desire follow from two modes of apprehension. First, there is sense apprehension, which we share with the animals. This is when we recognize something sensible and then have a sensible desire for it (if it is good) or a sensible repulsion from it (if it is perceived as harmful). Second, there is intellectual apprehension, unique to those with reason, by which we understand, at least partially, what a thing is and what are the principles by which it operates. Within the purview of reason, the person desires what is judged to be good as such and turns away from what is known to be evil. Thus a chocolate brownie might be sensibly good and sensibly desired, but the diabetic judges it to be bad and thus refuses the snack.

In his overview of the virtue of courage, Romanus Cessario offers this helpful summary of the two modes of desiring: "Sense appetite is aroused by values sensibly perceived or imagined, whereas intellectual activity, or will, is the power to enjoy things that come within the focus of understanding."[10]

---

[8] C. S. Lewis, *Mere Christianity* (New York: HarperCollins Publishers, 1980), 88–93.

[9] *ST* I, q. 80, a. 2.

[10] Romanus Cessario, OP, *The Virtues, or the Examined Life* (New York: Continuum International Publishing Group, 2002), 158. Cessario continues, "Rational love differs from sensitive love in that its object is the good as known by the intellect" (158).

This movement of intellectual desire is what Aquinas calls the will. It is at the level of the will that we become "masters of our own actions."[11]

Now the sense desires are normal reactions to our perceptions of the world around us. In human beings, however, they do not lead immediately to actions as they do in other animals since we typically do not act until those sense reactions are complemented with a decision of the will. Nonetheless, despite the necessary role of human freedom and rationality for human responsibility and morality, Aquinas neither collapses our sense emotions and reason into one another nor separates them.[12] Our emotions and reason remain distinct ways in which we respond as unitary persons both emotionally and rationally to the world.[13] Thus the human moral life is complex and complicated.[14] Following Aristotle, Aquinas observes that the sense desires may follow the guidance of the intellect but are not directly under its control—a political power versus a despotic power. He writes, "The intellect or reason is said to rule the irascible and concupiscible by a political power: because the sensitive appetite has something of its own, by virtue whereof it can resist the commands of reason."[15] The distinction between the sense and intellectual appetites means that sense desires or fears do not become properly moral until they fall under the guidance or consent of our will—and that it is part of the flourishing human life to have our emotions and intellects moving in harmony.[16]

---

[11] *ST* I, q. 81, a. 1, ad 3.

[12] Cessario, *The Virtues*, 164, writes, "For Aquinas, while the *passiones animae* remain neutral in themselves, they receive their true moral character from our personal determinations insofar as the virtuous man or woman authentically directs these sense urges toward the achievement of moral good."

[13] *ST* I, q. 82, a. 5, "Now the sensitive appetite does not consider the common notion of good, because neither do the senses apprehend the universal. . . . But the will regards good according to the common notion of good."

[14] For an insightful discussion of the implications of Aquinas's teaching on how the moral virtues are not only acquired by practice but also infused by grace, and how these complement one another, see Harm Goris, "Acquired and Infused Moral Virtues in Wounded Nature," in *The Virtuous Life: Thomas Aquinas on the Theological Nature of Moral Virtues*, edited by Harm Goris and Henk Schoot (Leuven: Peeters Publishers, 2017), 21–46.

[15] *ST* I, q. 82, a. 3, ad 2.

[16] *ST* I-II, q. 50, a. 3, ad. 1: "The sensitive powers have an inborn aptitude to obey the command of reason; and therefore habits can be in them: for insofar as they obey reason, in a certain sense they are said to be rational, as stated in *Ethic.* i, 13." See also *ST* I-II, q. 77, aa. 1–2, for some of Aquinas's key discussion of the complex ways in which the passions may influence or overwhelm the will and reason. Anthony Ross, OP, summarizes key aspects of this relationship: "Both reason and will may be powerless to guide a man's action, however clearly he sees what he ought to do, and even when he wishes to do it. . . . Commonly, there are two main ways in which the will may be hindered in following the reason, ways with

Aquinas distinguishes our passions or emotions, the chest in Lewis's imagery, into the concupiscible (desiring) and the irascible (fighting), numbering courage among the latter.[17] He says that the concupiscible passions focus on the "sensible good or evil . . . which causes pleasure or pain . . . [and include] joy, sorrow, love, hatred." The irascible passions add the dimension of difficulty and struggle in attaining the sensible good or avoiding the sensible evil and thus include "daring, fear, hope."[18] We ought not to imagine these desiring and fighting passions as separate parts of the living being. Instead, they function as a unified whole. As living embodied beings, we naturally desire pleasure and flee from pain; as living in a complex world with other beings, we quite often confront difficulties in obtaining pleasure or avoiding pain. Aquinas describes how the two sets of emotions complement one another: "The irascible faculty is bestowed on animals, in order to remove the obstacles that hinder the concupiscible power from tending towards its object, either by making some good difficult to obtain, or by making some evil hard to avoid."[19] Aquinas poetically describes the irascible desires as "the champion and defender" of the concupiscible desires since the irascible helps us strive to attain what is desirable but difficult to achieve and to fight against evils from which we might otherwise flee.[20]

---

which everyone is familiar without sharing the illness of alcoholism. Firstly, there may be a real pull against the influence of reason owing to the feeling aroused by something pleasurable. . . . It is the function of temperance to deal with this kind of problem. . . . Secondly, the will may be hindered from following reason by some natural revulsion from what is undeniably difficult, or dangerous. Courage then is required. It is this cardinal virtue which [sic] enables a man to face what is arduous in human life and to persevere through its dangers in accordance with the direction of right reason, and not simply through ignorance, or misguided fanaticism, or plain anger." See *Summa theologiae, Volume 42: Courage (2a2ae. 123–140)*, translated and edited by Anthony Ross, OP (London: Blackfriars, 1967), xxiii.

[17] For an overview of the complexity of meanings surrounding Aquinas's *"passiones animae"* and a defense of translating them primarily as "emotions" and secondarily as "passions," see the "Introduction" of *Summa theologiae, Volume 19: The Emotions (1a2ae. 22–30)*, translated and edited by Eric Darcy (London: Blackfriars, 1967), xxi–xxiii. With respect to the division of the concupiscible and the irascible, Romanus Cessario, *The Virtues*, 159, offers the helpful summary: "In Aquinas's account of the emotional life, the sense passions fall into two main categories: the contentious emotions of the irascible power and the impulse emotions of the concupiscible power."

[18] *ST* I-II, q. 23, a. 1.

[19] *ST* I-II, q. 23, a. 1, ad 1.

[20] *ST* I, q. 81, a. 2. The quote continues, "when it rises up against what hinders the acquisition of the suitable things which the concupiscible desires, or against what inflicts harm, from which the concupiscible flies. And for this reason, all the passions of the irascible appetite rise from the passions of the concupiscible appetite and terminate in them; for instance, anger rises from sadness, and having wrought vengeance, terminates in joy."

The Virtue of Courage amidst Fear, Sorrow, and Anger

Aquinas follows Aristotle in first defining the virtue of courage as the willingness to fall in battle. At times, Lewis will simply describe courage or fortitude as "guts."[21] We might call it "strength," "toughness," "grit," or "resilience." Romanus Cessario summarizes Aquinas's teaching: "True Christian fortitude is a form of spiritual bravery."[22] For Aquinas, courage habituates the irascible emotions—those of anger, daring, fear, and hope—to respond appropriately and in accord with reason. Perceived dangers and threats give rise to strong emotions in the human person. Courage faces such evils by both "aggression and endurance."[23] We will consider how Aquinas's teaching on courage offers a way of learning to live with the powerful passions of fear, sorrow, and anger.

Let us first consider the interaction of courage and fear. Aquinas does not reckon the willingness to confront an evil to be the best manifestation of courage but instead teaches that courage is especially apparent in endurance. He asserts that "the principal act of courage is to endure dangers, namely to stand immovable in their midst rather than to attack them."[24] Aquinas goes on to define the aspect of courage's endurance as "an action of the soul cleaving most resolutely (*fortissime*) to what is good, the result being that it does not yield to the threatening passion of the body."[25] Courage feels the fear yet does not yield to the fear but instead holds to the good. Aquinas describes such endurance as that by which "the brave man curbs fear."[26] This act of endurance, Aquinas states succinctly, "is more difficult than aggression."[27] To support this claim, he observes with great human wisdom that it is harder to calm fears than to check aggression since the presence of danger often mitigates aggression but exaggerates fears.[28] Aquinas knew that such overwhelming fears may be debilitating and harmful to our happiness.

Aquinas's attention to the dangers of fear is perhaps surprising. We tend

---

[21] Lewis, *Mere Christianity*, 79.

[22] Cessario, *The Virtues*, 167.

[23] *ST* II-II, q. 128, a.1, "As stated above (q. 123, aa. 3, 6), the act of fortitude is twofold, aggression and endurance." I leave the word "fortitude" in many translations since this is more common in translations of Aquinas and in the tradition. I use the word "courage" predominantly in this essay, however, since it carries a broader contemporary and less technical usage, in my judgment.

[24] *ST* II-II, q. 123, a. 6.

[25] *ST* II-II, q. 123, a. 6, ad 2.

[26] *ST* II-II, q. 123, a. 11, ad 1: "Daring and anger do not cooperate with fortitude in its act of endurance, wherein its steadfastness is chiefly commended: for it is by that act that the brave man curbs fear, which is a principal passion, as stated above [*ST* I-II, q. 25, a. 4]."

[27] *ST* II-II, q. 123, a. 6, ad 1.

[28] *ST* II-II, q. 123, a. 6: "It is more difficult to allay fear than to moderate daring, since the

to think of the Christian moral life as more focused on avoiding rash anger or disordered pleasures rather than avoiding harmful fears. As powerful as sensual passions and pleasures are for tempting us to abandon the good, even more powerful is fear of danger: "Fear of dangers of death has the greatest power to make man recede from the good of reason."[29] Aquinas insightfully observes that our hearts generate countless fears. As he puts it, "All fear arises from love; since no one fears save what is contrary to something he loves."[30] Moreover, evils that do not admit of remedy or of any easy solution "inspire the greatest fear."[31] These many fears can lead us to turn away from the good of reason.[32] Aquinas will even say that intense fears may compromise the free and voluntary character of human action since "when fear lays hold of a man he is under a certain necessity of doing a certain thing."[33] In terms of the earlier three-part structure of the human person, when fears become rampant, the chest turns away from the guidance of the head.

Contrary to what we might imagine, however, Aquinas goes out of his way to defend the proper role of fear of suffering and death within the life of the Christian. Fears are often warranted in this fallen world. People who experience no fear because they fail to see the true danger of a situation do not exemplify courage.[34] As he characterizes our situation, created goods

---

danger which is the object of daring and fear, tends by its very nature to check daring, but to increase fear."

[29] *ST* II-II, q. 123, a. 12: "Courage holds the first place, because fear of dangers of death has the greatest power to make man recede from the good of reason: and after fortitude comes temperance, since also pleasures of touch excel all others in hindering the good of reason."

[30] *ST* II-II, q. 125, a. 2. See also *ST* I-II q. 43, a. 1: "Since it is through his loving a certain good, that whatever deprives a man of that good is an evil to him, and that, consequently, he fears it as an evil."

[31] *ST* I-II, q. 42, a. 6.

[32] Romanus Cessario, *The Virtues*, 163, describes the role of the virtues in providing a harmony of the emotions and the will: "By connaturalizing the irascible and concupiscible appetites to reach out for the authentically good ends of human life, the virtues *circa passiones* steady a person for making the right prudential choice. . . . As real operative *habitus* of the human soul, the virtues *circa passiones* provide the actual operational principles for achieving any good action."

[33] *ST* II-II, q. 125, a. 4. Aquinas emphasizes, however, that such actions driven by fear remain disordered even if they lessen the culpability of the actor. See *ST* II-II, q. 125, a. 4, ad 1: "Fear excuses, not in the point of its sinfulness, but in the point of its involuntariness."

[34] *ST* II-II, q. 123, a. 1, ad 2. Josef Pieper aptly describes this phenomenon: "Whoever exposes himself to a danger—even for the sake of good—without knowledge of its perils, either from instinctive optimism ('nothing can possibly happen to *me*') or from firm confidence in his own natural strength and fighting fitness, does not on that account possess the virtue of fortitude." See his *The Four Cardinal Virtues* (Notre Dame, IN: University of Notre Dame Press, 1966), 126. Aquinas dedicates an entire article to showing how fearlessness is opposed to courage (*ST* II-II, q. 126).

remain true goods even if they are not the highest good. Thus, it is proper to love them and so fear their loss. The only sin is to turn away from the good of virtue on account of such fear.[35] Aquinas even defends the fear of death for Christians: "Although death comes, of necessity, to all, yet the shortening of temporal life is an evil and consequently an object of fear."[36] In fact, Aquinas observes that a person might not fear death simply because he no longer loves life from despair or because the person pridefully imagines that he is invincible.[37] With courage, it is not that we do not suffer, but that we live through sufferings and fears with endurance.

Just as courage thrives amidst fears, so also it does amidst sorrows. Aquinas describes sorrow as arising from present evils, whether they be bodily ills, small sins, the memory of serious sins, or the sins of others.[38] When we understand the due order that ought to be present in us and in those we love, it is proper to experience some sorrow and sadness when we recognize what is lacking both at the moral and physical levels. Against the view Aquinas attributed to the Stoics, namely, that the presence of sorrow is evidence of a lack of moral virtue, Aquinas argued that the emotion of sorrow is compatible with virtue. In his treatment of Aquinas's *Commentary on Job*, Fr. Brian Thomas Becket Mullady, OP, distinguishes between sadness in the emotions and sadness in the will. It is only sorrow in the will that indicates a turning from the good. According to Mullady, Aquinas holds that

> Job spoke in his lament about the suffering of the just from the point of view of the passions. Though his lament was loud and quite deep, he still did not curse God. Instead, he demonstrated his faith that in the providence of God material prosperity is not the final or the deepest good in man, though it is a good. This is a rehearsal for the lament of Christ in the Passion. . . . Job expresses the depth of his suffering in the name of the human race, but he shows that he is still a virtuous person on the level of his choosing and moral will by refusing to despair.[39]

---

[35] *ST* II-II, q. 125, a. 4, ad 3.
[36] *ST* II-II, q. 125, a. 4, ad 2.
[37] *ST* II-II, q. 126, a. 1.
[38] *ST* I-II, q. 59, a. 3.
[39] Brian Thomas Becket Mullady, OP, "Moral Principles in Thomas Aquinas's *Commentary on Job*," in *Reading Job with St. Thomas Aquinas*, edited by Matthew Levering, Piotr Roszak, and Jörgen Vijgen (Washington, DC: The Catholic University of America Press, 2020), 315–40, 339. See also Daria Spezzano, "The Hope and Fear of Blessed Job," in *Reading Job with St. Thomas Aquinas*, 261–314.

Job experiences tremendous feelings of sadness and, yet, continues to turn with his intellect and will to God. Unlike a certain cult of earthly happiness, Aquinas asserts that moderate sorrow is a sign of mental health: "the mark of a well-formed mind."[40] The word "moderate" here does not refer to the intensity of the sorrow but addresses the reality that the feeling of sorrow does not eclipse the movement of reason to what is true and good. Moderate sorrow thus refers to sadness under the moderation of reason. So in this life, we are not seeking a world without sadness. In the face of the evils in our world and in our own hearts, feelings of sadness are often appropriate. Courage ensures that these sorrowful feelings do not overwhelm us and lead us to turn away from the goodness of God and our reason as the direction for our actions.

We will examine last the interplay of courage and anger. In the face of attacks and injustices, courage helps us to avoid either shutting down and doing nothing or overreacting with destructive rage. Courage describes a spirited willingness to confront an external danger or even an internal obstacle. Aquinas holds that the confrontational side of courage at times may be assisted properly by anger in facing evils directly and attacking those who seek to do harm.[41] Perhaps just as important, courage *moderates* our anger and attack, ensuring that they do not overreact to the situation at hand or deepen into resentment.[42]

Aquinas's treatment of anger merits particular consideration. Aquinas criticizes the position he attributes to the Stoics, namely that anger is in itself a sinful passion. He holds, instead, that anger becomes sinful only when it turns from the good of reason or when its intensity overwhelms reason.[43] Nonetheless, this anti-Stoic justification of the potential appropriateness of anger does not entirely capture Aquinas's position. He fully understands just how dangerous anger can be in undermining the good life. Following tradition, he counts anger among the seven capital vices and

---

[40] *ST* I-II, q. 59, a. 3, ad 3: "Immoderate sorrow [*tristitia*] is a disease of the mind: but moderate sorrow is the mark of a well-conditioned mind [*ad bonam habitudinem animae pertinent*], according to the present state of life."

[41] *ST* II-II, q. 123, a. 10, ad 3.

[42] Max Scheler has a fascinating treatment of how resentment may lead to a revaluation of morals in his *Ressentiment* (Milwaukee, WI: Marquette University Press, 1998). In this book, Scheler criticizes Nietzsche's famous criticism that Christianity is rooted in the ressentiment of slave morality. Scheler holds that this is true for much of what he describes as modern bourgeois morality or humanitarian love but distinguishes this from Christian morality or Christian love, which stems from God's gift of creation and the fullness associated with love.

[43] *ST* II-II, q. 158, a. 2.

presents two main rationales for so doing: first, the goal of anger, restoring justice, is so desirable that it easily leads us astray; and, second, the mode of anger, its impulsiveness, is so powerful that it easily leads to immoderate actions.[44] Aquinas thus teaches that we are ever in need of meekness to curb anger: "For anger, which is mitigated by meekness, is, on account of its impetuousness, a very great obstacle to man's free judgment of truth: wherefore meekness above all makes a man self-possessed."[45]

Courage thus may feel anger at times but only for the proper reason and only to a limited extent. Meekness necessarily forms a part of true courage, ensuring that feelings of anger never overwhelm the person's "free judgement of truth." Anger cannot stand alone. Aquinas's presentation of the Christian moral life thus presents the emotions of anger, sadness, and fear as appropriate to our present condition and yet in serious need of the guiding influence of our rational judgment through the virtue of courage to find balance and genuine happiness.

The language of resilience and its contemporary studies in psychology provide a helpful way of capturing aspects of Aquinas's understanding of courage. Craig Steven Titus, a scholar of both Thomistic moral theology and contemporary psychology, describes how courage finds the mean between fear and daring by cultivating the proper influences of security and confidence.[46] Titus writes, "In between fear and fearlessness, we experience security, in which we hold firm in the face of fear. Fortitude calls immediately upon security to overcome fear or at least hold it at bay."[47] Titus shows that this same interplay is found amidst contemporary psychology: "Psychosocial researchers have shown that hope, self-confidence, self-assertiveness, and initiative taking help us to confront, to counter, and to correct difficulties. They can help us manage the obstructive and debilitating nature of fear."[48] At times, we risk thinking of the virtues merely in a taxonomical manner and forget that the virtues describe living strengths that have been developed so that the person is actively carrying out courageous actions and enduring great suffering.[49] Aquinas describes how courage and patience

---

[44] *ST* II-II, q. 158, a. 6.

[45] *ST* II-II, q. 157, a. 4.

[46] Craig Steven Titus, *Resilience and the Virtue of Fortitude: Aquinas in Dialogue with the Psychosocial Sciences* (Washington, DC: The Catholic University of America Press, 2006).

[47] Titus, *Resilience and the Virtue of Fortitude*, 169–70.

[48] Titus, *Resilience and the Virtue of Fortitude*, 168.

[49] Aquinas's technical way of expressing this existential dimension of the virtues is to say that virtues are "the mean between potency and act." See Vernon J. Bourke, "The Role of Habitus in the Thomistic Metaphysics of Potency and Act," in *Essays in Thomism*, ed. Robert E. Brennan, OP (New York: Sheed & Ward, 1942), 103–9.

respond and grow in the midst of challenges.[50] Resilience describes that ability to endure fears and overcome obstacles, to act with what Titus describes as "reasoned daring or patient perseverance."[51] With its sense of active and ongoing response to objective hardships, resilience describes the dynamic character of the virtue of courage.

Courage as a Gift of the Holy Spirit

Aquinas posits a gift of the Holy Spirit that complements the virtue of courage: the gift of courage. The virtue of courage maintains a perfection of the capacities of the human person in the face of achieving difficult goods and attacking and enduring difficult evils. Nonetheless, Aquinas is attentive to the ways in which the Christian life in which the person lives in the Spirit, according to the "law of the Spirit of life" (Rom 8:2). Following the traditional acceptance of Isaiah 11:2–3 as the enumeration of seven gifts of the Holy Spirit, Aquinas presents the gifts of the Spirit as higher perfections of the Christian life in which the person becomes disposed to be moved by the Spirit.[52] With respect to the virtue of courage, Aquinas presents the gift of courage as an even greater ability to stand firm in the midst of dangers. His summary is worth quoting at length:

> Now man, according to his proper and connatural mode, is able to have this firmness of mind in both these respects, so as not to forsake the good on account of difficulties, whether in accomplishing an arduous work or in enduring grievous evil. In this sense, fortitude denotes a special or general virtue, as stated above (q. 123, a. 2). Yet furthermore, man's mind is moved by the Holy Spirit, in order that he may attain the end of each work begun, and avoid whatever perils may threaten. This surpasses human nature: for sometimes it is not in a man's power to attain the end of his work, or to avoid evils or dangers, since these may happen to overwhelm him in death. But the Holy Spirit works this in man, by bringing him to everlasting life, which is the end of all good deeds, and the

---

50   Aquinas, *On the Virtues*, q. 5, a. 1, ad. 14: "Courage includes patience since courage shares this with patience, that it is not overwhelmed in the face of present evil, and even that it grows larger so as to push away the evil as is proper [*quod patientia includitur in fortitudine: nam fortis habet id quod est patientis, ut scilicet non conturbetur ex imminentibus malis; et etiam addit amplius, ut scilicet in mala imminentia exiliat secundum quod oportet*]."

51   Titus, *Resilience and the Virtue of Fortitude*, 177.

52   *ST* I-II, q. 68, a. 1, "These perfections are called gifts, not only because they are infused by God, but also because by them man is disposed to become amenable to the Divine inspiration."

release from all perils. A certain confidence of this is infused into the mind by the Holy Spirit who expels any fear of the contrary.[53]

In the face of the fear of suffering and death, the gift of the Holy Spirit allows us to remember the promise of eternal life. In remembering that salvation is a gift given and received of the same Holy Spirit indwelling our souls, we may confidently stand firm in the midst of the worst of evils knowing that even death will not prevent our attaining eternal life. Aquinas summarizes his view of the gift of courage in an almost poetic manner, "Fortitude, as a virtue, perfects the mind in the endurance of all perils whatever; but it does not go so far as to give confidence of overcoming all dangers: this belongs to the fortitude that is a gift of the Holy Spirit."[54] The virtue of courage yields endurance in the face of suffering; the gift offers confidence of victory over death. This is surely an understanding of courage that only comes from Christian revelation. No longer merely the willingness to fall in battle but the readiness to rise after death. In this holistic view of courage, we may have resilience in facing suffering and death in this life and confidence that we will overcome suffering and death in the next life.

C. S. LEWIS ON COURAGE

Lewis's writings initially may appear quite different from Aquinas's, and, yet, both rely on an interplay of the reason and the imagination. Aquinas would say that our human intellect requires imaginative representations (phantasms) in order to arrive at truth. Thus Aquinas often gives examples from the physical world to reinforce metaphysical principles of participation and causality. Lewis takes this imaginative principle of human understanding to a new level when he offers fictional stories to help us draw meaning from larger truths. Lewis writes, "For me, reason is the natural organ of truth; but imagination is the organ of meaning. Imagination, producing new metaphors or revivifying old, is not the cause of truth, but its condition."[55] Lewis's stories thus draw together reason and imagination, showing their necessary complementarity without reducing one to the other.

---

[53] *ST* II-II, q. 139, a. 1.
[54] *ST* II-II, q. 139, a. 1, ad 1.
[55] C. S. Lewis, *Selected Literary Essays*, (Cambridge: Cambridge University Press, 1969), 251–65.

Learning from Pain

As war broke out across Europe in the fall of 1939, C. S. Lewis returned
to teach at the University of Oxford. Lewis himself was no stranger to war.
He had fought in the trenches of World War I and had been injured by
a shell inadvertently dropped by English artillery. In that fall of 1939 in
Oxford, Lewis delivered a sermon "On Learning in War-Time" in which
he raised the pressing question: Why should anyone engage in university
studies during a war and, not just any war, but such a war in which National
Socialists in Germany threatened the very survival of England and the rest
of Europe? Lewis noted that the situation of the war raises questions "which
every Christian ought to have asked himself in peace-time."[56] Why should
we dedicate ourselves to building up human learning and culture when we
are in a spiritual war of cosmic proportions? Not only *why* should we do so
but, perhaps more importantly, *how* can we do so?

Lewis writes, "The war creates no absolutely new situation: it simply
aggravates the permanent human condition so that we can no longer ignore
it. Human life has always been lived on the edge of a precipice."[57] We have
always been amidst the specters of death, suffering, crime, poverty, war. The
very drama of being human is to live amidst such fears. Again, imagine
yourself arriving as a student at Oxford in the fall of 1939 and watching
Germany quickly take over most of Europe. Or imagine yourself attend-
ing college in the midst of a pandemic and unsure of finding employment.
Amidst these ever-present dangers, Lewis affirms that civilizations worthy
of the name have sought to build up human culture, to learn from those who
have lived before us about the meaning and purpose of life, to scrutinize
reality in all its splendor via the natural sciences and humanities.[58] Fighting

---

[56] C. S. Lewis, "On Learning in War-Time," in *The Weight of Glory and Other Address* (Grand Rapids, MI: Eerdmans Publishing, 1979), 43.

[57] Lewis, "Learning in War-time," 44. Lewis would offer a similar reminder in a 1948 essay, "On Living in an Atomic Age," in which he wrote, "In other words, do not let us begin by exaggerating the novelty of our situation. Believe me, dear sir or madam, you and all whom you love were already sentenced to death before the atomic bomb was invented: and quite a high percentage of us were going to die in unpleasant ways. . . . the first action to be taken is to pull ourselves together."

[58] Lewis defends the importance of the pursuit of learning and ordinary activities in the midst of war. He makes the commonsensical observation that it is nearly impossible to turn away from ordinary life and activities even when one enters the war directly. He recalls his own experience even in the trenches when very little time was spent actually fighting and much time was spent playing cards, cleaning uniforms, and such. Lewis observes that after a conversion to Christianity, much of one's daily life and work may well remain the same. Lewis does not, however, draw the conclusion that our efforts to make life war-directed or God-directed are in vain. Drawing on St. Paul's admonition in 1 Cor 10:31, "Whether you

a war or a pandemic entails more than the fear of death or the desire for physical survival; it is a defense of a way of life. He identifies specifically the challenges of *distraction* (or excitement), *frustration*, and *fear*.[59]

Lewis's book *The Problem of Pain* shows that pains and fears may have a positive role as well in breaking down our illusions of self-sufficiency. The ongoing presence of fears and pains reminds us that neither we nor our world is as good or perfectible as we like to think. Lewis writes, "Pain insists upon being attended to. God whispers to us in our pleasures, speaks in our conscience, but shouts in our pain: it is His megaphone to rouse a deaf world. We are most keenly aware of God's character in our suffering. It is when our self-sufficiency is peeled away that we see how weak we really are."[60]

As Lewis had mentioned, all human life is necessarily lived on a precipice. Lewis's friend J. R. R. Tolkien wrote, "Actually I am a Christian, and indeed a Roman Catholic, so that I do not expect 'history' to be anything but a 'long defeat'—though it contains (and in legend may contain more clearly and movingly) some samples or glimpses of final victory."[61] There is something wonderful in the admission that modern technological reasoning is finally incapable of making the world safe and secure and eliminating our paralyzing fears and anxieties. Recovering the courage calls for the recognition that evils, pains, and sufferings are an integral part of this present valley of tears. They are not temporary aberrations in an otherwise safe and secure world. Simply put: life is painful. Such a recognition allows us to see our need for courage in all circumstances in this life. We are freed from the illusion of achieving perfection in this life—in ourselves, our families, or our communities.

---

eat or drink, or whatever you do, do all to the glory of God," Lewis offers the homespun observation, "A mole must dig to the glory of God and a cock must crow." From "Learning in War-Time," 49.

[59] Lewis, "Learning in War-Time," 51–54. In addition to Aquinas's focus on fear and anger and the predominant emotions in the face of hardship and danger, Lewis insightfully adds a third one of distraction. Notice how contemporary anxiety tends to correlate with—and no doubt be exaggerated by—habits of continual distraction. The seventeenth-century Catholic author Pascal in his *Pensées*, trans. A. J. Krailsheimer (New York, NY: Penguin, 1995), 37–43 (nos. 132–39), dedicates much commentary to the role of distractions: "*Diversion.* Being unable to cure death, wretchedness and ignorance, men have decided, in order to be happy, not to think about such things" (37). The encroaching of digital distractions into all aspects of life has been the subject of much recent conversation. For example, see Cal Newport, *Digital Minimalism: Choosing a Focused Life in a Noisy World* (New York: Penguin Books, 2020).

[60] C. S. Lewis, *The Problem of Pain* (New York, NY: Touchstone Books, 1996), 83.

[61] J. R. R. Tolkien, *The Letters of J. R. R. Tolkien*, edited by Humphrey Carpenter (Boston, MA: Mariner Books, 2000), 255.

The imperfectability of this life and the resulting need for courage ought not to lead to quietism but instead may inspire us to act with greater boldness, leaving the results in God's hands. Lewis himself would go on to teach throughout the war, write many books and countless essays, give many talks in person and on the radio without any security that England would survive or that anyone would ever be around to read his books. In addressing workers of his age, Lewis suggested that Christianity tries to make the conditions of the world "as good as possible, i.e., to reform them" and "fortifies you against them insofar as they remain bad."[62] Projects of reform can never be an end in themselves. We must learn how to live amidst countless pains and evils that compromise life.

Stories of Courage in the Face of Fears, Weaknesses, and Death

Lewis presents in numerous stories the need for courage to overcome the debilitating character of fears. The role of courage thus forms part of his larger insistence that human life may not be reduced to its rational component, or the head, without dangerously falsifying human experience. In a scene from *The Voyage of the Dawn Treader*, one book from his *The Chronicles of Narnia* series, the characters in the story are sailing on a ship and encounter many different dangers and adventures. At one point, they sail near an island covered in complete darkness, an island on which they are told that all their dreams come true. At first, the sailors are excited, and then, all of a sudden, they begin rowing as hard as they can to get away from the island: "for it had taken everyone just that half-minute to remember certain dreams they had had—dreams that make you afraid of going to sleep again—and to realize what it would mean to land on a country where dreams come true."[63] Though the sailors are rowing with all their might, they remain trapped in the darkness and paralyzing fear.

In the midst of this panic, "Lucy whispered, 'Aslan, Aslan, if ever you loved us at all, send us help now.' The darkness did not grow any less, but she began to feel a little—a very, very little—better." Then, all of the sudden, a small beam of light enters the darkness and illumines the ship. "Lucy looked along the beam" and at first saw something like a cross, then an airplane, then eventually she saw it as an albatross.[64] The great bird landed on the

---

[62] C. S. Lewis, *God in the Dock: Essays on Theology and Ethics*, edited by Walter Hooper (Grand Rapids, MI: Eerdmans Publishing Company, 1976), 49, originally cited by Chris R. Armstrong, *Medieval Wisdom for Modern Christians: Finding Authentic Faith in a Forgotten Age with C. S. Lewis* (Grand Rapids, MI: Brazos Press, 2016), 137.

[63] C. S. Lewis, *The Voyage of the Dawn Treader* (New York, NY: HarperCollins, 1980), 197.

[64] Lewis, *The Voyage of the Dawn Treader*, 200–201. See C. S. Lewis, "Meditation in a

prow of the ship and then flew in front to guide them out of the darkness. As it circled the ship, the albatross whispered to Lucy, "'Courage, dear heart,' and the voice, she felt sure, was Aslan's, and with a voice a delicious smell breathed into her face."[65] Amidst overwhelming fears, the sailors had lost their direction. Their chests had overwhelmed their heads. Lucy's, however, did not. She used her head to ask Aslan, a symbolic parallel of Jesus Christ in the *Narnia* stories, for help.

By looking along the light and no longer along her fears, Lucy was able to remember that there is something higher than our fears. Something that Aquinas described as "the good of reason." Aslan in the story speaks to her, "Courage, dear heart." We often need help from others and from God not to let fears blind us to what is good and true in life.

Lewis calls the island of the fears of nightmares simply "the dark island." In contrast to truth, which enlightens the intellect, fear darkens the intellect. Into fear's darkness, courage brings light. Courage highlights the insufficiency of reason alone. With courage, we remember who we are, what makes for our true good and happiness, God and his promises of mercy. As Lewis writes in *Mere Christianity*, "Faith is the art of holding on to things your reason has once accepted, in spite of your changing moods. For moods will change, whatever view your reason takes."[66] It is not only that faith dispels fears, but, perhaps much more overlooked, it is courage that allows faith to do so.

What happens when someone gives in to fears and fails to act in accord with the truth of faith that reason once accepted? In another scene from one of *The Chronicles of Narnia: Prince Caspian*, we hear of Susan, who refused to listen to her sister, Lucy, when Lucy had seen Aslan the great lion telling them to go in a different direction. Later, when Susan is finally able to see Aslan herself, she confesses to Lucy that deep down, she knew it was Aslan leading them all along but did not want to follow him. She just wanted to get out of the woods. In this instance, she did not lack knowledge of the right thing to do; she lacked the courage to do it, the willingness to bear the difficulty and associated fears. Aslan eventually speaks directly to Susan:

> After an awful pause, the deep voice said, "Susan." Susan made no answer but the others thought she was crying. "You have listened

---

Toolshed" for his distinction between two modes of knowing: *looking at* the human experience itself and *looking along* the experience to its object in *God in the Dock: Essays on Theology and Ethics*, 212–15.

[65] Lewis, *The Voyage of the Dawn Treader*, 201.

[66] C. S. Lewis, *Mere Christianity*, 125.

to fears, child," said Aslan. "Come, let me breathe on you. Forget them. Are you brave again?"

"A little, Aslan," said Susan.[67]

The assent of our minds to faith may not bear fruit when we listen to our fears. It is courage—and often asking God for courage—that allows faith to dispel fears.

Enduring suffering without giving in to terror or despair, confronting evil without giving in to panic or fear, all of these actions require the strength of courage. It is not enough to know the right thing to do since we must also be able to act in the midst of situations that occasion intense fears. Love alone cannot be the answer since, as we observed with Aquinas earlier, fears rise in proportion to our loves, for the more we love things, the more we fear to lose them. If this is true with respect to the love of security and comfort, how much more with respect to the love of our own life and that of our loved ones.

It is not simply the case that life is worth living; it is also the case that death is worth dying. At a key point in Lewis's story *The Last Battle*, at a point when all the earthly hopes of the Narnians have fallen, Roonwit the Centaur offers these last words to the last king of Narnia: "Remember that all worlds draw to an end and that noble death is a treasure which no one is too poor to buy."[68] What does it mean to buy a noble death? A noble death requires courage and toughness in the face of suffering.[69] None of us knows how our courage may hold up in the face of some deaths. Nonetheless, we do know how our courage is holding up right now and how it has held up in the face of past sufferings and trials. First Peter 4:19 teaches, "Let those who suffer according to God's will do right and entrust their souls to a faithful Creator." In *The Last Battle*, Lewis presents this truth with imaginative richness. As the last king of Narnia approaches his last battle, one which they will almost certainly not survive, he offers the following encouragement to the child Jill: "But courage, child: we are all between the paws of

---

[67] C. S. Lewis, *Prince Caspian* (New York, NY: HarperCollins, 1994), 162.

[68] C. S. Lewis, *The Last Battle* (New York, NY: HarperCollins, 1994), 113.

[69] Jesus's own death provides an example. Mark describes Jesus's intense anguish in the garden of Gethsemane prior to his impending betrayal and passion: "My soul is very sorrowful, even to death" (Mark 14:34). And, yet, on the Cross, Jesus prays a line from Psalm 31, "Father, into your hands I commit my spirit" (Luke 23:46). The psalm continues, "you have redeemed me, O LORD, faithful God" (v. 5). In a noble death, one turns to God. It is not the absence of fear but feeling the fear and still turning with our intellects and wills to God the Father.

the true Aslan."[70] Courage comes at least in part from embracing our status as creatures in the hands of our Creator. Michael Ward, a noted C. S. Lewis scholar, describes how Lewis powerfully portrays the profundity of suffering in this particular book:

> Lewis was impatient with clerical bromides about death being a small thing, and in *The Last Battle* he takes his readers down to the very bottom rung of the ladder of sadness as he orchestrates a story of apocalyptic terror. He dares to do something hardly associated with so-called "children's literature": he kills off every single character with whom the story opens.[71]

And, yet, it is in the same book, just before King Tirian and the child Jill die, that Lewis the author calls for courage. What else do we have in the face of such suffering and death? Surely neither our own ingenuity nor any so-called "march of progress" will allow us to evade death at some point. As in *The Last Battle*, so each character in the story of our life will die. Courage here finds its home in trusting in God's providential and redemptive care: "Courage, child: we are all between the paws of the true Aslan."

Lewis presents a unified image of how courage in the face of death is elevated by trusting that Christ has overcome death. In the character of Roonwit the Centaur's dying words, Lewis reminded us that "noble death is a treasure which no one is too poor to buy." Lewis believed that Christ has already purchased that noble death for us. At the beginning of his *The Problem of Pain*, Lewis quotes one of his favorite Christian authors, George MacDonald: "The Son of God suffered unto death, not that men might not suffer, but that their sufferings might be like His." No Christian need ever suffer or die alone since we now live and die through him, with him, and in him. In this same book, Lewis eventually places all suffering within a cruciform, Christological, and Trinitarian setting:

> For in self-giving, if anywhere, we touch a rhythm not only of all creation but of all being. For the Eternal Word also gives Himself in sacrifice; and that not only on Calvary. For when He was crucified He "did that in the wild weather of His outlying provinces which He had done at home in glory and gladness." From before

---

[70] Lewis, *The Last Battle*, 134.
[71] Michael Ward, *Planet Narnia: The Seven Heavens in the Imagination of C. S. Lewis* (Oxford: Oxford University Press, 2008), 198.

the foundation of the world He surrendered begotten Deity back to
the begetting Deity in obedience.[72]

Lewis here is not suggesting that the divine nature suffers properly speaking.[73] Instead, the crucifixion is the traditional theological temporal mission of the Son that reveals the Son's eternal procession. As such, "surrender" may be spoken of in both but must mean different things when spoken of temporal created being versus eternal uncreated being. In the context of suffering, the key point is that the eternal order of filial self-gift has entered our temporal order through the Incarnation up to its culmination in the Cross and its inherent suffering and death. This is what now allows our suffering and death to partake in Christ's and so also attain his everlasting homeward return to the Father. This highest Christological view of a noble death echoes Aquinas's understanding of the Spirit's gift of courage by which we have confidence that all suffering and death shall finally be overcome.

Not only is a noble death something which no man is too poor to buy, Lewis's character Roonwit also teaches that all worlds come to an end. In an essay, "The World's Last Night," Lewis observes that the doctrine of the Second Coming is likely one of the hardest for modern Christians to take seriously into their lives. With this difficulty in mind, he nonetheless explores what we need to learn from the revealed knowledge that this world will end. The end of the world challenges our assumptions that we either are—or should be—in control of the world around us. Lewis reminds us that this is not the case:

---

[72] Lewis, *The Problem of Pain*, 136, citing George MacDonald, *Unspoken Sermons: 3rd Series*, 11–12. Michael Ward cites this same passage in his persuasive argument that the fundamental theme of *The Problem of Pain* is the painful self-giving expressed in the crucifixion as opposed to some who have claimed that it primarily views pain as an instrument of moral improvement. See his "On Suffering," in *The Cambridge Companion to C. S. Lewis*, ed. Robert MacSwain and Michael Ward (Cambridge: Cambridge University Press, 2010), 203–22. Perhaps it is the self-giving of the crucified Christ that makes possible our eschatological moral improvement in the ability to love God in heaven. Michael L. Peterson offers the helpful philosophical clarification to avoid God as the direct cause of evil: "While suffering is intrinsically evil, Lewis argues that God can use it for our benefit." See his "C. S. Lewis on the Necessity of Gratuitous Evil," in *C. S. Lewis as Philosopher: Truth, Goodness, and Beauty*, 2nd ed., eds. David Baggett, Gary R. Habermas, and Jerry L. Walls (Lynchburg, VA: Liberty University Press, 2017), 211–27.

[73] Lewis extensively defends the distinction between created reality and the uncreated being of God in his *Miracles*. The entire burden of *Miracles* (New York, HarperOne, 2009) ch. 11, "Christianity and 'Religion,'" is to distinguish the belief in God as the Creator from the more commonly held view of the god of pantheism, in which whatever god exists remains part of the whole of nature and thus ultimately subject to the same processes as nature.

The doctrine of the Second Coming teaches us that we do not and cannot know when the world drama will end. . . . We keep on assuming that we know the play. We do not know the play. We do not even know whether we are in Act I or Act V. We do not know who are the major and who the minor characters. The Author knows. . . . When it is over, we may be told. We are led to expect that the Author will have something to say to each of us on the part that each of us has played. The playing it well is what matters infinitely.[74]

Lewis here contrasts two ways in which we think about reality: the prideful ego-centric view that assumes that we are the originator of meaning, authors of our own supposed mini-universes, or, alternately, the humble God-centered view in which we recognize God as the true author and take responsibility for the unrepeatable yet limited role assigned to us. As Lewis repeats throughout his writings, this latter view is only made possible in Christ.[75] So we may come to recognize a Creator greater than ourselves, we come to recognize someone in whose providence we may trust, and, what is most important, we actually do so in Christ.

Even when Lewis does not make explicit reference to Jesus Christ, he habitually connects courage in the face of death with trust in divine providence. In an essay on Hamlet, Lewis points out that Hamlet asked the question of "to be or not to be" early in the play in Act III when he had lost his way and that by the end Hamlet had found his way again. Lewis quotes Hamlet's more mature view in the final scene of Act V as he is approaching his final combat, "There's a special providence in the fall of a sparrow. If it be now, 'tis not to come. If it be not to come, it will be now. If it be not now, yet it will come—the readiness is all."[76] As Lewis describes Hamlet, finding his way meant learning to see that God's hand is at work even in the face of his own death. Courage thus is perfected in trust in divine providence: "the readiness is all."

Perhaps Lewis's most beautiful description of courage and trust in God in the face of fear and uncertainty comes in his work of science fiction called *Perelandra*.[77] In this imaginative retelling of Genesis, the first man and the

[74] C. S. Lewis, "The World's Last Night," in *The World's Last Night and Other Essays* (San Francisco: HarperOne, 2017), 99–122.
[75] Lewis, *Mere Christianity*, bk. II, ch. 4, "The Perfect Penitent."
[76] C. S. Lewis, "Hamlet: The Prince or the Poem?" in *Selected Literary Essays*, ed. Walter Hooper (Cambridge: Cambridge University Press, 1969), 88–106.
[77] Lewis would describe *Perelandra* (1943) as his favorite among his books—at least until he

first woman created on Venus undergo extensive temptation. Deploying his imagination to assist reason, Lewis describes turf-like islands that float on the surface of the oceans of the planet Venus. These islands instantly conform to the shape of the waves, an image of the rational creature perfectly conforming to God's will. On Venus, the man and the woman are commanded not to sleep on the fixed lands but only on the floating islands. Here is how Lewis has the unfallen woman describe her eventual acceptance of the command:

> And why should I desire the Fixed except to make sure—to be able on one day to command where I should be the next and what should happen to me? It was to reject the wave—to draw my hands out of Maleldil's, to say to him, "Not thus, but thus"—to put in our own power what times should roll towards us.[78]

Lewis is not advocating a thoughtlessness about tomorrow or suggesting that we ought not plan and prepare. It is a recognition that the waves of divine providence—and the waves of countless other free wills and natural events—will come at us regardless. Although we can resist these waves with our wills, we cannot refuse them.

Amidst all fears and anxieties, those surrounding death above all call for courage and trust in God's providence. Lewis has the unfallen man summarize his temptation in terms of facing suffering and death:

> "Though a man were to be torn in two halves. . . though half of him turned into earth. . . . The living half must still follow Maleldil. For if it also lay down and became earth, what hope would there be for the whole? But while one half lived, through it He might send life back into the other." Here he paused for a long time, and then spoke again somewhat quickly. "He gave me no assurance. No fixed land. Always one must throw oneself into the wave."[79]

---

wrote *Till We Have Faces* (1956). See Alan Jacobs, *The Narnian: The Life and Imagination of C. S. Lewis* (San Francisco, CA: HarperCollins, 2005), 243. *Perelandra* is an imaginative retelling not only of Genesis but certainly of Milton's *Paradise Lost* as well. Published in 1942, Lewis's *Preface to Paradise Lost* treats similar themes of rebellion, temptation, and obedience.

[78] C. S. Lewis, *Perelandra* (New York: Charles Scribner's Sons, 1996), 179. In the fictional story of *Perelandra*, Maleldil parallels certain features of the Son of God in the Christian faith, one who is fully divine, from the Father, and the one through whom all worlds have been created.

[79] Lewis, *Perelandra*, 180.

This image of being torn "in two halves" refers to the separation of body and soul that is the death of the living whole. The reality of the creature is one of awaiting the waves of divine providence. It takes courage to throw oneself into the wave, especially waves that may well drown and overcome us. As Lewis describes it here, the soul of man may continue to find life in Christ, or the parallel Maleldil in *Perelandra*, awaiting a promised final resurrection. Wisdom and happiness come in ceasing to fight those waves and learning to trust them as part of the ever greater waves of divine providence that will eventually restore life.

CONCLUSION: PRACTICES IN COURAGE

To conclude, let us consider some practices proposed by Aquinas and Lewis. In doing so, we will complete our limited goal of helping to show how those recovering their understandings of courage might respond in the midst of the current pandemic of anxiety and depression. Virtues are like muscles: they grow through practice and repetition, through our cooperation with God's grace. Lewis would use the image of virtues to show that God does not want particular actions from us but instead wants us to become people of a particular sort—not merely doing a brave action here or there but becoming brave people—or even more precisely to allow the courage of Christ to take root in our lives.[80] In this way, virtues describe a healthier integration of our initial distinction among the three parts of human nature—head, chest, and belly—we seek a healthier integration. Sorrows and fears overlap significantly in the dynamic unity of the human person. Aquinas himself offers five distinct remedies for sorrow or sadness.

One of Aquinas's remedies for sorrow is that we should try going to sleep or taking a warm bath![81] What we do with our bodies matters. We might try to become sleep ninjas: folks who take their sleep seriously and banish the phone from the bed.[82] As the saying goes, move a muscle, change a thought. When we are feeling anxieties and fears, we might go for a walk,

---

[80] Lewis, *Mere Christianity*, bk. III, ch. 2, "The Cardinal Virtues"; bk. II, ch. 5, "The Christ Life."

[81] *ST* I-II, q. 38, a. 5.

[82] A recent study on college students in *Psychology Today* found that 50 percent reported that they woke up at night to answer texts, resulting in poorer sleep quality, resulting increase of anxiety and depression. See J. Roen Chiriboga, PhD, and David Rosenberg, M.D., "Anxiety and Depression in College Students: Some Potential Reasons Why 1 in 5 College Students Have Anxiety or Depression," *Psychology Today*, July 30, 2020, https://www.psychologytoday.com/us/blog/changing-times-changing-mental-health/202007/anxiety-and-depression-in-college-students.

hit the gym, do yoga. Even a minute of deep breathing can lower our blood pressure and heart rate.[83]

Another of Aquinas's remedies concerns pleasures. Aquinas suggests that pleasures alleviate pains and sorrows.[84] Perhaps a small dessert or a little chocolate, a hot coffee or espresso, or even one or two funny videos that help us laugh. Notice that Aquinas does not find anything virtuous in trying to cultivate sad or painful feelings. Instead, he presumes we ought to seek their remedy and find small measures of pleasure. He distinguishes these wholesome pleasures from sinful pleasures that eventually lead to greater sorrow. Lewis proffers a similar principle in *The Screwtape Letters* when he affirms that all genuine pleasures come from God and that sin is always a twisted pleasure.[85] Such positive pleasures may be found even in work. Lewis encouraged the students during World War II to focus on their present vocation. Today this means studying when we are studying, eating when we are eating, texting when we are texting, etc. In other words, banish the phone for an uninterrupted hour of work each day. Courage is rarely shown in running into a burning building. Courage is more likely to be practiced in resisting the urges of distraction and boredom and finding the pleasures of work well done.

Aquinas offers another remedy for sorrows in giving in to their outward expression. Recall that our emotions and chests are part of us. Aquinas writes that "tears and groans naturally assuage sorrow."[86] Rather than trying not to have them, which never seems to work, we might learn about them. We might learn to notice our fears. Lewis suggests that when we are dealing with fears or temptations, we should stop *looking along* the fear and instead *look at* the fear. Thus the emotion loses the power to dominate our thoughts. Recall that Aquinas said that fears come from loves. So instead of thinking of fears as bad, consider the underlying love at work. Perhaps a student feels anxiety about tests; such fears might come from a love of doing well in studies.

In another remedy for sorrow, Aquinas says that "sorrow is lessened

---

[83] We might get in the habit of at least twenty minutes of sustained movement each day—not as an effort to achieve bodily perfection but to achieve emotional calmness and equilibrium.

[84] *ST* I-II, q. 38, a. 1.

[85] C. S. Lewis, *The Screwtape Letters* (New York, NY: Macmillan Publishing, 1982), 41: "Never forget that when we are dealing with any pleasure in its health and normal and satisfying form, we are, in a sense, on the Enemy's ground. . . . He made the pleasures: all our research so far has not enabled us to produce one." Note that Lewis writes this work of fiction from the point of view of diabolical temptation so that "the Enemy" is God.

[86] *ST* I-II, q. 38, a. 2. Perhaps you might recall the "Hail Holy Queen" prayer in which we pray, "mourning and weeping in this valley of tears."

by sympathizing friends."[87] Let us have the courage to open our hearts to others and to offer support to others in turn. Aquinas, moreover, observed that courage's aggression comes easier than courage's endurance of suffering. We might focus on the courage to change ourselves, our attitudes, our actions, our words. Anxieties can multiply because we focus on things outside of our control. Let us draw in the focus on ourselves and our growth. If our depression and anxiety become overwhelming, let us have the courage to seek help from professionals and support groups.

Aquinas's final remedy for sorrow is the contemplation of truth, specifically praying about the good "things of God and of future happiness."[88] Toward the end of Lewis's *The Problem of Pain*, he attempts to lead our reason and our imagination home to this reunion with God our Creator and Redeemer:

> The golden apple of selfhood, thrown among the false gods, became an apple of discord because they scrambled for it. They did not know the first rule of the holy game, which is that every player must by all means touch the ball and then immediately pass it on. To be found with it in your hands is a fault: to cling to it, death. But when it flies to and from among the players too swift for eye to follow, and the great master Himself leads the revelry, giving Himself eternally to His creatures in the generation, and back to Himself in the sacrifice, of the Word, then indeed the eternal dance "makes heaven drowsy with the harmony." All pains and pleasures we have known on earth are early initiations in the movements of that dance: but the dance itself is strictly incomparable with the sufferings of this present time. As we draw nearer to its uncreated rhythm, pain and pleasure sink almost out of our sight.[89]

Beyond our bellies and chests, we might foster courage amidst fears and sorrows in our heads through prayer and meditation—remembering that a great dance of love and sacrifice holds together the cosmos. We might begin practicing the virtue of courage by admitting our fears and simply asking God to increase our courage. When we remember that God has a plan for each person and for the whole cosmos that has already been realized in Jesus Christ, we can see that events do not happen *to* us but rather for us. Amidst the darkness of paralyzing and often-imagined fears, with Lucy in Narnia,

---

[87] *ST* I-II, q. 38, a. 3.
[88] *ST* I-II, q. 38, a. 4.
[89] Lewis, *The Problem of Pain*, 137.

we are invited to stop looking along our fears and call out for Christ and hear his words to us: "Courage, dear heart."

"It's a Cold and It's a Broken Hallelujah":
Thomistic Reflections on Hopeless Faith

JEFFREY M. WALKEY
Ave Maria University, FL

IN THE LYRICS to his 1984 song "Hallelujah," musician Leonard Cohen—whose song is repeatedly covered by others, most notably John Cale and Jeff Buckley—strikes a somber note when he proclaims: "It's a cold and it's a broken Hallelujah." What does it mean for a "Hallelujah" to be "cold"? What does it mean for it to be "broken"? It seems that it approaches something like hopelessness. It is a hopeless "Hallelujah!"[1]

The proclamation "Hallelujah" has entered the Christian lexicon and liturgy as "Alleluia." It comes from the Hebrew, meaning "Praise to you, YHWH." What, though, could a "cold and broken" praise of YHWH be? Is it possible? Can a Christian who believes God and believes what God has revealed proclaim such an "Alleluia"? Can a Christian experience such hopelessness while retaining faith? Might one offer a cold praise to the Lord because of some perceived distance from the source of light and love? Might one offer a broken praise to the Lord because of some perceived disconnect from the one in whom we live and move and have our being?

These are not merely idle curiosities. First, one can imagine, or perhaps

---

[1] I am not here claiming that the meaning that Cohen might have intended in his lyrics is identical to what I have to say about hopelessness and faith. His words simply provide a point of departure for reflecting on the possibility of hopelessness in the life of faith.

knows, a Christian in such a valley that faith itself may be incapable of offering the consolation by virtue of which their "Hallelujah" might become less cold and less broken. Said differently, the consolation of faith might not *of itself* be capable of transforming despair concerning their plight or their future into hope. As C. S. Lewis retorts to a would-be comforter: "Talk to me about the truth of religion and I'll listen gladly. Talk to me about the duty of religion and I'll listen submissively. But don't come talking to me about the consolation of religion or I shall suspect that you don't understand."[2] In the depths of grief, anxiety, or depression—all of which might approach or contribute to complete despair—what one believes to be true, what one affirms in faith, often does not—and, in some circumstances, cannot—at that moment, heal the human person.

Second, and here I speak mostly from experience, certain Christian traditions give the impression that robust faith makes no room for feelings of anguish or despair. If our faith is operative, it is supposed, our existence cannot be anything other than joy-filled or hopeful, and in perpetuity. For some, faith ought to lead to our being "healthy, wealthy, and wise."[3] You "believe God" for the good, and it is granted. This is not typical of the Catholic tradition, of course, in which the "dark night of the soul" is recognized as a real possibility, a possibility that does not negate the faith of the believer. The sentiment that faith precludes sorrow or despair, though, can creep into even the Catholic outlook on faithful existence.

This sentiment does not, I would argue, take seriously the sense of anguish and darkness felt and expressed by Lewis, not to mention St. John of the Cross or St. Teresa of Calcutta, among others. It does not adequately account for the experiences of innumerable Christians who seek to serve the Lord even in the midst of anxiety, depression, and despair. In fact, in presuming that faith precludes such experiences, such sentiments could, and often do, exacerbate the situation by contributing a sense of guilt to the suffering already felt. It suggests that there is no place for hopelessness in the life of faith; it suggests that there is no place in the life of faith for a "cold and broken Hallelujah!"

In this essay, drawing on St. Thomas Aquinas, I shall argue against such a sentiment. Although I would like to discuss anxiety, depression, and the like, for sake of space, I shall focus my attention on the experience of despair in the life of faith. Nevertheless, the complicated interrelationships between the various passions, the priority of some to others, will make unavoidable

---

2   C. S. Lewis, *A Grief Observed* (New York: HarperCollins, 2001), 28.
3   One need only look at certain "prosperity" gospels to see such things.

the mention of other passions besides despair.[4] Moreover, any consideration of despair is complicated, most especially because there are two senses of despair for St. Thomas: the irascible passion of despair and the sin against theological hope. The focus of this essay is the former—namely, the passion of despair. To this end, the following discussion will be fourfold. First, I shall discuss the passions of the soul (*passiones animae*) in general. Here, I shall focus on St. Thomas's definition of the passions while also addressing certain potential misunderstandings. Second, I shall discuss St. Thomas's "taxonomy"[5] of the passions. This will include a discussion of the eleven principal passions, both concupiscible and irascible. Third, I shall narrow the focus and discuss the passion of despair, especially in its relationship to the passion of hope and its causes. Lastly, fourth, I shall conclude the essay with some reflections on the relationship between the passion of despair and the virtue of theological faith. Ultimately, as we shall see, the passion of despair need not involve sin, against neither faith nor charity. The passion of despair, then, allows for what I am calling "hopeless faith." Consequently, it leaves room for the possibility of a "cold and a broken Hallelujah!"[6]

THE PASSIONS IN GENERAL

According to St. Thomas, all passions of the soul pertain to the sensitive appetite. As St. Thomas notes rather directly, "Passion is a movement of the sensitive appetite."[7] In order to situate the discussion, it will be helpful to draw attention to key aspects of this definition. But first, let us be clear about what the passions are not. They are not, at least for St. Thomas, identical to what some would today call "emotions." The connotation in English misses the mark. Remarking on the different senses of "passion," at least as it is

---

4   There are other complications as well. In English, words like "passions," "emotions," "feelings," and even "affections" are often used as synonyms or at least something approximating synonyms. This is problematic in the context of a discussion of St. Thomas's use of *passiones*. Although *passiones* is sometimes translated as "emotions" or "feelings," this is imprecise and for reasons that will be noted below.

5   The language of "taxonomy" is borrowed from Peter King. See his "Emotions," in *The Oxford Handbook of Aquinas*, ed. Brian Davies and Eleonore Stump (Oxford: Oxford University Press, 2014), 209–26.

6   Although my focus is on despair, it seems that an account analogous to that which I offer below could be given for other "negative" passions (e.g., fear, sorrow), or certain other annexed passions (e.g., anxiety, depression). This is worth discussing, but such considerations are beyond the scope of the present essay.

7   *Summa theologiae* I-II, q. 22, a. 3, sc. All English translations of the *ST* come from *Summa theologiae*, 5 volumes, trans. Fathers of the English Dominican Province (Allen, TX: Christian Classics, 1981). See also, *De veritate*, q. 26, a. 3.

used in the Christian tradition, and the English term "emotion," Gondreau notes, "[S]upport for this [distinction] is found in the fact that Christ's own suffering on the Cross is termed his 'Passion,' while never being called his 'Emotion.'"[8] This observation about the inadequacy of translating *passiones animae* as "emotions" is echoed by Thomas Dixon. He suggests, "[I]t was in fact the recent departure from traditional views about the passions (not the influence of those views) that led to the *creation* of a category of 'emotions' that was conceived in opposition to reason, intellect and will."[9] This new (modern) category, and especially given its conception of the "emotions" as in opposition to reason, intellect, and will, is not what St. Thomas means by *passiones animae*.

Also, the passions are not, again, at least for St. Thomas, identical to what we call "affections." While St. Thomas's use of *affectiones* might designate, at times, acts or movements of the sensitive appetite, his employment of the term is often broader. As Robert Miner observes, "Thomas consistently reserves *passiones* for acts of the sensitive appetite. He uses *affectiones* (and, less frequently, *affectus*) for acts that may or may not belong to the sensitive appetite."[10] Thomas Dixon notes that "[*affectus* refers] to acts of the will, both in Augustine and Aquinas, and are contrasted with *passiones*,

---

8 Paul Gondreau, *The Passions of Christ's Soul in the Theology of St. Thomas Aquinas* (Providence, RI: Cluny Media, 2018), 174. In spite of my hesitations, the reader should be aware that it is not uncommon to find *passiones animae* translated as "emotions." Peter King, for instance, in his contribution to *The Oxford Handbook of Aquinas*, renders *passiones* as "emotions." See King, "Emotions," in *The Oxford Handbook of Aquinas*, 209–26. I worry, however, that speaking of "emotions" remains problematic. The word "emotions" comes with its own history. The development of what is often now called "emotion" is in some ways a development from the positions of St. Thomas and other pre-modern authors. To translate *passiones* as "emotions," and without sufficient attention to the latter's historical development, leaves us open to equivocation. For discussions of the historical developments between pre-modern and modern uses of *passiones* and "emotions," see, for instance, Thomas Dixon, *From Passions to Emotions: The Creation of a Secular Psychological Category* (Cambridge: Cambridge University Press, 2005), and Susan James, *Passion and Action: The Emotions in Seventeenth-Century Philosophy* (Oxford: Oxford University Press, 2003). For others works that talk about "emotions" in St. Thomas, see, for instance, Nicholas E. Lombardo, *The Logic of Desire: Aquinas on Emotion* (Washington, DC: The Catholic University of America Press, 2011); Brian Davies, *Thomas Aquinas's Summa Theologiae: A Guide & Commentary* (Oxford: Oxford University Press, 2014); Nicholas Kahm, *Aquinas on Emotion's Participation in Reason* (Washington, DC: The Catholic University of America Press, 2019). In principle, if we are clear about how we are using the word "emotions," it could be unproblematic. Because of potential misunderstandings, I shall continue to speak of "passions" rather than "emotions."

9 Dixon, *From Passions to Emotions*, 3, emphasis added.

10 Robert Miner, *Thomas Aquinas on the Passions: A Study of* Summa Theologiae *1a2ae 22–48* (Cambridge: Cambridge University Press, 2010), 35.

which for both writers were not active movements of the will but passive movements of the lower, sensory appetite."[11] That St. Thomas maintains this distinction between passions and affections is clear from the fact that he has no difficulty employing the language of affectivity when speaking about God, one who, for St. Thomas, cannot suffer passions.[12] St. Thomas states, "When love and joy and the like are ascribed to God or the angels, or to man in respect of his intellectual appetite, they signify simple acts of the will having like effects, but without passion."[13] Again, God suffers no passions. He is not passive with respect to anything. Nor does God have a sensitive soul, and consequently, a sensitive appetite that might be moved by some bodily change. And yet, in God, there is love and joy and the like. If God has such affections, which St. Thomas seems to affirm, but God cannot have passions, then it is safe to say that, for St. Thomas, *passiones* and *affectiones* are not synonymous terms.[14] One might modify Gondreau's words above, saying, "Support for this distinction is found in the fact that Christ's own suffering on the Cross is termed his 'Passion,' while never, I suppose, being

---

[11] Dixon, *From Passions to Emotions*, 48.

[12] Of course, Christ, who is God incarnate, suffers on the Cross. This "Passion," however, pertains to his humanity and not his divinity. Unlike many contemporary "kenotic" Christologies, for St. Thomas, there is no place for the suggestion that the Cross, for instance, changes God in his divinity. For responses to the claim that kenosis, as well as other attributes like humility and obedience, enter into the divine life or are eternally present, see Guy Mansini, "Can Humility and Obedience Be Trinitarian Realities?" in *Thomas Aquinas and Karl Barth: An Unofficial Catholic-Protestant Dialogue*, eds. Bruce L. McCormack and Thomas Joseph White (Grand Rapids, MI: Eerdmans, 2013), 71–98; Bruce Marshall, "The Dereliction of Christ and the Impassibility of God," in *Divine Impassibility and the Mystery of Human Suffering* (Grand Rapids, MI: Eerdmans, 2009), 246–98; Thomas Joseph White, *The Incarnate Lord: A Thomistic Study in Christology* (Washington, DC: The Catholic University of America Press, 2015) and "Intra-Trinitarian Obedience and Nicene-Chalcedonian Christology," in *Nova et Vetera*, English Edition 6 (2008), 377–402.

[13] *ST* I-II, q. 22, a. 3, ad 3. Remarking on this passage, Miner observes, "Aquinas thinks that while they [i.e., the love and joy of God, angels, and man in respect of his intellectual appetite] are not *passiones*, they are *affectiones*." Miner, *Thomas Aquinas on the Passions*, 37.

[14] Thomas Dixon draws attention to a particular text that is helpful in this context, namely, *ST* I, q. 82, a. 5, ad 1. There, St. Thomas states, "Love [*amor*], concupiscence [*concupiscentia*], and the like can be understood in two ways. Sometimes they are taken as passions [*passiones*]—arising, that is, with a certain commotion of the soul. And thus they are commonly understood, and in this sense they are only in the sensitive appetite. They may, however, be taken in another way, as far as they are simple affections [*affectum*] without passion [*passio*] or commotion [*concitatio*] of the soul, and thus they are acts of the will. And in this sense, too, they are attributed to the angels and to God. But if taken in this sense, they do not belong to different powers, but only to one power, which is called the will." See Dixon, *From Passions to Emotions*, 46.

called his 'Affection'—though Christ's Passion might reveal something about God's affection."[15]

Rather than "emotion" or "affection," the most appropriate synonym or approximation for *passio* in modern English, it seems to me, is "suffering." When we suffer, we are passive with respect to some agent (real or imagined) acting upon us.[16] Strictly speaking, however, for St. Thomas, "suffering" denotes the negative passions, such as hatred, sorrow, despair, and so on. In these passions, we are properly said to suffer. As Gondreau remarks, "The notion of 'suffering' best conveys what Thomas wishes to express by the term *passio* . . . inasmuch as suffering always comprises a loss and a change to a contrary or unsuitable disposition."[17] So, while "sufferings" might capture what St. Thomas means by *passiones*, for the sake of clarity and for the reason just noted, it is better simply to employ "passion."

Even if we remain clear about our use of terms, another potential misunderstanding arises. For some thinkers, the passions have a predominantly, if not entirely, negative connotation. The Stoics, for instance, held that "all passions are evil," and Cicero in particular held them to be "diseases of the soul" (*animae morbos*).[18] Moreover, as evil, the Stoics, according to St. Thomas, held also that "every passion of the soul lessens the goodness of an act."[19]

---

[15] The differentiation between *passiones*, on the one hand, "emotion" or *affectiones*, on the other, could also be made between *passiones* and the English word "feelings." Although there may be overlap between the two notions, even in our usage, "feelings" seems to be a rather vague term. As such, I worry that it could lead to misunderstanding given its wide application and imprecision vis-à-vis, for instance, the body and the sensitive appetite. For these reasons, in this essay, *passiones* will not be used as a synonym for "feelings."

[16] Matthew Lapine calls passions a certain "responsiveness" or "receptivity." See Matthew A. Lapine, *The Logic of the Body: Retrieving Theological Psychology* (Bellingham: Lexham Press, 2020), 65.

[17] Gondreau, *The Passions of Christ's Soul*, 188

[18] *ST* I-II, q. 24, a. 2, resp. In the same response, St. Thomas notes that the passions are also sometimes called "disturbances" (*perturbantiones*) of the soul. This negative appraisal continues into the present. The observation concerning the negativity of the passions/emotions is echoed in Dixon's work. He points to, for example, Robert Solomon's book *The Passions: Emotions and the Meaning of Life*, 2nd ed. (Indianapolis: Hackett Publishing, 1993), 2. There, according to Dixon, Solomon argues "that Western thinkers have been prone, right up to the late twentieth century, to take a negative view of the emotions and to think of them as inherently bodily, involuntary and irrational."

[19] *ST* I-II, q. 24, a. 3, resp. Although St. Thomas critiques the Stoics, his critique of certain aspects of the Stoic position is not wholly negative. For instance, in his discussion of the relationship between moral virtue and the passions, he notes in *ST* I-II, q. 59, a. 5, resp.: "If we take the passions as being inordinate affections [*affectiones*], as the Stoics did, it is evident that in this sense perfect virtue is without the passions [*manifestum est quod virtus perfecta est sine passionibus*]." If by "passions" we mean inordinate affections, then the Stoics are on to something. But this understanding of the passions is not the operative understanding in

Neither position is the position of St. Thomas.[20] The latter recognizes the potential evil of the passions but says that this is so only "when they are not controlled by reason" (*cum carent moderatione rationis*).[21] Moreover, the passions qua passions do not lessen the goodness of an act. St. Thomas observes, "[I]f we give the name passions to all movements of the sensitive appetite, then it belongs to the perfection of man's good that his passions be moderated by reason. . . . [I]t belongs to the perfection of moral good, that the actions of the outward members be controlled by the law."[22] For St. Thomas, then, the passions are not in themselves evil, nor do they lessen the goodness of an act. Rather, they are potentially perfective of man. Only when the passions are not moderated by reason are they evil and the moral goodness of the acts that occur lessened.

Having cleared the path of potential distractions, let us return to St. Thomas's definition of "passion." First, as a movement of the *sensitive* appetite, the passions are found where there is bodily modification or changes that come through the senses. By virtue of the sensitive power, for instance, one might see a predator with the eye. The bodily organ is modified by the color or shape of some object, and this constitutes our seeing that

---

St. Thomas's treatment of the passions. The integration of the moral virtues and the passions, then, involves the passions that are movements of the sensitive appetite. In the same *respondeo*, St. Thomas continues in *ST* I-II, q. 59, a. 5, resp.: "[I]f by passions we understand any movement of the sensitive appetite, it is plain that moral virtues, which are about the passions as about their proper matter, cannot be without passions."

[20] For a discussion of the moral neutrality of the passions, and in particular, whether despair is neither good nor evil in itself, see Michael R. Miller, "Aquinas on the Passion of Despair," in *New Blackfriars* 93 (July 2012), 387–96. See especially p. 396 where Miller concludes: "Aquinas is wrong when he states that none of the passions are essentially good or bad. Despair never causes the soul to move to even a mutable good since this passion alone essentially stops all movement, both of the body and the soul. If one filled with despair acts toward a good it is not because they felt the passion in accord with reason, but because some initial hope inherent in one of his current activities remains in spite of his despair. The passion of despair is not morally neutral; it always works to an evil end and never is felt rightly." I do not have space to do justice to Miller's claim, but it does seem overstated. Conceivably, there are instances in which despair—which does stifle movement—is suffered but without being morally evil. The hope of seeing a loved one again but realizing that it would be difficult and, in fact, deeming it impossible, could lead to despair. It is true that the good end is not attained, but the passion itself does not yet seem to have a moral quality. The apprehension that it would be difficult and ultimately impossible could be accurate. Also, it is not clear why the passion in this instance could not be under the control of reason. Moreover, it might not be voluntary. As such, it is difficult to see how it could be truly morally evil. For a response to Miller, see Jeffrey Froula, "Aquinas on the Moral Neutrality of the Passion of Despair," in *New Blackfriars* 97 (May 2016), 308–24.

[21] *ST* I-II, q. 24, a. 2, resp.

[22] *ST* I-II, q. 24, a. 3, resp.

object. Corresponding to this sensitive power is a sensitive appetite, and this is different from other appetites. Remarking on the distinction between, for example, the sensitive and intellectual appetites, St. Thomas states, "[I]t must be observed that the sensitive appetite differs from the intellective appetite, which is called the will, in the fact that the sensitive appetite is a power of a corporeal organ, whereas the will is not. . . . Every act of a power that uses a corporeal organ, depends not only on a power of the soul, but also on the disposition of that corporeal organ."[23] Also, he observes, "[P]assion is properly to be found where there is corporeal transmutation. This corporeal transmutation is found in the act of the sensitive appetite, and is not only spiritual, as in the sensitive apprehension."[24] So, the sensitive power detects some object. The sensitive appetite will, in one way or another, respond to this object as passively sensed.

The involvement of the body is crucial for understanding St. Thomas on the passions. As Gondreau notes, "[B]ecause the sensitive appetite acts in conjunction with the body, passion necessarily involves a bodily change or 'transmutation,' without which there can be no movement of passion. Passion, in other words, requires a bodily modification for its operation."[25] Though the passions involve, and even require, bodily change, they cannot be reduced to a bodily phenomenon.[26] Because human beings are composites of body and soul, the passions are passions not merely of the body but of the whole human person. The person "suffers" this or that passion. Other powers of the soul (e.g., common sense, cogitative power, memory) are operative even in the passions beyond merely bodily operations. More on that below. Grasping this bodily—though not merely bodily—aspect of St. Thomas's account of the passions will be helpful for thinking through the nature of the passion of despair and our culpability for it.

Second, if the passions are movements of the sensitive *appetite*, it is worth briefly considering the way in which they are appetitive (and how this involves other powers of the soul). Quite simply, an appetite is a power ordered toward or away from some object under a certain formality. It names that "in respect of which the soul is referred to something extrinsic as to an end"[27] and "something suitable to itself."[28] More specifically, in the case

---

[23] *ST* I-II, q. 17, a. 7, resp.

[24] *ST* I-II, q. 22, a. 3, resp.

[25] Gondreau, *The Passions of Christ's Soul*, 170.

[26] The passions are not merely bodily transmutations. They involve certain immaterial aspects of the human person as well.

[27] *ST* I, q. 78, a. 1, resp.

[28] *ST* I, q. 78, a. 1, ad 3.

of the sensitive appetite, the soul is "responsive to the estimation of the sensitive apprehensive power."[29] In the passions, then, some object is not merely sensed but also apprehended and under a certain formality. There is an apprehensive power that corresponds to the appetitive power. The latter does not occur apart from the former. As St. Thomas notes, "[T]he appetible does not move the appetite except as it is apprehended."[30]

This sensitive apprehension, then, involves something beyond the senses, beyond the body alone. As noted, it involves other powers: common sense, imagination, estimative power, and memory—though the estimative power in animals is replaced by the cogitative power in humans. The passions, then, in which case something is apprehended, involve certain higher operations by means of which judgments might be made. One does not merely "sense" (by way of some bodily organ) a dangerous animal *as dangerous*. Rather, the eye, for instance, sees the color, shape, and so on of some object and subsequently judges this object to be dangerous. Such estimations occur in humans through the cogitative power, or what St. Thomas also calls "particular reason." He remarks, "[T]he power by which in other animals is called the natural estimative, in man is called the 'cogitative,' which by some sort of collation discovers these intentions [*intentiones*]. Wherefore it is also called the 'particular reason.'"[31] Regarding this "cogitative" power, Kevin White observes, "Its actuation [i.e., the passions], in keeping with the rule that appetite follows apprehension, is directed by the universal apprehension of reason acting through the intermediary of the 'cogitative' power or 'particular reason,' an inner sense-power that apprehends and compares invisible *intentiones* or 'values,' such as danger, in objects of the outer senses."[32] In short, that the passions are movements of the sensitive *appetite* implies the operation of some sensitive *apprehension*.

Third, that the passions are *movements* of the sensitive appetite could lead to misunderstandings of various sorts. One such misunderstanding

---

[29] Lapine, *The Logic of the Body*, 45.

[30] *ST* I, q. 80, a. 2, ad 1. Although the passions involve something beyond mere sensing, that is to say, apprehension by way of the cogitative power or particular reason, it is conceivable, as I shall suggest below, that the bodily disposition of a particular organ might affect the apprehension of some appetible object, possibly distorting that apprehension, while contributing to certain passions, like despair.

[31] *ST* I, q. 78, a. 4, resp. See also, *ST* I, q. 81, a. 3, resp.

[32] Kevin White, "The Passions of the Soul (Ia IIae, qq. 22–48)," in *The Ethics of Aquinas*, ed. Stephen J. Pope (Washington, DC: Georgetown University Press, 2002), 105. For a book-treatment of the relationship between the passions and other (higher) powers of the soul, see Nicholas Kahm, *Aquinas on Emotion's Participation in Reason* (Washington, DC: The Catholic University of America Press, 2019).

is to reduce St. Thomas's sense of "motion" (*motus*) here to merely local or physical motion. For instance, in the context of the passions, Eric D'Arcy suggests, "[I]t is physical movement, involving local motion in the ordinary sense, that St. Thomas plainly has in mind."[33] According to Miner, D'Arcy and others who interpret St. Thomas in this way "impose a univocal sense of motion upon Aquinas."[34] Given that the Angelic Doctor has recourse to "movements of the will" (*motus voluntatis*) and the language of "rational movements" (*rationabilem motum*),[35] neither of which can be reduced to physical or local motion, it is clear that St. Thomas employs *motus* analogically. As Gondreau notes in this context, "By 'movement' Aquinas means the passage from potency to act or, in this case, the passage from the sense appetite's *potential* inclination towards some object to its *actual* inclination towards a specific object."[36] "Motion" involves all manner of movement from potency to act; as such, it can be said in many ways. While the passions involve the body and bodily change, one must take care to avoid reducing the sort of movement at issue to physical or local motion.[37]

The passions, then, are movements of the sensitive appetite. As movements, they involve actualization of some potency in the sensitive appetite. Insofar as this potency is actualized by some agent external to the appetite itself, this movement is passive; it is receptive. As sensitive, the passions involve the body and bodily change. For a passion to occur, there must be some bodily transmutation. As appetitive, the passions are ordered to some object—namely, the object sensed, the object that brings about some bodily

---

[33] Eric D'Arcy, introduction to *Summa Theologiae*, vol. 19 (Cambridge: Cambridge University Press, 2006), xxvii–xxviii (quoted at Miner, *Thomas Aquinas on the Passions*, 39).

[34] Miner, *Thomas Aquinas on the Passions*, 39

[35] See *ST* I-II, q. 24, a. 2, resp.

[36] Gondreau, *The Passions of Christ's Soul*, 175, original emphasis. Of course, the word *passio* concerns something that is passive with respect to some agent as well. In the case of the sense appetite, the passive power is moved by some sensible object that is apprehended. St. Thomas states at *ST* I, q. 80, a. 2, resp.: "For the appetible power is a passive power, which is naturally moved by the thing apprehended: wherefore the apprehended appetible is a mover which is not moved." That apprehension is involved here, and in human beings this involves the cogitative power or particular reason, one cannot, again, reduce the movement involved in the passions to physical or local motion.

[37] Thomas Dixon, *From Passions to Emotions*, 43–45, similarly notes the broader use of "movement" (*motus*) in the context of the passions. He observes: "One of the principal ways in which Aquinas defined the passions was as movements (*motus*) of the lower appetite. This metaphor derived from the idea in Aristotelian physics that each sort of object had a natural tendency to move in a certain direction. . . . This was extended to the passions, which were seen as expressions of the natural tendency of the lower appetite (or sensory love) to move towards sense-goods and away from sense-evils, and of the higher appetite (or rational love) to move towards or away from intellectual goods or evils."

change. And yet, appetites are not moved apart from some apprehension. The apprehensive power that corresponds to the appetitive power estimates or judges the object under some formality. In the passions, at least for humans, this estimation comes by way of the cogitative power or particular reason. An estimation of an object is made, the appetite responds, and its movement is passion. This is what a passion is in general.

THE PASSIONS IN PARTICULAR

Having described the passions in general, what are they in particular? That is, what are the particular passions? For St. Thomas, there are eleven principal passions.[38] The eleven principal passions are of two kinds. They either pertain to the concupiscible appetite or they pertain to the irascible appetite. As St. Thomas notes,

> [T]he object of the concupiscible power is sensible good or evil,
> simply apprehended as such, which causes pleasure or pain. But,
> since the soul must, of necessity, experience difficulty or struggle
> at times, in acquiring some such good, or in avoiding some such
> evil, in so far as such good or evil is more than our animal nature
> can acquire or avoid; therefore this very good or evil, inasmuch as
> it is of an arduous or difficult nature, is the object of the irascible
> faculty.[39]

The concupiscible passions pertain to the good or evil simply, while the irascible passions pertain to the good or evil as specified under the formality of arduousness or difficulty. Each of the eleven principal passions, again, are either of these two kinds.

Now, there are six passions that pertain to the concupiscible appetite—namely, love (or like), desire, pleasure (or joy), hatred (or dislike), aversion, and sorrow. St. Thomas states,

> In the first place, therefore, good causes, in the appetitive power,
> a certain inclination, aptitude or connaturalness in respect of
> good: and this belongs to the passion of "love": the corresponding

---

[38] Although St. Thomas identifies eleven principal passions that might be suffered by the human person. There are others, but they would be "annexed," so to speak, to one of the eleven principal passions. This is similar to how St. Thomas treats various virtues (and vices) as annexed under, for instance, the four cardinal virtues. We see this in the *Secunda Pars*.

[39] *ST* I-II, q. 23, a. 1, resp.

contrary of which is "hatred" in respect of evil. Secondly, if the good be not yet possessed, it causes in the appetite a movement towards the attainment of the good beloved: and this belongs to the passion of "desire" or "concupiscence": and contrary to it, in respect of evil, is the passion of "aversion" or "dislike." Thirdly, when the good is obtained, it causes the appetite to rest, as it were, in the good obtained: and this belongs to the passion of "delight" or "joy": the contrary of which, in respect of evil, is "sorrow" or "sadness."[40]

Note that the six are, in fact, three opposing pairs. While one loves a good object that is suitable, one hates an evil object that is not suitable. Both of these passions are a kind of "simple inclination."[41] One is either inclined toward some object and under the formality of goodness, or one is disinclined and under formality of bad or evil. The second pair implies a kind of movement towards or away from some object. While one desires a good object that attracts us, one experiences an aversion to an evil object that repels us. The last pair, as St. Thomas notes, involves rest. While one experiences pleasure in the possession of some good, one feels sorrow for having succumbed to some evil.

Recall, however, that the estimation of the formality under which the object is apprehended is partially determinative of the passion that is suffered. If the object is judged *good* and *not yet possessed*, one suffers the desire to attain to the object. If the object is judged *evil* and *not yet possessed*, one suffers the aversion to that object. Because the sensitive apprehension is involved, and our "apprehensions" can in fact be *mis*-apprehensions, one might suffer the "wrong" passion.[42] That is to say, based on a misapprehension, one might respond inappropriately. If one apprehends some good as evil, one might hate what should be loved. If one apprehends some good not yet possessed as evil, one might suffer aversion to an object that should be desired. Also, because the passions involve the body or bodily dispositions, the sensitive apprehension might be adversely affected by some defect in the body. These aspects of the passions should be kept in mind when we turn to the irascible passions, and specifically, the passion of despair. Although not

---

[40] *ST* I-II, q. 23, a. 4, resp.

[41] I borrow the language of "simple inclination" from Lapine, *The Logic of the Body*, 70.

[42] Of course, though negative passions, like despair, might arise because of a misapprehension of some good, it does not follow that such passions will always be based on misapprehension. One might rightly apprehend some good that is loved that it is arduous or difficult and that it is impossible. Moreover, all bodily dispositions might be properly functioning such that there is no bodily defect to which blame might be cast.

all despair arises due to some bodily defect or misapprehension, there are, as I suggest below, instances in which bodily defect and misapprehension play a significant role in the life of one who suffers the passion of despair.

Having considered the concupiscible passions in general, and before considering the irascible passions, it is worth noting the significance of love (*amor*) for St. Thomas. His language of "connaturality" (*connaturalitatem*) is helpful here. When one is connatural with something, one is attuned to that thing, one is sympathetic to it. When one lacks such connaturality, one lacks attunement, lacks sympathy. As such, one is inclined toward those things with which they are connatural and disinclined with respect to those things for which there is no such connaturality.[43] Though more might be said about love, at minimum it must be recognized that love plays a role in St. Thomas's account of *all* the passions, including, as we shall see, despair. It holds first place, in a certain sense. As St. Thomas notes, "Now in each of these appetites [i.e., natural, sensitive, and rational], the name 'love' [*amor*] is given to the principle [*principium*] movement towards the end loved."[44] Elsewhere, he states, "In the first place . . . good causes, in the appetitive power, a certain inclination, aptitude, or connaturalness in respect of good: and this belongs to the passions of 'love' [*amor*]."[45]

We love that to which we are attuned. We desire that which we love. We pleasure in those things that are loved and possessed. As Servais Pinckaers observes, "[L]ove is indeed the first change . . . that is caused in the appetite by what appears to be good. It provokes desire and is brought to

---

[43] The notion of connaturality is important for St. Thomas in a variety of contexts. There is the connaturality that obtains in the life of virtue, for instance. In *ST* II-II, q. 45, a. 2, resp., St. Thomas remarks, "Now rectitude of judgment is twofold: first, on account of perfect use of reason, second, on account of a certain connaturality [*connaturalitatem*] with the matter about which one has to judge. Thus, about matters of chastity, a man after inquiring with his reason forms a right judgment, if he has learnt the science of morals, while he who has the habit of chastity judges of such matters by a kind of connaturality [*connaturalitatem*]." In the same article, St. Thomas notes other contexts in which connaturality provides this function. He states, "Now this sympathy or connaturality [*connaturalitas*] for Divine things is the result of charity, which unites us to God." Through acquired virtue, which is to say habituation, or infused virtue, one might become connatural with the relevant object such that they are attuned to or sympathetic with the right course of action. This is distinct from the one who reasons to the right course of action. With respect to divine things, also, one might become connatural with God such that one is attuned to or sympathetic with the things of God, thus making recognition of such things possible. This occurs with charity, of course, but also faith.

[44] *ST* I-II, q. 26, a. 1, resp.

[45] *ST* I-II, q. 23, a. 4, resp.

completion in the experience of joy."[46] He continues, "[Love] is the source of the other passions."[47]

Let us return to St. Thomas's elevenfold taxonomy of the passions. In addition to the six passions of the concupiscible appetite, there are five that pertain to the irascible appetite—namely, hope, despair, courage (or daring), fear, and anger. As St. Thomas observes,

> Now the good which is difficult or arduous, considered as good, is of such a nature as to produce in us a tendency to it, which tendency pertains to the passion of "hope": whereas, considered as arduous or difficult, it makes us turn from it; and this pertains to the passion of "despair." In like manner the arduous evil, considered as an evil, has the aspect of something to be shunned; and this belongs to the passion of "fear": but it also contains a reason for tending to it, as attempting something arduous, whereby to escape being subject to evil; and this tendency is called "daring."[48]

Like the concupiscible passions, the first four irascible passions are, in fact, pairs. While one hopes to attain the arduous good that is possible, one might despair that it is impossible. While one might have courage in the face of some evil that can be avoided, one might fear it as though it were

---

[46] Servais Pinckaers, *Passions and Virtue*, trans. Benedict M. Guevin (Washington, DC: The Catholic University of America Press, 2017), 14. Although here I focus on *amor* as the basis of the passions, one should note some complications with doing so. First, there is a definite sense in which the concupiscible passions are the basis of the irascible passions. As St. Thomas maintains in *ST* I, q. 81, a. 2, resp.: "[T]he irascible is, as it were, the champion and defender of the concupiscible when it rises up against what hinders the acquisition of the suitable things which the concupiscible desires, or against what inflicts harm, from which the concupiscible flies. And for this reason all the passions of the irascible appetite rise from the passions of the concupiscible appetite and terminate in them." Recall, the concupiscible power considers the good (and evil) absolutely, while the irascible power considers the good (and evil) under the formality of arduous or difficult. Second, the language of concupiscence or concupiscible desire could be distracting if not properly defined. Some authors only take it in a negative sense, for instance. St. Thomas does not. Also, third, for St. Thomas there are diverse kinds of love. The love of concupiscence (*amor conupiscentiae*) is distinct, for St. Thomas, from the love of friendship (*amore amicitiae*). See *ST* I-II, q. 26, a. 4; also *Quaestio disputata de spe*, a. 3. There are also *dilectio* and *caritas*, both of which are called love. According to St. Thomas, however, *amor* is the broader term—"*Amor* names a genus" (Miner, *Thomas Aquinas on the Passions*, 116). As St. Thomas states in *ST* I-II, q. 26, a. 3, resp.: "For love [*amor*] has a wider signification than the others, since every dilection [*dilectio*] or charity [*caritas*] is love, but not vice versa."
[47] Pinckaers, *Passions and Virtue*, 14.
[48] *ST* I-II, q. 23, a. 2, resp. See also *ST* I-II, q. 23, a. 4, resp.

impossible to avoid. Unlike the concupiscible passions, the fifth irascible passion—namely, anger—is unique, having no opposite. It is merely the experience of some object that is present and recognized as being against us. St. Thomas describes this as follows: "Evil already present gives rise to the passion of 'anger' . . . which has no contrary passion."[49]

Like the concupiscible passions, the irascible passions have love for their source. We are inclined to what we love. We desire what we love. We pleasure in what we love. We also hope for that which we love, believing it possible though difficult. We despair of the good we love because it is hard and deemed impossible. We have courage against that which threatens the good that we love even if this is difficult. We fear that evil that threatens the good that we love and has been deemed impossible. Lastly, we are angry toward some evil that threatens the good that we love and is present.[50]

These are the eleven principal passions, according to St. Thomas. They pertain either to the concupiscible or the irascible appetites. The former concern some good (or evil) simply, while the latter concern some good (or evil) under the formality of arduous or difficult. Despair is among the latter. Let us now turn our attention to it.

THE PASSION OF DESPAIR, ITS RELATIONSHIP TO THE PASSION OF HOPE, AND ITS CAUSES

As we narrow our focus to the passion of despair, it will be helpful to say a few words about hope. As Pinckaers observes, "Hope adds to desire the sense of being able to obtain what we want, either by oneself, or with the help of another."[51] Concerning hope, its object, and its conditions, St. Thomas notes the following,

> First, that it [the object of hope] is something good; since, properly speaking, hope regards only the good. . . . Secondly, that it [the object of hope] is future; for hope does not regard that which is present and already possessed. . . . Thirdly, that it [the object of hope] must be something arduous and difficult to obtain, for we do not speak of anyone hoping for trifles, which are in one's power to

---

[49] *ST* I-II, q. 23, a. 4, resp.

[50] For specific discussions of the operative distinctions between the passions, see, for instance, *ST* I-II, q. 23, aa. 1, 2, and 4, especially. For St. Thomas's discussion of the order of the passions, both the order between the concupiscible and the irascible and the order between the various passions within the two principle categories, see *ST* I-II, q. 25

[51] Pinckaers, *Passions and Virtue*, 35.

have at any time. . . . Fourthly, that this difficult thing is something possible to obtain: for one does not hope for that which one cannot get at all.[52]

Hope, then, is that passion which intends—at a distance—some attainable good that is loved. Moreover, attaining this good that is loved is deemed possible though difficult.[53]

Such hope is crucial for human existence. We hope for the good. We hope for growth in virtue. We hope for the good of others. And this hope can be an impetus for action. As St. Thomas states,

> Hope of its very nature is a help to action by making it more intense: and for two reasons. First, by reason of its object, which is good, difficult but possible. For the thought of its being difficult arouses our attention; which the thought that it is possible is no drag on our effort. Hence it follows that by reason of hope man is intent on his action. Secondly, on account of its effect. Because hope . . . causes pleasure; which is a help to action. . . . Therefore hope is conducive to action.[54]

Regarding this aspect of hope, Pinckaers remarks that hope is "like the soul of action; we cannot act without a minimum of hope."[55]

This observation brings to the fore the significance of despair. If hope has the role it does as "the soul of action," then despair has a significant role as well, though as something that stifles action. If we love that to which we

---

[52] *ST* I-II, q. 40, a. 1, resp. See also *ST* I-II, q. 40, a. 2, resp.: "[H]ope is a movement of the appetitive power ensuing from the apprehension of a future good, difficult but possible to obtain; namely, a stretching forth of the appetite to such a good."

[53] Note that here our primary concern is the passion of hope and not the virtue. A virtue is a habit or stable disposition ordered to certain kinds of perfective action. Virtue is a disposition or "quality of mind" (*ST* I-II, q. 55, a. 4, resp.) which makes both the possessor and the action good; see *ST* I-II, q. 56, a. 3, resp. Also, as a stable tendency, it is not, according to St. Thomas, something that can be "easily changed"; see *ST* I-II, q. 49, a. 2, ad 3. Though the virtue of hope is not unrelated to the passion of hope, the latter does not name a habit or stable disposition for perfective action. Moreover, virtues, in the strict sense, pertain to the will or rational appetite and not the sensitive appetite. The will is the principle of action. The passions are not principles of this sort. St. Thomas maintains that the virtues of the irascible or concupiscible powers, if we are to call them virtues, are only such in a relative way (*secundum quid*). For St. Thomas's general discussion of habits and virtues, see *ST* I-II, qq. 49–70. For virtues considered in a relative sense, see especially *ST* I-II, q. 56, a. 3.

[54] *ST* I-II, q. 40, a. 8, resp.

[55] Pinckaers, *Passions and Virtue*, 35.

are inclined, that with which we are connatural or sympathetic, then we hope for those goods that we love and stretch forth toward them. When we despair, however, we deem of some good that is loved and deemed difficult, that it is also impossible. If we deem the loved good not only difficult but impossible, we will not act. There will be no "stretching forth of the appetite to [the good loved]."[56] If our despair is rooted in bodily defect or misapprehension, we will not act toward some good that one ought.

Another aspect of despair worth noting is that it has the character of withdrawal. As noted above, all the passions, with the exception of anger, are opposing pairs. The nature of the opposition or "contrariety" in the concupiscible passions, however, is different than the contrariety in the irascible passions. In the latter, there are opposing movements with respect to the same term. In the former, there are movements with respect to two opposing terms—namely good and evil. St. Thomas states,

> [T]here is a twofold contrariety of movements. One is in respect of approach to contrary terms: and this contrariety alone is to be found in the concupiscible passions, for instance between love and hatred. The other is according to approach and withdrawal with regard to the same term; and is to be found in the irascible passions.[57]

Regarding hope and despair in particular, he continues,

> Now the object of hope, which is the arduous good, has the character of a principle of attraction, if it be considered in the light of something attainable; and thus hope tends thereto, for it denotes a kind of approach. But in so far as it is considered as unobtainable, it has the character of a principle of repulsion. . . . And this is how despair stands in regards to this object, wherefore it implies a movement of withdrawal: and consequently it is contrary to hope, as withdrawal is to approach.[58]

When someone apprehends (or misapprehends) some loved good that is difficult, that it is, in fact, impossible, they suffer the passion of despair. They suffer from a tendency to withdrawal from the loved good. They suffer from a lack motivation to respond or act by way of approach to the loved good. As St. Thomas notes, "Despair implies not only privation of hope, but

---

[56] *ST* I-II, q. 40, a. 2, resp.
[57] *ST* I-II, q. 40, a. 4, resp. See also *ST* I-II, q. 23, a. 2.
[58] *ST* I-II, q. 40, a. 4, resp.

also a recoil from the thing desired, by reason of its being esteemed impossible to get."[59]

How does this happen? How does one despair of some good that is loved, deeming it difficult and impossible to attain? In spite of the differences between them, each of these eleven principal passions names an experience "suffered" by the individual in the sensitive appetite. Moreover, as noted above, each of these passions names something suffered in the sensitive appetite that is due to bodily modification or change. That is to say, though experienced in the sensitive faculties of the soul, the passions originate in the body, whether due to real or perceived circumstances in the external world. The passion of despair is no different in this regard. Having recognized some object as appetible, which is to say as a good to be sought and hopefully attained, one might despair of the possibility of actually attaining that good. One might believe that attaining the good is impossible, at least for themselves. Such despair is experienced in the irascible appetite due to some modification or change in the body. Conceivably, this experience of despair could be due to bodily modification or change that has for its cause something real or perceived in the external world. Equally conceivable is that this experience of despair could be due to a certain bodily disposition over which they had little or no control.[60] Let us focus on the latter.

For example, one might be predisposed to apprehend (or misapprehend) certain attainable though arduous goods as impossible. For example, a vitamin D deficiency in the body may cause Seasonal Affective Disorder, a mood disorder that could affect one's apprehension, contributing to a lack of hope with respect to some arduous good. Any number of things might contribute to our possibly misapprehending the arduousness or possibility of attaining to some good, leading to despair. In *ST* I-II, q. 40, a. 6, resp., St. Thomas mentions some examples of circumstances that could lead to certain (mis)apprehensions concerning some good. "Youths," for instance, look more to the future than the past, they tend toward those things that are arduous due to their being "full of spirit," and are inexperienced, having "not suffered defeat, nor had experience of obstacles to their efforts," which makes them "prone to count a thing possible to them." Also, there is the "drunkard" who is fully of "high spirits" such that he is prone to "heedlessness of dangers and

---

[59] *ST* I-II, q. 40, a. 4, ad 3.

[60] The question of control is a complicated one. There is a certain sense in which one might have control of his bodily disposition. One might, for instance, know about some bodily defect and seek to do something about it. Other times, however, some bodily disposition—defective or not—might not be something of which the person is aware and, indeed, sometimes may be something for which he has no control.

shortcomings."[61] While his examples concern hope, one can easily imagine other circumstances that might make one prone to despair. The bodily disposition of the drunkard has affected his capacity for apprehending the arduousness and possibility of the loved good. The bodily disposition of one who has consumed a depressant might have also affected his capacity for apprehending the arduousness and possibility of the loved good. The former, according to St. Thomas, suffers the passion of hope; the latter suffers the passion of despair.

Among the other causes of such apprehensions, one might include historical context, formation or habituation, and even brain chemistry. Depending on our neurophysiology, for instance, whether certain synapses fire or certain neurotransmitters are present, one might be disposed to apprehend that which is attainable as though it were not. Consequently, some people might be disposed to the passion of despair and, very often, through no fault of their own.[62] Again, the body or bodily dispositions can be partially determinative of our hoping or despairing. Because of one's body, he or she might despair of some good that is loved that it is difficult or impossible to attain even though, in fact, it is not.[63] This can be debilitating. One who suffers despair, whether through proper apprehension or misapprehension, might be paralyzed.

Despair, then, is a *movement* of the sensitive appetite. In it, the sense appetite is moved from potency to act such that what was previously in potency—namely, the sensitive appetite—actually responds to the object of sensation. That object is apprehended, of course. First, it is apprehended as a good that is loved and something for which to hope. Second, as apprehended as a good that is loved, it is also desired. One wishes to possess it. Third, it is deemed difficult. Fourth, and ultimately, it is deemed impossible. As a movement of the *sensitive* appetite, however, it concerns the body. The passions, including despair, are rooted in the body or bodily change (or bodily disposition). The body might affect the apprehension of the object

---

[61] *ST* I-II, q. 40, a. 6, resp.

[62] Of course, there could be a behavioral component to this as well. Cognitive behavior can have a drastic effect on the perception of the possibility or impossibility of some good. For many, the disposition to despair might be mitigated by cognitive behavioral therapy. In the case of those for whom brain chemistry contributes, medication (in addition to counseling) could be advantageous.

[63] One's despair might arise from a right apprehension of the arduousness and modality of the loved good. Though my emphasis is despair as something caused by a misapprehension rooted in bodily disposition, there are certainly instances in which despair is not due to misapprehension. Nonetheless, much that I have to say about the passion of despair vis-à-vis the presence of faith would obtain in either case, it seems to me.

given by the senses. As such, it might affect the *appetite* to which that apprehension corresponds. If the apprehension is right or true, then the passion that follows should be right. If the apprehension, possibly due to the body, is wrong, then the passion that follows is wrong. In such cases, one apprehends wrongly the good or the difficulty or the modality of the object. One might apprehend what is good as if it were not. One might apprehend what is not difficult as if it were. One might apprehend what is possible as if it were impossible. All of this could be influenced, at least in principle, by the body or bodily dispositions. As such, these apprehensions of sensible realities can lead to one passion rather than another, for instance, to despair instead to hope.

CONCLUSION: DESPAIR AND FAITH

In this conclusion, let us briefly reflect on the relationship between the passion of despair and the theological virtue of faith. As described above, according to St. Thomas, the passion of despair of itself might not be sinful but rather something truly "suffered," in both the technical and the existential senses of the word. Insofar as it pertains to the sensitive appetite, in which case the role of the will is not primary, it is not (or not necessarily) a voluntary act.[64] Nothing involuntary is a properly human act such that it might be sinful. Moreover, insofar as there might be some defect in one's bodily disposition, about which culpability might be mitigated or absent, negative passions like despair need not be sinful.

As such, the passion of despair is not something that would undermine the faith of the individual who suffers, as if it were a sin against charity. Part of—and only part of—the reason that the passion of despair does not imply or entail a loss of faith has to do with the faculties involved. Faith, according to St. Thomas, is intellectual assent that is moved by the will. Both of these operations pertain to the rational aspects of the soul rather

[64] This is, admittedly, a disputed claim. For instance, see Jeffrey Froula, "Aquinas on the Moral Neutrality of the Passion of Despair," 310: "In man, the passions are, to some extent, subject to reason and will, and are therefore voluntary." There remains some ambiguity, however. Froula also notes, I think rightly, "Insofar as the passions are movements of the essentially non-rational sense appetite, they are neither morally good nor evil. For, considered simply as movements of a non-rational faculty, the passions are not voluntary." Yet, this is, as he points out, according to its "natural genus." Froula observes, "Yet in man, the passions are, to some degree, subject to the rational powers of reason and will. Because of this, the passions in man can be voluntary 'either from being commanded by the will, or from not being checked by the will' [*ST* I-II, q. 24, a. 1]." A key term here is "can." The passions *can* be voluntary though they need not be, it seems to me.

than the sensitive aspects. The will, or rational appetite, is distinct (though not entirely separated) from the sensitive appetite, being based on a different sort of apprehension. Though the senses certainly contribute to the operations of the rational soul, they are not determinative. In faith, the healing and elevating presence of grace—namely, in the form of the *lumen fidei* (in the intellect) and the *divina instinctus* (in the will)—makes for, again, a different sort of apprehension. The light of faith attunes one to supernatural truth; the divine instinct attunes one to the supernatural Good who God is. Because the light of faith (in the intellect) and the divine instinct (in the will) have their source in God and not the senses,[65] the assent that occurs in faith need not be negated somehow by the sensitive apprehension and sensitive appetite that is, at least in part, rooted in bodily disposition. The healed/elevated intellect and will might "override" the sensitive apprehension or movement of the sensitive appetite. This is not to say that the body cannot affect faith, but it certainly need not.

One who experiences the passion of despair, then, one who lacks hope due to the passive response of the sensitive appetite to whatever is apprehended, and in conjunction with the bodily change or disposition, is no more guilty of unbelief than one who is fearful or anxious or depressed. This position is strengthened by the observation that, for St. Thomas, not even the sin of despair, the sin against theological hope, of itself negates one's faith. St. Thomas notes,

> Unbelief pertains to the intellect, but despair, to the appetite, and the intellect is about universals, while the appetite is moved in connection with particulars, since the appetitive movement is from the soul towards things, which in themselves, are particular.[66]

He continues,

> [A] man while retaining in the universal, the true estimate of faith, namely, that there is in the Church the power of forgiving sins, may

---

[65] It is more complicated than this, of course. For St. Thomas, there is certainly an external, or one might say sensitive, component to the act of faith. There is the internal cause of faith, which is grace, including both the *lumen fidei* and the *divina instinctus*. There is also an external component—namely, the preached word that is heard. One's sensitive apprehension of what is heard could be impacted by one's bodily disposition, and consequently, the preached word could be misapprehended. Nevertheless, because the role of the will is ambiguous in the context of the passions, the culpability for its effects might still be mitigated or absent.

[66] *ST* II-II, q. 20, a. 2, resp.

suffer a movement of despair, to wit, that for him, being in such a
state, there is no hope of pardon, his estimate being corrupted in a
particular matter. In this way there can be despair, just as there can
be other mortal sins, without unbelief.[67]

Again, what St. Thomas has in mind when speaking of the despair that
one might have while retaining faith pertains to the particular estimation of
one's own salvation. It is not a doubt or denial of the universal principle that
sins may be forgiven and salvation obtained.

Of course, one ought not think too well of faith without hope. Despair
that opposes theological hope is, after all, a mortal sin. It constitutes a loss
of charity and sanctifying grace. To put it bluntly, the sin of despair is something of which to repent. It is not, however, something that of itself removes
faith. As St. Thomas states, "He who receives faith from God without charity [which is to say, apart from sanctifying grace], is healed from unbelief
[*sanatur ab infidelitate*], not entirely (because the sin of his previous unbelief
is not removed) but in part, namely, in the point of ceasing from committing
such and such a sin."[68] Here, we have confirmation of the earlier passage in
which St. Thomas affirms that one who lacks theological hope may, nevertheless, remain a believer. One remains "healed from unbelief" even apart
from charity and sanctifying grace, which is to say, in the state of mortal
sin, even as a consequence of the sin of despair.[69] There is, of course, much
more that could be said about the sin of despair and the presence or absence
of faith and even the relationship between the passion of despair and the sin
of despair.[70] Those discussions must wait for another occasion. It suffices for
our purposes to recognize that even the mortal sin of despair does not, of
itself, negate faith, and the passion of despair need not either.

Ultimately, then, in one who suffers the passion of despair, faith can

---

[67] *ST* II-II, q. 20, a. 2, resp.
[68] *ST* II-II, q. 6, a. 2, ad 3.
[69] For a more thorough discussion of the relationship between faith and charity, the possibility of faith apart from charity, see my essay, "Can Dead Faith Assent to God? A Brief
Reflection on Saint Thomas's Account on the Relationship between Living and Lifeless
Faith," in *Nova et Vetera*, English Edition, 18, no. 4 (2020).
[70] Regarding the relationship between the passion of despair and the sin of despair, I simply
note that one might suffer the passion of despair without committing the sin of despair;
one might lack the passion of hope while retaining the theological virtue of hope. In fact,
one might suffer many of the negative passions and yet still retain hope. For a discussion of
Job's hoping in the face of his suffering, see Daria Spezzano, "The Hope and Fear of Blessed
Job," in *Reading Job with St. Thomas Aquinas*, ed. Matthew Levering, Piotr Roszak, Jorgen
Vijgen (Washington, DC: The Catholic University of America Press, 2020), 261–314.

remain . . . though it is a "hopeless" faith. The despairing believer can still believe God and what God has revealed. From the depths of despair, that one might still proclaim a cold and a broken "Hallelujah!"—a cold and a broken "Praise to you, YHWH!"

The Role of Suffering
in the New Evangelization

JOHN RZIHA
Benedictine College, KS

DURING THE 2021 Benedictine college graduation ceremony, the keynote speaker, Bishop Andrew Cozzens, challenged the graduates to recognize that the love of Christ can transform any suffering into an act of love. He stated that the graduates should not be afraid of embracing the suffering that accompanies authentic love, for this is the secret to a joyful life. Upon hearing these words, one of the non-Catholic nursing professors remarked, "Now I understand why the students regularly talk about suffering in their papers." I was surprised by her comment. After all, even when I was a young child, my parents (echoing Paul in Col 1:24) had instilled in me the idea that when I endured my suffering out of love for Christ, I participated in his act of redemption.

My parents' common Catholic response to the existence of suffering follows a much longer tradition of explaining how suffering fits into God's plan of salvation history. Long before Christ, the existence of suffering was seen as a challenge to faith in a good and powerful God. In response to this challenge, the Catholic Church throughout the centuries has usually embraced the role of suffering as a key aspect of living a holy life. Unfortunately, when this embrace was built on a poor theology of God and his interaction in the world, the result was spiritually unhealthy actions focused on fear of God and on suffering as a punishment for sins.

However, in recent times, some personalist philosophers and theologians have noted the close link between suffering and the complete gift of self that gives true personal identity. These scholars root their theology of suffering in an understanding of a Trinitarian God who creates humans to participate in the complete giving and receiving that manifests the personal identity in the Trinity. From this perspective, suffering is closely coupled to love and, when done out of love for God, results in humans becoming more like God. Because of this important role of suffering in the life of sharing in God's love and happiness, St. John Paul II even spoke of the Gospel (or good news) of suffering.[1] Suffering allows humans to transcend themselves through a sincere gift of self in a particularly profound way. It allows humans to discover themselves more and more fully.[2] In a similar vein, St. Josemaría Escrivá spoke of suffering as the "touchstone of love."[3] A touchstone is used to determine the purity of gold. Escrivá explained that when someone loves through suffering, "the tenderness of a person's gift of himself takes root and shows itself in a true and profound affection that is stronger than death."[4]

A detailed study of the role of suffering in making humans more like God through a loving gift of self is certainly a worthwhile endeavor, but in this paper I am going to draw out another implication of suffering found in some of these more recent theologians: the very important role of suffering in the new evangelization. To explain this role, I will first note what is meant by the new evangelization. Then I will show the key role of suffering in evangelization in the writings of Pope St. John Paul II and Fr. Luigi Giussani. Finally, I will look at a very different role of suffering in the writings of Alasdair MacIntyre.

WHAT IS THE NEW EVANGELIZATION?

Because we live in a post-Christian society, the recent popes have referred to the effort to evangelize traditionally Christian areas as a "new evangelization." The original evangelization focused on bringing Christian beliefs and practices to cultures that were not familiar with Christianity. The new evangelization seeks to reintroduce Christianity to a society that, although

---

[1] Pope John Paul II, On Human Suffering *Salvifici Doloris* (Feb. 11, 1984). Section VI is titled the "Gospel of Suffering," but the whole document presents a Gospel of suffering.

[2] John Paul II, Salvifici Doloris, §23. St. John Paul states: "The more he shares in this [God's] love, man rediscovers himself more and more fully in suffering: he rediscovers the 'soul' which he thought he had 'lost' because of suffering." See also John Paul II, The Gospel of Life *Evangelium Vitae* (March 25, 1981), §81.

[3] Josemaría Escrivá, "Marriage: A Christian Vocation," in *Christ Is Passing By* (New York: Scepter, 1974), 55.

[4] Escrivá, "Marriage," 55.

familiar with Christian beliefs and practices, either misunderstands these beliefs or has lost its understanding of their deeper meaning. These post-Christian societies often equate Christianity with an antiquated superstition that results in illogical rules that suppress their true individuality. As a consequence, many either reject Christianity completely or have a "sort of secularist interpretation of the Christian faith"[5] that distorts traditional Christian morality.

The new evangelization seeks to counter these deeply flawed understandings of Christianity by showing how faith in Christ answers the fundamental questions of life and results in true and lasting happiness. John Paul II explains how all are called to transform culture by drawing others to the faith by radiating "joy, love and hope" so that others may see that the Christian message gives meaning to every aspect of life.[6] The message of Jesus Christ is the antidote to the unhappiness that comes from many anthropological errors in modern and postmodern society. In a society that often considers suffering to be the antitheses of happiness, the Christian message teaches that a participation in the Crucifixion of Christ is the way to true happiness.

Joseph Ratzinger further explains the new evangelization by noting that all people ask the question of what is the path toward happiness. He replies, "To evangelize means to show this path—to teach the art of living. At the beginning of his public life Jesus says, I have come to evangelize the poor (Luke 4:18); this means: I have the response to your fundamental question; I will show you the path of life, the path toward happiness—rather: I am that path."[7] The new evangelization focuses on showing that Jesus is the path to true life and happiness. Since suffering is a key aspect of living, in teaching the art of living, the new evangelization also teaches the art of suffering and how trials and setbacks are important milestones on the path to happiness (see John 15:10–13).

---

5   John Paul II, The Church in Europe *Ecclesia in Europa* (June 28, 2003), §47: "Everywhere, then, *a renewed proclamation is needed even for those already baptized*. Many Europeans today think they know what Christianity is, yet they do not really know it at all. Often they are lacking in knowledge of the most basic elements and notions of the faith. Many of the baptized live as if Christ did not exist: the gestures and signs of faith are repeated, especially in devotional practices, but they fail to correspond to a real acceptance of the content of the faith and fidelity to the person of Jesus. . . . [O]ne encounters a sort of secularist interpretation of Christian faith which is corrosive and accompanied by a deep crisis of conscience and of Christian moral practice."

6   John Paul II, *Ecclesia in Europa*, §§48 and 58.

7   Joseph Ratzinger, Address to Catechists and Religion Teachers (December 2000).

A METHOD OF EVANGELIZING

To fully understand the role of suffering in the new evangelization, it is necessary to understand the method of evangelization. Because the method of John Paul II and Luigi Giussani are relatively similar, I will describe their methodology together and then talk about the role of suffering in their methodology. I will then explain the methodology and role of suffering in the works of Alasdair MacIntyre in a separate section.

Although there are many different ways that one can effectively spread the Gospel in a post-Christian culture, both Saint John Paul II and Fr. Luigi Giussani (1922–2005, founder of the Communion and Liberation Movement) use a phenomenological methodology. Phenomenology is a philosophical method that seeks to find truth by an examination of one's experiences. Although John Paul and Giussani used the method in their own unique ways, they both began with an examination of human experiences in order to find true meaning and happiness in peoples' lives. In other words, both believed that by thinking about our past experiences and deeply examining what made us truly happy or unhappy within those experiences, we can find moral and spiritual truths.

Giussani believed that a thorough examination of one's experiences will result in a recognition that only God will fulfill one's deepest needs and desires. He called this innate inclination to God "the religious sense."[8] He believed that a deep look at human experiences reveals that humans cannot fulfill their true needs on their own. When real inner suffering strikes (and all people will experience this in their own unique ways), humans find that they are helpless to fulfill their true needs.[9] They find themselves in a state of "solitude" (even amidst others) and seek community based on this commonality of helplessness. In other words, this interior suffering causes people to feel all alone in a constantly moving world, and it drives them to search for others who share in their sufferings.

Yet, even in these communities, there is still an emptiness in their lives. They realize that they need something "beyond their own situations that can resolve" their inner suffering. This expectation that only something greater than humans can resolve their suffering leads to prayer[10] and ultimately to

---

[8] Luigi Giussani's book *The Religious Sense* (Montreal: McGill-Queen's University Press, 1997), is dedicated to showing that all humans have an adherence to an ultimate thing in all of their gestures, actions, and relationships. This ultimate thing is God, who is the ultimate meaning of human existence.

[9] Luigi Giussani, *The Journey to Truth Is an Experience* (Montreal: McGill-Queen's University Press, 2006), 53–54.

[10] Guissani, *The Journey to Truth*, 55–58.

an *encounter with Christ* where they find meaning in their interior suffering.[11] This encounter with Christ takes place through an encounter with the Church which is the face "that the reality of Christ takes in our lives."[12] Through a deep look at their experiences, humans can determine that only in the Church can they discover their true selves.[13] In order to help others discover their true selves, all Catholics should become the face of Christ to those who desire greater meaning and happiness in their lives. To evangelize, Catholics must constantly be open to an encounter with others.

After reading this brief explanation of Giussani's methodology, one might be tempted to ask, "How does this examination of experiences not lead to a purely subjective morality?" After all, a look at one's subjective experiences hardly seems like a good source of objective truth. John Paul II provides the answer to this question. Early in his academic formation, he learned the teachings of St. Thomas Aquinas and recognized how these teachings offered the answers to the questions asked by an unfulfilled and selfish modern world.[14] However, he also realized that modern Europeans no longer looked for moral truths outside of themselves (like in God or in the order of nature); they sought to find morality within themselves.

Because this practice of seeking morality within oneself normally ends in disaster, the future Pope John Paul II sought to find a way to teach people how to discover traditional Catholic moral truths within their own experiences. He was able to do this by grounding the phenomenological methodology of Max Scheler in Thomas Aquinas's understanding that humans are naturally inclined to perform actions that fulfill them. Aquinas

---

[11] Guissani, *The Journey to Truth*, 65–68, 92.

[12] Guissani, *The Journey to Truth*, 93.

[13] Giussani states, "Lived experience means to be immersed in a present that involves our whole personality, engaging all the factors that make up a human being. It is the evidence of a living experience. And no proposal or experience exists that corresponds to the factors making up the self in a way that can be compared to the Christian experience." *Why the Church?* (Montreal: McGill-Queen's University Press, 2001), xi.

[14] Several authors have provided an intellectual biography of St. John Paul II that explains in detail how and why he used a phenomenological approach rooted in the anthropology and moral theology of Thomas Aquinas. The author that I have found to be the most helpful is Michael Waldstein. He has several works that address this topic, including the recently published, *The Glory of the Logos in the Flesh: St. John Paul's Theology of the Body* (Washington, DC: The Catholic University of America Press, 2020). Other authors include Brian Pedraza, *Catechesis for the New Evangelization* (Washington, DC: The Catholic University of America Press, 2020); W. Norris Clarke, "The Integration of Personalism and Thomistic Metaphysics in Twenty-First-Century Thomism," in *The Creative Retrieval of Thomas Aquinas* (New York: Fordham University Press, 2009); and Thomas Petri, *Aquinas and the Theology of the Body: The Thomistic Foundations of John Paul II's Anthropology* (Washington, DC: The Catholic University of America Press, 2018).

believed that because God created all things for purpose, all things were created to become more like God by performing specific types of actions. Humans, in particular, were created to become like God by entering into loving relationships with God and others. Hence, God imprinted on human nature an interior drive to perform those actions that fulfill them and allow them to participate in God's happiness. Karol Wojtyła, the future Pope John Paul II, recognized that because all humans have this interior drive to perform their proper actions, when humans deeply examine their actions, they will find moral truth. He explained, "If *operari* results from *esse*, then *operari* is also—proceeding in the opposite direction—the most proper avenue to knowledge of that *esse*."[15] In other words, because a person's actions follow his mode of being, by studying his actions you can learn about the person himself and discover how that person can find his true identity.

Although using the phenomenological method divorced from a teleological understanding of human nature will lead to moral relativism,[16] by grounding his use of the phenomenological method in a robust account of the natural inclinations, Wojtyła is able to guide humans to discover objective moral truths by looking within their experiences. For example, all humans are made to transcend themselves and ultimately discover their true identity by giving the gift of themselves. Wojtyła believed that if humans examine their experiences at a deep enough level (especially the experience of performing actions), they will find that they are fulfilled in personal relationships (as made in the image of the Trinity). The evangelizer seeks to help humans properly interpret their experiences to find the truth. John Paul's *Theology of the Body* is a good example of this methodology. In this work, he covers a topic from multiple different perspectives in hopes that one or more of these perspectives will resonate with the experiences of the audience. He believes that, deep down, everyone can find experiences that confirm that

---

[15] Karol Wojtyła, "The Person: Subject and Community," in *Person and Community* (New York: Peter Lang, 1993), 223. Pedraza in *Catechesis for the New Evangelization*, 152, explains this quote by noting: "If the reality of the human person is expressed in human acts, then these acts, in turn, can provide access to the reality of the person."

[16] Ronald Modras, "The Moral Philosophy of John Paul II," in *Theological Studies* 41, no. 4 (1980): 684, explains how John Paul recognized that, ultimately, the phenomenological system of Scheler is not a sufficient philosophical system to ground a moral philosophy. He notes, "Although Scheler's system includes some objective tendencies, its objectivity breaks down, Wojtyla contends, because of its phenomenological principles; good and evil only 'appear' as phenomena of intentional feelings. Scheler's 'emotional intuitionism' considers values in isolation from the context of human action; Wojtyla rejects it as unable to determine acts as good or evil in themselves. For moral values to be real and objective, they must be based on principles that are 'meta-phenomenological, or, frankly, meta-physical.'"

true happiness comes from recognizing the proper role of the body in loving relationships.

THE ROLE OF SUFFERING WITHIN THEIR NEW EVANGELIZATION METHODOLOGY

Since the evangelizer guides people to discover their inclination to God within their experiences, and suffering is a key aspect of human experience, for both Giussani and John Paul, suffering has a key role in evangelization. I will first treat the role of suffering for the person hearing the Gospel message, and then I will examine the importance of suffering for those proclaiming the Gospel.

In the post-Christian Western culture, many people have an incorrect understanding of the Christian message and believe that it is either false or will not fulfill any of their needs. As a consequence, when it comes to evangelizing, one of the big problems in the modern world is that very few people want to hear the message of Christ. Even if their life seems to lack meaning, they have plenty of distractions to keep them from dwelling on these deeper issues. If they are able to avoid evaluating their experiences through constant distraction, then a phenomenological methodology will not be effective. However, suffering has a way of cutting through the distractions and forcing people to ask questions about the meaning of life. John Paul explains that when people suffer, "even the most heedless person is prompted there to wonder about his own life and its meaning."[17] He also notes, "[I]t is precisely in times of sickness that the need to find adequate responses to the ultimate questions about human life is the most pressing: questions on the meaning of pain, suffering and death itself."[18]

Not only does suffering move people to wonder about the meaning of their lives, it also helps open a soul closed in on itself. John Paul notes, "It is suffering, more than anything else, which clears the way for the grace which transforms human souls."[19] Once suffering causes people to reexamine the meaning of their experiences, an encounter with Christ, who loves us and

---

[17] John Paul II, Address on the Ninth World Day of the Sick (Aug. 22, 2000), §3. See also *Salvifici Doloris*, §§9 and 26; *Evangelium Vitae*, §32.

[18] John Paul II, Address on the Thirteenth World Day of the Sick (Feb. 11, 2005), §6. Here is the full quote: "[I]t is precisely in times of sickness that the need to find adequate responses to the ultimate questions about human life is the most pressing: questions on the meaning of pain, suffering and death itself, considered not only as an enigma that is hard to face, but a mystery in which Christ incorporates our lives in himself, opening them to a new and definitive birth for the life that will never end."

[19] John Paul II, *Salvifici Doloris*, §27.

brings us hope, gives meaning to this pain and suffering.[20] In other words, often humans with a false interpretation of their experiences have "hardened" their interpretation and are not open to other viewpoints. Unless something significant happens in their lives, they have little reason to reevaluate their experiences and seek a loving relationship with God. Physical, emotional, or spiritual suffering can be a catalyst that causes humans to reevaluate their lives and search for meaning by reevaluating their interpretation of their experiences.[21] Thus, suffering serves as a preamble for the Gospel message since it motivates people to search for answers that can best be explained by the self-gift of Christ in the Incarnation and Crucifixion.

By overcoming the distractions of a comfortable life, suffering allows the Gospel to be spread to those who would normally not be open to it. However, if those who are suffering are going to incorporate the Gospel in their lives, *there must be someone there to accompany them* and help them interpret their experiences in light of this interior inclination to give of themselves to God and others. The experience of suffering forces people to ask deeper questions in their life, but how they interpret this experience will depend upon whether or not someone is there to guide them to the Crucifixion and to give an explanation of how a relationship with Christ will bring true meaning and happiness to their lives.[22] This guide can show them how suffering, when endured willingly, can be an act of great love and a true gift of self.[23]

Through their actions and words they seek to show those who are suffering that when someone loves God, a life lived in pain can become very "attractive." Giussani explains: "How can a life lived in pain become so attractive? The energy deriving from adherence to the ultimate reality of things means that even what the world around us sees as useless has its use . . . if all life is being lived in relation to true reality—'if it is offered to God'" as an act of love. "In truth . . . man's sanctification through suffering introduces him, even down here, to a better world."[24] However, suffering is

[20] Luigi Giussani, "Woman, Do Not Weep!" in *Christ, God's Companionship with Man* (Montreal: McGill-Queen's University Press, 2015), 75–78.

[21] Jeffry Bishop, *The Anticipatory Corpse: Medicine, Power, and the Care of the Dying* (South Bend, IN: The University of Notre Dame Press, 2011), prelude; gives a good example of how cancer can cause someone to reevaluate her life.

[22] John Paul notes in *Evangelium Vitae*, §92: "The work of education cannot avoid a consideration of suffering and death." See also §89.

[23] John Paul II, *Salvifici Doloris*, §29, states that suffering is "present in order to unleash love in the human person, that unselfish gift of one's 'I' on behalf of other people, especially those 'who suffer.'"

[24] Luigi Giussani, *Why the Church?*, 221. Giussani takes the last part of this quotation from

only attractive when someone understands the "Gospel of suffering" and is guided to look deep into their experiences to find that suffering really can be a key component of loving others. There is always suffering in the world, and the members of the Church must seek out those who are suffering physically, emotionally, and spiritually in order help them discover true happiness amidst their afflictions.[25]

Suffering also plays an important role for those seeking to evangelize others. In a world where false beliefs bombard people from every direction, others need a reason to take Catholicism seriously. Giussani notes that when Christians suffer joyfully, the faith is "verified" within us.[26] Joyful endurance of suffering shows that the totality of who we are is bound to Christ. When humans are willing to suffer out of love for someone else or for a particular cause, the suffering shows that their love is real. These people are authentic to the core of their being—fully living what they believe. Furthermore, as already seen, Giussani believed that suffering forces people to recognize that they cannot fix their problems by themselves and causes them to seek others who suffer like them. When those without faith have an encounter with Christians who suffer, the Christians' very act of suffering with hope and love points to something greater than themselves. These Christians become a "sacrament" that communicates the deeper meaning of Christianity: that the nature of God as love is most revealed when he sacrificed his life for us at Calvary. Because the suffering of Christ reveals this love of God, John Paul II speaks of the "Gospel of suffering" as part of God's plan for humans to discover their true identity in a sincere gift of self.[27] When those within the Church suffer with joy, they become a beacon of light to others who are also suffering and struggling to find meaning in their lives.

Furthermore, because the phenomenological method is focused on the proper interpretation of experiences, those who have found meaning in their suffering bring valuable insight into the process of evangelizing others. Their suffering brings them into solidarity with those who suffer and becomes a commonality between them and the one they seek to help.[28] In other words,

---

Charles Moeller's *Sagesse grecque et Paradoxe chrétien.*

[25] As Giussani notes, "The greatest joy in a man's life is to feel Christ alive and beating in his heart, taking flesh in his thoughts." *Christ, God's Companionship with Man*, 13. See 70–71 and 75–78 for more on suffering and happiness.

[26] See Giussani's description of the "encounter" in *The Journey to Truth Is an Experience*, 91–106. For a more explicit citation, see Josemaría Escrivá, *Saint Paul's Letters to the Corinthians.* (Ireland: Four Courts Press, 2005), 147.

[27] John Paul II, *Salvifici Doloris*, sec. VI.

[28] John Paul II, *Salvifici Doloris*, §29 states, "Suffering . . . is also present in order *to unleash love in the human person*, that unselfish gift of one's 'I' on behalf of other people. . . . [E]very

when suffering causes people without faith to seek greater meaning in their lives, someone who has already experienced a similar type of suffering can more effectively guide them to properly interpret their experiences. For example, I just had a student write a beautiful paper about how her experiences of struggling with her faith after losing her best friend allowed her to very effectively bring meaning to the life of a young woman who had recently lost her father. The genius of the phenomenological method is that those who struggle with temptation, loss, anxiety, pain, or other illnesses have an invaluable role in evangelization because they have insight into how to help others properly interpret their similar experiences. When their afflictions help them to enter into solidarity with Christ, they are able to help others with similar afflictions enter into solidarity with Christ.

People have asked me why God allows them to be plagued by various conditions, such as depression, same-sex attraction, chronic pain, or a toxic home life. Without purporting to explain the depths of God's plan, I can always assure them that God allows these afflictions in their lives so they can help guide others with a similar condition. These people have unique experiences and insights that will help them guide others to understand the Gospel of suffering as a manifestation of their true personal identity. These very afflictions that make their life hard can be ways to manifest the type of love necessary for true loving relationships with God and others and the resulting true freedom and happiness.

A study of the writings of John Paul and Giussani shows that two features especially highlight the role of suffering in the new evangelization. The first is the important role of suffering within the phenomenological method. Because this method helps humans discover moral and spiritual truths by looking within their experiences, suffering has a particularly important role both for the one with and the one without a loving relationship with God. For those without this relationship, suffering opens people up to the Gospel by causing them to question their understanding of their experiences. For those with this relationship, suffering allows them to enter into solidarity with others who need the Gospel since they have experienced similar things. The second feature is the close link between suffering and the complete gift of self through which humans discover their true personal identity. When humans suffer out of love for God or others, they transcend themselves

individual must feel as if *called personally* to bear witness to love in suffering. . . . This refers to physical sufferings, but it is even more true when it is a question of the many kinds of moral suffering, and when it is primarily the soul that is suffering" (emphasis in original); see also §30 where the pope states that suffering should transform the whole of civilization into a "civilization of love."

through an act of love. This gift of self causes and enhances relationships that shape and define their true personal identity. When others guide them to understand the role of the Gospel of suffering in their relationships, suffering brings meaning and happiness to their lives.[29]

THE ROLE OF SUFFERING IN THE THOUGHT OF ALASDAIR MACINTYRE

Alasdair MacIntyre (1929–present) is probably the most influential contemporary Catholic philosopher in America. He is most famous for his use of intellectual history to show that the teleological understanding of the world found in the Thomistic/Aristotelian tradition is the most intellectually coherent of all philosophical options. Although he is certainly not an evangelist in the normal sense of the term, MacIntyre has played a role in the new evangelization (even if unintentionally). Although he is writing to a different audience (scholars) and using a different methodology, a type of suffering is also involved in an intellectual "conversion" to a more coherent tradition (or in his terms: rational justification of a more coherent position). Furthermore, recognizing the intellectual consistency of the Thomistic/Aristotelian tradition also means recognizing the intelligibility of the Gospel as found in the Thomistic tradition. MacIntyre himself had an intellectual and spiritual conversion during the late 1970s and early 1980s, where he gradually moved from working within the Marxist tradition to the Aristotelian tradition to eventually the Thomistic/Aristotelian tradition (although one can still find Marxist elements in his writings).

MACINTYRE'S METHODOLOGY

MacIntyre's methodology is especially seen in his books *Three Rival Versions of Moral Inquiry* and *Ethics in the Conflicts of Modernity*.[30] MacIntyre believes that people mature philosophically through intellectual problems and challenges. By examining their personal narrative (a history of the development and exercise of their rational powers), a person is able to justify his or her practical decisions. In other words, to live a rationally consistent moral life, humans must have good reasons for why they perform their actions. To find these reasons, they should study the narrative of their moral development. Through this narrative, they will often discover an epistemological crisis in

---

[29] See John Paul II, *Evangelium Vitae*, §81.

[30] Alasdair MacIntyre, *Three Rival Versions of Moral Inquiry* (South Bend, IN: University of Notre Dame Press, 1990) and *Ethics in the Conflicts of Modernity: An Essay on Desire, Practical Reasoning, and Narrative* (Cambridge: Cambridge University Press, 2016).

their lives. The crisis comes from the realization that they live with one set of norms in one area of their life and another set of norms in another area of their life.[31] For example, they might find that their actions at work are not rationally consistent with their actions at church or with their family. This intellectual "suffering" motivates them to discover the theoretical presuppositions that motivate their practical reasoning in order to overcome these problems of intellectual incoherence.[32] They seek to determine whether they are acting from conflicting presuppositions or whether they are just irrational in applying these presuppositions.

If they find that they have conflicting presuppositions, then they must seek the source of their theoretical (metaphysical) presuppositions. The source can be found within a community narrative (a framework). In other words, since they were formed within a particular tradition (or traditions) within their community, they must now examine the development of the moral, political, and spiritual frameworks within their community. Yet, this community narrative must also be justified through another historical narrative—a history of the philosophical framework itself. For example, if they find that they were most influenced by a framework of moral relativism, they must study the history of how moral relativism developed due to the attempt over the centuries to find moral justification outside of a teleological system. Only through a detailed study of the historical narrative of their tradition can they see if their tradition was able to answer and overcome its own inconsistencies as well as the objections and challenges posed by other competing traditions (a type of societal intellectual suffering).

MacIntyre has written several historical narratives tracing the development of multiple philosophical traditions to show that the Thomistic/Aristotelian tradition has a coherence and adaptability that no other traditions have.[33] In other words, he is able to show that the societal and philosophical challenges of other traditions are not only answered within the Thomistic/Aristotelian tradition but that they actually strengthen this tradition since the truths found in these challenges are incorporated into this tradition, making it even more coherent. Just as people mature philosophically through intellectual problems and challenges, so also do traditions. Throughout the different narratives that he has written, MacIntyre has covered nearly every relevant Western philosopher and has shown

---

[31] MacIntyre, *Ethics in the Conflicts of Modernity*, 207.
[32] MacIntyre, *Ethics in the Conflicts of Modernity*, 209.
[33] MacIntyre, *Three Rival Versions*, 144–46.

how the Thomistic/Aristotelian tradition gives a more rationally coherent account of reality.[34]

In *Ethics in the Conflicts of Modernity*, MacIntyre gives four examples of his methodology in practice. In these examples, he shows how one would find moral contradictions in the historical narrative of one's life and the strengths and weaknesses of the traditions his or her thoughts are derived from. In his narrative of Sandra Day O'Connor, he writes a personal narrative for her that shows the development of her moral and political thought and the moral and political tradition she was drawing from when she made decisions. The following quotation shows the rational crisis that he believes O'Connor should have found in her life if she had properly examined her actions and the traditions they were flowing from:

> Of any tradition we may ask what resources it provides for critical scrutiny of its own beliefs and practices when these [beliefs] are put into question. Lack of such resources inevitably leads to significant failures, to an inability to renew the tradition by rethinking and reformulating its commitments in the face of inescapable questions. . . . *But there is a type of tradition that is peculiarly and unsurprisingly prone to such failure, that which counts among its deepest commitments a rejection of the possibility of radical self-criticism by educating its adherents into thinking in terms of a false opposition between abstract reasoning on one hand and reckoning with the particularities of social life on the other.*[35]

MacIntyre is placing Sandra Day O'Connor's actions within the tradition of political liberalism and notes that, historically, this tradition has been especially prone to failure and that those within this tradition have been unable to act consistently and overcome political challenges. This story serves as an example of how incoherence (intellectual suffering) within either one's personal moral narrative or the moral tradition this narrative is derived from should lead to a reevaluation of one's moral presuppositions and beliefs.

---

[34] Some of his more important intellectual historical narratives are *After Virtue, Whose Justice? Which Rationality?, Three Rival Versions of Moral Inquiry,* and *Ethics in the Conflicts of Modernity.*

[35] MacIntyre, *Ethics in the Conflicts of Modernity,* 272 (emphasis added).

THE ROLE OF SUFFERING IN THE NEW EVANGELIZATION

I am not sure that MacIntyre would be happy with my use of the term "evangelization" when referring to his work of helping others navigate the challenges of looking for the moral inconsistencies in their lives and traditions. Nonetheless, at its deepest level, his work is at the very least a preparation for the Gospel and in most cases an actual spreading of the Gospel. After all, the Thomistic/Aristotelian tradition that MacIntyre considers to be the most coherent affirms the Gospel message of a wise and loving God who creates an ordered world filled with rational humans that can understand this order and act accordingly by entering into loving relationships with God and others. Aristotle helped prepare people for the acceptance of this message, and Thomas Aquinas directly proclaims this message and shows that it is rationally coherent. Others within the Thomistic tradition (like John Paul II) have further developed the narrative by responding to challenges made by competing philosophical systems. Because MacIntyre shows the rational consistency of the Gospel message and answers objections of other philosophical traditions, I believe he is an important part of the new evangelization—even if he is more focused on building the foundation than actually evangelizing.

Despite these reservations, I will show what evangelization would look like when using MacIntyre's methodology. In this methodology, to evangelize means getting others to see that they will grow philosophically only by overcoming inconsistencies and problems in their moral life. Evangelizers will help people "write" their own personal moral narrative that evaluates their own moral development and actions. They will then guide others to find the inconsistencies in their moral thinking and get them to recognize the intellectual suffering that comes from living these inconsistencies.[36] Evangelizers must further guide them to see the tradition that their moral thinking comes from. Finally, they must help others learn the intellectual history of their tradition so they can determine whether its conclusions are rationally justified. Last of all, the evangelizer must be able to show the greater intellectual coherence of the traditions that correctly embody the Gospel message. MacIntyre recommends the Thomistic tradition because it has consistently overcome the challenges of competing traditions and embraced the truths within these competing traditions to become even more coherent, unlike some other "Christian" traditions that have not been able to overcome the challenges of other philosophical systems. Although

---

[36] This is very similar to the suffering that Plato alludes to when he quotes Socrates as saying, "The unexamined life is not worth living." *Apology*, section 38a.

MacIntyre is focused on this specific tradition, the most coherent of all philosophical systems are those guided by divine Revelation. Hence, other philosophical traditions that properly correspond to the Gospel message would be valid alternatives.

Obviously, using this methodology is not a project for everyone. Unlike in other forms of evangelization, which can be done by nearly any Catholic who knows the fundamentals of the faith and exhibits great love and humility, these evangelizers must be highly educated. They will need to be well educated in practical reasoning, in the relation between actions and their theoretical presuppositions, in the history of the development of various philosophical traditions, and finally in a tradition that embodies the Gospel message in an intelligible way.

However, from MacIntyre's perspective, after experiencing a lifetime of dialogue with intellectuals in other moral traditions, this exercise is exactly what is needed to get someone to change intellectual traditions. Yet, even with the proper guide, "conversion" (rational justification of a more coherent position) will not happen unless others experience an intellectual crisis. This suffering is essential to motivate the person to begin the arduous process of learning the history of their own moral tradition as well as one that embodies the Gospel message. Since this exercise is so difficult, a great deal of intellectual angst (and grace) is necessary to inspire a person to adopt a different moral tradition. In a world filled with leaders and scholars who live, teach, or enact morally inconsistent principles, there must be wise and educated people who challenge them to see these inconsistencies and exhort them to feel the proper intellectual angst that should accompany them.[37]

Like John Paul and Giussani, MacIntyre also believes that there need to be people within the Christian tradition to guide others to interpret their experiences. Only for MacIntyre, these experiences center on an examination of how they are enacting their moral presuppositions. Furthermore, this examination must be followed by a look at how these presuppositions flow from a particular tradition and an examination of the tradition itself.

---

[37] For example, the whole COVID-19 response of 2020 and 2021 was filled with intellectual inconsistencies. For MacIntyre, different traditions rank goods differently. Many people (even in the Church) ranked spiritual, social, and psychological goods as very high in some areas of life (like in advocating for pro-life causes or helping those with mental illness) but ranked them as less important than physical goods in other areas of life (like in certain extreme COVID-19 protocols). For MacIntyre, this type of inconsistency should bring "intellectual suffering" and cause a deeper search for truth. However, for most people, a recognition of this suffering can only come about if scholars and leaders are challenged to look at health in a more teleological way.

CONCLUSION

Giussani, John Paul II, and even MacIntyre give suffering an important role in their methodology. For Giussani and John Paul, suffering motivates people to reexamine their lives, opens them up to the grace of God, and allows people to grow in solidarity with others. For MacIntyre, it also causes people to reevaluate their lives but in the context of an evaluation of a particular moral tradition. Joseph Ratzinger emphasizes the close link between suffering and the gift of self within the act of evangelization in a quotation from Augustine: "St. Augustine comments on the text of John 21:16 in the following way: 'Tend my sheep,' this means to suffer for my sheep. . . . A mother cannot give life to a child without suffering. Each birth requires suffering, is suffering, and becoming a Christian is a birth. . . . We cannot give life to others without giving up our own lives."[38] Because the new evangelization includes a gift of self, it will also include suffering.

---

[38] Ratzinger, "Address to Catechists and Religion Teachers," §1.2.

Hope & Eternity

PART THREE

Purgatory:
A Place of Christian Satisfaction*

ROMANUS CESSARIO, OP
Ave Maria University, FL

I. AN UNEXPECTED VISITOR

In the year 1273, at the Dominican convent in Naples, St. Thomas Aquinas received an unexpected visit from a fellow Dominican.[1] At first, the Angelic Doctor thought that this confrere, who had succeeded him in Paris as regent-master in theology from 1272 to 1273, had just returned from the City of Lights.[2] "Welcome brother," said St. Thomas. "When did you arrive?" Recall that Thomist thought, all in all, prefers ordinary explanations of phenomena over whatsoever extraordinary ones. However on this occasion, something most extraordinary was at work in old Naples. The Dominican, whose name was Romanus, replied to Thomas, "I am, in fact, dead."

Now, this thirteenth-century Romanus was a politically well-connected Dominican of Roman origins, a member, in fact, of the very prominent

---

* This paper was delivered orally as a keynote address at the "Hope & Death: Christian Responses" conference at The Aquinas Center, Ave Maria University, on Friday, February 12, 2021.

[1] I follow the account given in Bernard Gui, "Life of St. Thomas Aquinas," no. 19, as found in *The Life of Saint Thomas Aquinas: Biographical Documents*, trans. and ed. Kenelm Foster (London: Longmans, Green, & Co., 1939), 40, 41.

[2] See Jean–Pierre Torrell, OP, *Saint Thomas Aquinas*, vol. 1: *The Person and His Works*, rev ed., trans. Robert Royal (Washington, DC: The Catholic University of America Press, 2005), 143.

Orsini clan. The recently deceased Romano de' Rossi Orsini, known in Latin as Romanus, went on to explain that God had granted him permission to visit St. Thomas because of the saint's "merits." For his part, St. Thomas suffered a momentary astonishment at the news of his successor's death, but he quickly regained his wits and took advantage of what he now realized was a vision to query his celestial guest. Never waste a good vision, so to speak. So Aquinas proceeded to seek answers from Romanus about unresolved theological questions that perhaps only someone in heaven could answer.

First, however, Aquinas asked a personal question, "How do I stand with God?" "Well," replied Romanus. Then Thomas posed the next logical question: "And what about you?" At this juncture in the narrative, we join the topic of this book. Romanus replied, "I am now in eternal life though I was kept fifteen days in Purgatory for neglecting to attend promptly to a will for which the bishop of Paris had made me responsible." This detail of Romanus's reply seems to have caused no surprise to Brother Thomas. On the contrary, Aquinas at once launched into full-time research mode with his heavenly guest.

What did Aquinas ask of his unexpected visitor? Our saint posed questions both about how human knowing works in heaven and how immediately the soul beholds God in the Beatific Vision. These questions, however, appear to have taxed Romanus's patience. So he explained simply that he does indeed see God, as if that should suffice to satisfy St. Thomas's intellectual curiosity. The extraordinary vision, we are told, ended with Brother Romanus's hinting that Thomas would soon discover for himself the answers to his questions about how the blessed see God.[3] And as it happened, Aquinas died the next year.

This essay concerns hope in the face of death. So let us return to Romanus's remark about his after-death, so to speak, experience. *"Fui in purgatorio quindecim diebus propter negligentiam."* The medieval Latin of Bernard Gui, from whose account of St. Thomas's life this charming incident is taken, spells out Purgatory time in twenty-four hour days. Romanus endured fifteen days, 360 hours, in Purgatory on account of his having been dilatory. Now, a moral theologian might question whether Romanus's Purgatory sentence covered all of his sins. Otherwise put, is negligent execution of a will the only misdeed of this noble Dominican that would have required his spending time in Purgatory? Consider the throes of everyday life. Was Romanus ever impatient? Did he allow distractions to creep into his prayers?

---

3   This detail is found in Tolomeo of Lucca's account of the vision in his "Historia Ecclesiastica," no. 16, as found in Foster, *The Life of Saint Thomas Aquinas*, 139.

Did he ever undergo, however briefly, an Abelard and Heloise moment? He had been living in Paris, after all. (Italians, of course, don't engage in that sort of behavior.) To the best of my knowledge, no account of Romanus's personal life exists. We do, however, know something about his family.

This Romanus was the nephew of Pope Nicholas III (d. 1280), whom the poet Dante, in his epic *The Divine Comedy*, places in hell for, among other reasons, the pope's nepotism: "I was a son of the She–Bear, so sly and eager to push my whelps ahead, that I pursed wealth above, and myself here."[4] Dante sees the Pope's feet locked (pursed) in stone. In any event, there is no need to infer from Pope Nicholas's medieval papal politics that the career of his nephew, one of his putative "whelps," had benefitted unduly from his uncle's largesse. At the same time, to cover a lifetime of rough and tumble Dominican apostolic activity, fifteen days in Purgatory for neglecting a legal obligation does appear somewhat, well, jejune. Truth to tell, Dominicans daily encounter all sorts of at least venial temptations. So if one assumes that Romanus Orsini did sin more than by succumbing only once to dilatoriness, how did he escape the punishment due for those sins? In other words, why only fifteen days in Purgatory? Even without knowing what other sins this Dominican master may have committed, the theological answer to this admittedly hypothetical question can be summarized by one word from the Church's theological dictionary: satisfaction.[5]

II. THE CHURCH IN PURGATORY

Before we treat of the role that Christian satisfaction plays in the spiritual perfection of the deceased, we should pause to consider the place where Brother Romanus spent his short fifteen days, that is, Purgatory. Purgatory, a place of punishment where, as Dante again puts it, "God wills the debt be paid."[6] Purgatory, a place of waiting. Purgatory, a place with only temporary occupants, like the waiting room in an Amtrak station. Indeed, Dante himself receives this good counsel from his guide, the Roman poet Virgil: "Do not think of the torments; think, I say, / of what comes after them: think that at worst / they cannot last beyond the Judgment Day."[7] Purgatory, a

4 See Dante, *Inferno*, trans. John Ciardi (New York, NY: Mentor Books, 1961), canto 10, beginning with line 61.
5 For a general treatment, see my *The Godly Image: Christian Satisfaction in Aquinas* (Washington, DC: The Catholic University of America Press, 2020).
6 Dante, *Purgatorio*, trans. John Ciardi (New York, NY: Mentor Books, 1961), canto 10, line 105.
7 Dante, *Purgatorio*, canto 10, lines 106–8.

place for the imperfect just, where, as Dante explains, elect souls "make their beauty perfect."[8]

Purgatory holds a key position in Catholic teaching about the composition of the Church. Indeed, the faith of the Church holds that at the present time, that is, before the Last Judgment, some of the Lord's disciples continue their pilgrimage on earth whereas others who have died are being purified while still others are in glory.[9] The *Catechism of the Catholic Church* further affirms that the "constant faith of the Church" holds that the communion between those who remain wayfarers and those who have died in the peace of Christ is "reinforced by an exchange of spiritual goods."[10] So we can speak of the Church in Purgatory.

Sadly, the reformers of the sixteenth century saw things very differently. To choose one theme that bears upon what the Church holds about satisfaction, consider what Euan Cameron, an Episcopalian priest, has written about the views of these reformers: "There remained no place in reformed teaching for the cycle of sin, sacramental confession, priestly absolution, and ritual penance. . . . If there was no penance, there was no purgatory: the souls of the saved 'paid all their debts by their death,' as Luther said."[11] This reformed teaching continues to suffuse most Protestant thought. Suffice it to remark that such alterations to Catholic faith affect seriously the practice of ecclesial communion, especially the exchange of spiritual goods among the members of Christ's Body.

Catholic teaching remains clear: Purgatory as a state in which souls find purification from the remnants of sin holds an indispensable place within the sacramental account of the Church's constitution. Catholic ecclesiology does not first of all concern itself with an adjudication of the differences among Christian denominations, as they are called, or their tenets. Instead, Catholic theology recognizes that the Seven Sacraments and divine charity as transformative of persons identify the true Church of Christ. What the sixteenth-century reformers rejected was that this very communion in charity binds together all members of the Church, whether on earth, in heaven, or in Purgatory.[12] Of course their doctrine of extrinsic justification would have made it difficult for them to make these connections. Further, their decided distaste for sacramental efficaciousness, and especially for the

---

[8] Dante, *Purgatorio*, canto 2, line 75.
[9] See CCC 954, on "The Communion of the Church of Heaven and Earth."
[10] CCC 955.
[11] Euan Cameron, "The Power of the Word: Renaissance and Reformation," in *Early Modern Europe: An Oxford History*, ed. Euan Cameron (Oxford: Oxford University Press, 1999), 91.
[12] See CCC 953.

priests who absolve and transubstantiate, did not help them to acknowledge the full mystery of communion, the *communicatio sancti Spiritus*.[13]

Catholics, as Aquinas's vision of Brother Romanus indicates, embrace the Church as a living communion of persons. They recognize that the Church on earth—once called militant, that is, on the march—the souls in Purgatory, and the saints in heaven remain bound together under one Headship, that of Christ's capital grace, and that among these members there exists an exchange of spiritual goods. You do not need to study theology to discover these truths. Pay close attention to a proper Catholic funeral. Or observe the daily celebration of the Liturgy and the liturgical feasts that mark the calendar year. Catholic fellowship grows out of the Eucharist; it does not replace it. To sum up: the Church of Christ includes Purgatory until the consummation of all things.[14]

What does Purgatory provide for those who die in friendship with Christ but who are not ontologically disposed for the Beatific Vision? The simple answer is purification. But how? In order to answer this question, Catholic teaching appeals to a metaphor. St. Gregory the Great, for example, speaks about a "purifying fire."[15] The *Catechism*, in turn, describes the purpose of Purgatory as a purification for the deceased "so as to achieve the holiness necessary to enter the joy of heaven."[16] Or, in Dante's phrase, to "make their beauty perfect." The abovementioned *Catechism* text includes a cross reference to another of its sections, namely at §1472, which falls under the heading of Indulgences. In this section, we discover, among other useful things, why we need a certain holiness or beauty to see God. Indulgences then provide a sort of back door into our seeing what Christian satisfaction for the dead accomplishes.

Indulgences exist because of sin. Sin, so states the *Catechism*, entails both fault and punishment. Fault arises from the willful violation of God's law. When this fault concerns grave or serious matters, we exclude ourselves altogether from beatific communion with the saints, both here below and in heaven. Forgiveness, in a word, comes ordinarily with sacramental absolution. Less grave faults, such as venial sins, also require repentance, though such can be forgiven apart from sacramental absolution. However, even absolution from fault (*culpa*) does not complete the reconciliation of the sinner to God. There still remains the punishment (*poena*), or the liability

---

[13] See the *Roman Missal*, The Introductory Rites: "Gratia Domini nostri Iesu Christi, et caritas Dei, et communicatio Sancti Spiritus sit cum omnibus vobis."

[14] See CCC 681.

[15] See Saint Gregory, *Dialogues* 4.39 (cited in CCC 1031).

[16] See CCC 1030.

for punishment that disordered acts incur. To take one example, in Canto 13 of his *Purgatorio*, Dante sees the envious with their "eyelids pierced and sewn with iron wires."[17] In other words, they cannot look around and gaze invidiously at what others possess and enjoy.

Punishment for serious unforgiven sin results in what the catechetical literature calls "eternal punishment." At the same time, every sin, whether forgiven mortal sins or even venial sins, whether actual or overcome by acts of charity, brings with it a "temporal punishment." The phrase "temporal punishment" points to the fact that the punishment does not last forever, as Virgil reminded Dante, but only for a period measured by earth time. So, as we have seen, Brother Romanus spent fifteen days in Purgatory for his tardiness.

Some people wrongly believe that punishment for sin puts God in a very bad light. Luther apparently held some such view, and so he simply eliminated all punishment for the believer in the sweet hereafter. God, however, does not take on the identity of an Avenger, though people freighted with servile fear think of him in this way. Truth and mercy identify God, as the psalmist says, "Mercy and truth have met each other: justice and peace have kissed" (Psalm 84:11,[18] Douay–Rheims).[19]

In any event, the ordinary Catholic sinner who frequents the Sacraments is left with "temporal punishment." This punishment results from the very nature of sin itself. St. Augustine sets the tone when he remarks that every disordered affection brings its own punishment. St. Thomas quotes this text from the first book of the *Confessions* in an objection to question 87, article 1, of the *prima secundae*: "In *Confessiones* 1, [12] Augustine says, 'Every disordered affection [*inordinatus animus*] is its own punishment.'"[20] What does this mean? In brief, disorder strikes against the truth about the good of the human person. Say a man purposefully harbors a lecherous desire for another man's wife. This adulterous inclination, even without his having committed adultery, does not dispose such a man to see the God who created marriage as the loving union of one man and one woman. Or to take the example from Dante, those who waste their time regretting that they do not possess what they see others enjoying fail to express thanks to God for the gifts that they have received.

---

[17] Dante, *Purgatorio*, canto 13, lines 70–71.

[18] Ps 85:10, RSV2CE: "Mercy and faithfulness will meet; righteousness and peace will kiss each other."

[19] For further discussion, see Romanus Cessario and Cajetan Cuddy, "Mercy in Aquinas: Help from the Commentatorial Tradition," *The Thomist* 80 (2016): 329–39.

[20] See *Summa theologiae* I-II, q. 87, a. 1.

In the *Summa* text cited above, Aquinas goes on to outline the three ways that punishment for sin can arise. This division corresponds to the three divinely established orders to which the human will is subject: reason, spiritual and temporal governance, and divine law. The exegesis of this text from Aquinas, which is complex, need not detain us for the present discussion. Suffice it to remark that each of the punishments that follow a departure from divine rule aims to reverse the lack of due order that sin introduces into the sinner's inclinations—that is, the powers that remain subject (or reside) in the soul (*inordinatus animus*). Drunkenness provides a good example of a subversion of the order of reason. Fines for financial misconduct that violates civil laws aim to compensate the common good for the harm that the unjust man perpetrates against it. Canonical punishments respond to the damage caused to the supernatural common good of the Church by, oftentimes, unscrupulous clerics such as simoniacal prelates. Many other examples suggest themselves. Each punishment would share a common feature, namely, that it arises as a result of a disordering of the human person from the good of Beatitude.

An important thing to remember about sin and the liability for punishment concerns Aquinas's psychology. The disorder that sin introduces into the human person affects the powers of the human soul even though the effects of the disorder may appear in a person's outward behavior. In the concupiscible appetite, because of the familiar results that accompany sins like drunkenness and gluttony, these punishments appear more patently. There are parallels in certain sins of unchastity—for example, the exaggerations that pornographers aim to orchestrate. The irascible appetite also exhibits outwardly this lack of due order, for example, in the inconveniences that the coward causes in battle or that the impatient person afflicts on those around him. Sins against the rational appetite sometimes appear less blatantly. Still, even the thief who does not get caught suffers a disorientation with respect to the common good. He suffers from the fact that he detests the moral truth that justice renders to each person what is his due. The *Catechism* summarizes the possible ways that sins introduce disorder into the soul when it says that "every sin, even venial, entails an unhealthy attachment to creatures, which must be purified either here on earth, or after death in the state called Purgatory."[21] Attachments belong to the appetitive orders. Even those, however, who sin against intellectual virtues, such as prudence and faith, find their punishment in their attachment to these errors. The

---

[21] CCC 1472.

foolishly impetuous person refuses to seek sound counsel.[22] The thickheaded heretic refuses to recant his heresy.

Recall that a discussion of the punishments for sin appears in the *Catechism* under the heading of "Indulgences." The practice of granting indulgences opens up what the Church teaches about the effects of sin and their healing by satisfaction. An indulgence, so states the *Catechism of the Catholic Church*, brings "remission before God of the temporal punishment due to sins whose guilt [*culpa*] has already been forgiven."[23] Catholics can gain indulgences for themselves or apply them to the dead. Indulgences work under the general authority of the Church that, again in the words of the *Catechism*, "dispenses and applies with authority the treasury of the satisfactions of Christ and the saints."[24] In other words, indulgences apply the good deeds of Christ and the saints to those who fulfill the conditions for obtaining the said indulgence, such that the indulgenced sinner receives remission either of all temporal punishment or of some.[25]

To return to St. Thomas's vision, one explanation as to why Brother Romanus spent only fifteen days in Purgatory could be that he had obtained indulgences for whatever other sins he may have committed in a life that included a teaching stint in Paris.

III. SATISFACTION AND INDULGENCE

Indulgences are not scams, as certain reformers asserted.[26] To gain an indulgence one must possess true interior contrition for past sins and already have confessed these sins to a priest. No one excluded from communion with God by grave sin can expect to receive the total gift of his mercy. On the other hand, to remove the arrow and to heal the wound are not the same ("*non est idem abstrahere telum, et sanare vulnus*").[27] This metaphor means that it is one thing to forgive sin—to remove the arrow—and another thing to heal the wounds caused by sin. The infraction of a divine rule disregards the inbuilt purposes of human nature, and so it puts the human person in a state

---

[22] See *ST* II-II, q. 53, a. 5.

[23] CCC 1471.

[24] CCC 1471.

[25] The traditional practice of the Church assigned periods of time, e.g., seven years or three hundred days, to various partial indulgences. In 1967, Pope Paul VI, by means of his Apostolic Constitution *Indulgentiarum Doctrina*, eliminated these distinctions in favor of two categories: plenary and partial (see Norms 2 and 3).

[26] For further discussion, see Romanus Cessario, "St. Thomas Aquinas on Satisfaction, Indulgences, and Crusades," *Medieval Philosophy & Theology* 2 (1992): 74–96.

[27] St. Augustine, *De Trinitate*, bk. 15.

of disorder. Sinful actions affect adversely the psychology and character of the whole person. Each sinner, therefore, needs a remedial discipline that can redirect his or her human energies towards engaging in virtuous activity. We call this remedy satisfaction.

The "temporal punishment" due to sin results from sin itself. Recall that St. Augustine taught that every disordered action brings about its own punishment. Sin conforms man's psychological powers to purposes that fall short of those that perfect human lives and that incarnate God's goodness in the world. Since this sinful deformation implies disordered attachments to created goods, Christian conversion ordinarily entails the willing acceptance of satisfactory works: abstinence from even legitimate pleasures, such as wine or beer; fasting; useful donations of one's time or money; and similar privations. These satisfactory works are required because of the very human need to order one's affective life toward good deeds and away from bad ones. Pope St. John Paul II explained at the time of the Great Jubilee of the Year 2000 that a sinner needs not only forgiveness but also restoration, which implies "a real change of life, the gradual elimination of evil within, a renewal of our way of living."[28]

Healing the wounds that sin causes in the human person falls outside of our own abilities. We need Our Lord. By his Passion, death, and Resurrection, Christ accomplished full satisfaction for our sins: "He himself bore our sins in his body on the tree, that we might die to sin and live to righteousness. By his wounds you have been healed" (1 Pet 2:24). The sovereign dignity of Christ's person means that his work possesses a kind of infinite value. Christ's work proves so great that the Church announces a treasure trove—the *thesaurus ecclesiae*.[29] Indulgences draw upon this spiritual treasure chest that contains the good works of Christ and the saints.

The personal actions of Christ and the saints make up the *thesaurus ecclesiae*, the treasury of the Church. Because Catholics form one Body in the Church, they can participate in this spiritual treasure, which is constantly augmented by the good deeds of holy men and women. Of course, what the saints accomplish takes on satisfactory value only because they themselves remain united with Christ and in particular with his Passion and death. By bearing evils and practicing charity, each holy Catholic becomes an active participant in healing the world, completing, as the Letter to the Colossians reminds us, "what is lacking in Christ's afflictions for the sake of his body" (Col 1: 24).

[28] See Pope John Paul II, Bull of Indiction of the Great Jubilee of the Year 2000 *Incarnationis Mysterium*, §9.
[29] See CCC 1446, 1447.

In the Church, everything exists in a communion of charity. This fact of faith explains the canonical rule that the one who presides over the universal Church on earth possesses authority to dispense the treasures of the Church. When the Successor of Peter grants an indulgence, he exercises the "power of the keys." St. Thomas Aquinas demonstrates the biblical foundation for this prerogative of the Roman Pontiff:

> Therefore, dispensation of this treasure belongs to the one who is in charge of the whole Church; hence the Lord gave to Peter the keys of the kingdom of heaven (Matthew 16:19). Accordingly, when either the well-being or absolute necessity of the Church requires it, the one who is in charge of the Church can distribute from this unlimited treasure to anyone who through charity belongs to the Church as much of the said treasure as shall seem to him opportune, either up to a total remission of punishment or to some certain amount. In this case, the Passion of Christ and of the other saints would be imputed to the member as if he himself would have suffered whatever was required for the remission of his sins, as happens when one person satisfies for another.[30]

Note that our union in charity with Christ and the saints grounds our sharing in their meritorious and satisfactory works.

One may inquire how an indulgence can change our psychological dispositions. The Church teaches that Christ's love remains powerful enough to alter what the sinner himself did not have the occasion (or perhaps even the will) to do for himself. In other words, Christ brings the full gift of the Father's mercy. The Church recognizes that, because he is the very Son of God, Christ's sufferings communicate exceeding value to every member of the Church. A spiritual reading of the Gospels reveals the supreme charity and obedience with which Christ lived his life. An indulgence provides a concrete way for Catholics to participate in this obedient love.

Christ's heroic love can overcome even the habitual sinner's psychological resistance to godly living. Of course indulgences do not provide an excuse for spiritual laziness. Still, the duly indulgenced sinner who rejoices in the gift of the Father's mercy is made ready for ultimate communion. The divine mercy also explains that an indulgence can be obtained on behalf of the souls of the deceased. Because the elect who await final purification belong

---

[30] Thomas Aquinas, *Quodlibetal* 2, q. 8, a. 2, from *Mediaeval Sources in Translation*, trans. Sandra Edwards (Ontario: Pontifical Institute of Mediaeval Studies, 1983).

to the one communion of the Church, those on earth still on the march can apply an indulgence to the faithful departed. The Incarnate Son establishes a wide communication of divine goodness that can overcome whatsoever indisposition sin may leave in the living or the dead. Only the mystery of the Incarnation can explain such a wondrous exchange whereby Christ's satisfaction takes the place, as it were, of the satisfactory works a sinner did not accomplish. Why such divine indulgence, so to speak? St. Thomas Aquinas gives the reason: "The labor of Christ's sufferings suffices."[31] In the mystery of a vicarious life, the eminent satisfaction of Christ and the superabundant satisfaction of the Blessed Virgin Mary and the saints become ours. As I have said, the repentant sinner receives the fullness of the Father's mercy and if dead, can sin no more.

IV. SATISFACTION FOR THE DEAD

Confessio oris, contritio cordis, and *satisfactio operis.* The medieval rhyme recounts the constituent parts of the Sacrament of Penance and Reconciliation. Confession of the mouth, contrition of the heart, satisfaction of works. Aquinas discusses these parts in the last question of his *Summa* that he composed, namely, *tertia pars,* question 90, article 2. Satisfaction performed by penitent Catholics here below contributes to the reformation of their godly images—that is, to make their beauty perfect. The satisfaction does not reach completion with the recital of the few prayers that priests often assign as "penances" in the Sacrament of Penance. Satisfaction should carry over into Catholics' everyday lives such that whatever good they do and evil they endure contributes to the strengthening of their Catholic virtue. Some less Dantesque examples stand out: fasting cures gluttony. Almsgiving corrects the tendency to hoard. Spending time in prayer before the Blessed Sacrament mollifies urges to satisfy the concupiscence of one's eyes. (One learns not to let appearances distract.) In other words, doing penance forms an integral part of Catholic discipline.

Satisfaction accomplished by the living seems clear enough, but what about the dead? How can spirits without bodies, that is, the Holy Souls in Purgatory, undergo satisfaction that leads to a reformation of their persons? Throughout his *Purgatorio,* Dante illustrates the punishments of those in Purgatory with examples that mainly involve the bodies of these souls. The Envious have their eyes sewn tight. Still, how can satisfaction work on souls

---

[31] Thomas Aquinas, *Quodlibetal* 2, q. 8, a. 2, ad 4.

without bodies? This question remains for our consideration. Fortunately, St. Thomas again comes to our assistance.

In about Advent of 1269, some intelligent student at Paris actually posed to Aquinas the question of how corporeal fire can affect immaterial souls. The query comes in this form, "Whether a separated soul can be acted upon by corporeal fire?"[32] Aquinas entertains objections that reflect both philosophical and theological points that would seem to indicate that corporeal fire cannot act on separated souls. Then he begins his reply with distinctions that bring him to the point where he identifies a meaning of acted upon that can apply to immaterial substances. "We say," Aquinas affirms, "that all that is in any way kept from its proper impetus or inclination is acted upon." Then he gives an example: "As we say a falling stone is acted upon when it is impeded in such a way that it cannot fall down, and as we say a man is acted upon when he is detained or bound so he cannot go where he wants." Note when Aquinas speaks of a proper inclination, he draws our attention to the powers of the soul that suffer from every sin, whether corporeal or not. Impurity does not affect only the body. Impurity extends its harm to the sense powers of the soul.

With an eye to the authority of St. Augustine, Aquinas announces to his quodlibetal inquirer that, "in this way, through a kind of binding the soul is acted upon by corporeal fire as Augustine says in *De civitate Dei* 21." Such binding should not seem strange, Aquinas goes on to explain, to one who considers that the soul is bound to the human body as long as the person lives a terrestrial existence. "All the more then," says Aquinas, "can spirits be bound to corporeal fire by means of divine power, not so as to give life but so as to receive punishment, as Augustine says." This reply offers an example of the scholastic method at its best. Well does the *Catechism* remind us that the "Church, by reference to certain texts of Scripture, speaks of a cleansing fire."[33] Dante seems to have understood not only the biblical texts but also the tradition that both Aquinas and St. Augustine upheld.

Consider this illustrative example. When Dante arrives at the highest level of Purgatory, he finds those being punished for lust. "We are so many," cries one of the Poor Souls. These faithful departed are required to cry out the names of their sins—for example, Sodom, "that by their shame," as the *Purgatorio* says, "they aid the fire that makes them fit to rise."[34] These lustful shades also shout out praise to those who have lived chaste lives. Even so, as Dante observes, "they [lustful shades] were ever careful to stay within

---

[32] Thomas Aquinas, *Quodlibetal* 2, q. 7, a. 1. The quotations that follow are from this text.

[33] CCC 1031.

[34] Dante, *Purgatorio*, canto 26, lines 80–81.

the fire that burned them there."[35] Perhaps one finds no better illustration of how Aquinas sees corporeal fire function in Purgatory. The flames' constraints cure the disordered inclinations and wayward impetuses of the immaterial souls detained in Purgatory. Today, of course, Dante would have to reconsider whether crying out, "Sodom!" would produce shame immediately in the repentant sodomite.

V. CONCLUSION

What lessons might we draw from this overview of Christian satisfaction and the dead? Three seem the most important for Catholic life and devotion. First, Catholics should aid their deceased brothers and sisters in Purgatory by performing satisfactory works for them. As Aquinas sees it, the Poor Souls cannot act on their own.[36] Thus, the Magisterium has urged living Catholics to help those souls in Purgatory who, in the words of Pope Sixtus IV, "are less (than ever) able to help themselves."[37]

Second, Catholics should learn from the punishment that Purgatory inflicts that sins, even those that require bodily organs, such as unchastity, do not affect only the bodies of the sinners. Indeed, sinful disorder leaves its mark on the soul and its powers. Disordered souls are not ready to see God just as gravely disordered persons on earth are not ready, without repentance, for Eucharistic communion. The adulterer, for instance, must undergo purification of his lingering attachment to the pleasure that accompanied the adulterous intercourse of which he now repents.

Third, sinners who are both honest and wise will keep what the Church holds about satisfaction, *satisfactio operis*, and indulgences uppermost in their Catholic consciences. God has provided a way, by the merits and satisfaction of Christ, to heal the wounds that sins leave in the Catholic believer even after the arrow of fault has been removed by absolution within the Sacrament of Penance and Reconciliation. All in all, what the Church holds about Purgatory, satisfaction, and the dead should inspire Catholics to embrace Catholic life joyfully even when they find themselves burdened by sin or its remnants. Dante assures us that Christ's mercy suffices to make us

---

[35] Dante, *Purgatorio*, canto 26, lines 14–15.

[36] See *ST* II-II, q. 83, a. 11: "Those who are in Purgatory though they are above us on account of their impeccability, yet they are below us as to the pains which they suffer: and in this respect they are not in a condition to pray, but rather in a condition that requires us to pray for them."

[37] See the Bull of Sixtus IV, *Salvator Noster* (August 3, 1476), in Denzinger 1398 (43rd edition).

"new, / remade, reborn, like a sun–wakened tree / that spreads new foliage to the Spring's dew / in sweetest freshness, healed of Winter's scares; / perfect, pure, and ready for the Stars."[38]

---

[38] Dante, *Purgatorio*, canto 33, lines 142–46.

The Foundationally Natural Intelligibility of the *Imago Dei* in the Human Person

and Its Implications Regarding the Knowledge of the Separated Soul

STEVEN A. LONG
Ave Maria University, FL

IT IS A VIEW FREQUENTLY and not implausibly held today that there is no firm basis for any knowledge of the incorruptibility or immortality of the soul apart from revelation that could suggest any real activity of the rational soul after death, naturally speaking, or provide any slightest light with respect to human destiny. However, I will argue to the contrary that the doctrine of the *imago dei* in the human creature, which is central for the understanding of human nature and destiny and for the elevability of the human person to grace and glory, fulfills these theological purposes only because, and insofar as, the *dynamism* of the *imago* in man to grace and glory is *founded upon* the natural knowability of the intellectual nature of man as a subsistent, positively immaterial, incorruptible, and immortal principle,[1]

---

[1] Of course, the teaching of the Church is that the rational soul of the human person is spiritual and immortal. See the *Catechism of the Catholic Church*, §366: "The Church teaches that every spiritual soul is created immediately by God—it is not 'produced' by the parents—and also that it is immortal: it does not perish when it separates from the body at death, and it will be reunited with the body at the final Resurrection." See also Pius XII, *Humani Generis*

and implicitly a principle whose intelligible activity is not entirely nullifiable by death.

This requires a treatment of the *imago dei* in the human person. The stakes at hazard are suggested by St. Thomas Aquinas's teaching in question 93 of the prima pars of the *Summa theologiae* that the *imago dei* in the human person essentially consists in the intellectual nature. Thomas understands intellectual nature as intrinsically and positively immaterial and the *imago* as pertaining to all else merely by "trace."[2] For Thomas, the *imago* essentially consists in the intellectual nature (the *imago naturae*[3]) as an intrinsically spiritual principle that is the foundation for the specific obediential potency of the human person for grace and glory. Here it is important to address the critical distinction between *imago* in the human person and the human person *integrally considered*, a distinction that I believe insightful minds have confused in diametrically opposed ways. Not only the possibility of the elevation of the human person to grace, but the very intelligibility of the Christian doctrine of God, as well as any objective knowledge whatsoever, would be negated by the possibility of a complete reduction of intelligence

---

(Aug. 12, 1950), §36; Paul VI, *Credo of the People of God* (June 30, 1968), §8. And note Lateran Council V (1513), for example Session 8: "Consequently, since in our days (which we endure with sorrow) the sower of cockle, the ancient enemy of the human race, has dared to scatter and multiply in the Lord's field some extremely pernicious errors, which have always been rejected by the faithful, especially on the nature of the rational soul, with the claim that it is mortal, or only one among all human beings, and since some, playing the philosopher without due care, assert that this proposition is true at least according to philosophy, it is our desire to apply suitable remedies against this infection and, with the approval of the sacred council, we condemn and reject all those who insist that the intellectual soul is mortal, or that it is only one among all human beings, and those who suggest doubts on this topic. For the soul not only truly exists of itself and essentially as the form of the human body, as is said in the canon of our predecessor of happy memory, pope Clement V, promulgated in the general council of Vienne, but it is also immortal; and further, for the enormous number of bodies into which it is infused individually, it can and ought to be and is multiplied." See Denzinger, 1440.

2   In *Summa theologiae* I, q. 93, a. 2, ad 3, Thomas argues that the intellectual nature alone is to the image of God, "sola natura intellectualis est ad imaginem Dei," while in *ST* I, q. 93, a. 3, resp., he argues that every other likeness to God in the human creature is an "accidental quality" of the *imago* rather than constituting the essential and principal analogical likeness of the *imago*.

3   In *ST* I q. 93, a. 9, the first objection is framed in terms of the *imago naturae, imago gratiae, and imago gloriae*, and nothing in Thomas's response suggests an objection to this formulation (which conforms to his own account of the *imago* principally and essentially consisting in the intellectual nature) but rather points out that it is consistent with the analysis of the *Sentences* (*Super Sent.*, lib. 2, d. 16, q. 1, a. 4, corp.) holding "that the image is taken from the memory, the understanding and the will, while the likeness is from innocence and righteousness."

and will to functions of material nature. But our knowledge of intellectual nature is not principally through revelation but through natural reason, although the dynamism of the created *imago* to grace and glory is a matter of revelation. There may be reason to think that more can be known naturally of the separated soul than first meets the eye.

Secondly, this paper adverts briefly to questions 75, 76, and 89 of the prima pars of the *Summa*, explicating the nature, subsistence, incorrupt-ibility, and separable natural activity of the soul. Thomas's treatment is not detached from the actual synthesis of providence ordaining the integral human person to the supernatural end of the beatific vision. But he does show a principal concern regarding the natural intelligibility of the rational soul and its knowledge in precision from the beatific vision.

Thirdly, and finally, this paper treats Thomas's teaching regarding the natural knowledge of the separated soul as implied by sound philosophic anthropology affirming the limited but real transcendence of human spirit, a teaching that seems necessary to the intelligibility of the doctrine of the *imago dei* in the human person.

Because of the distinctive role of metaphysical reasoning in this theolog-ical consideration, however, a brief preamble about the role of metaphysics within theology precedes these considerations.

PREAMBLE

Classical civilization, as part of the divine providence preparing the world for Christian revelation, laid the foundation for certain metaphysical insights into the truth of being and nature and the relative but real tran-scendence of human spirit. These insights have been developed and elevated further by a long process of intellectual refinement and assimilation to the understanding of revelation. Articulated in what are called the preambles of faith, arguably they enter into the secondary object of revelation, that is, the conditions requisite to the intelligibility of the promulgation of the Gospel.[4] Christ did not come to preach the message of the metaphysical principle of contradiction, but if the principle does not pertain to the real—a metaphysical premise—the entirety of the realism of the assent of faith is

---

[4]   See the Congregation for the Doctrine of the Faith, "Doctrinal Commentary on Conclud-ing Formula of *Professio fidei*" (June 29, 1998), §§6, 7, issued by Cardinal Ratzinger, who mentions logical and historical necessities for the intelligibility of the promulgation of the faith: but clearly and more fundamentally there are metaphysical necessities for the intelli-gibility of the promulgation of the faith. The principle of contradiction as applying to being is not merely a logical but a metaphysical principle.

denied in one breath. Similarly, whatever the structure of created being is, it is—by divine decree rather than by human assertion—a prerequisite for and a conditioning element of supernatural revelation. Thus theology that lacks metaphysics and philosophy of nature—or even lacks realist ontology of knowledge—seems in danger of converting divine truths into a species of glossolalia.

To put it as St. Thomas does, we do not possess quiditative or direct essential knowledge of God, who is the subject of theology. How then can theology proceed? His answer is clear: on the basis of all the effects of God in nature and grace.[5] But the proper and first effect of God is being in the sense of *esse* or actual existence.[6] It follows that metaphysics has a privileged instrumentality within *sacra doctrina*, and the theologian who proceeds without metaphysical wisdom risks either absorbing revealed truths into contingent conceptual constructs or social ideology or else converting the contemplation of the truth of revelation into a species of fideist poetry or only aspirationally connected historical moments.

Further, the Church has consecrated certain principles and insights in formulating her teaching. For example, to mention only a few: relation and procession, person, nature, and substance with respect to the Trinity; substance and nature with respect to the Person of Christ; form with respect to sanctifying grace, justification, and the sacraments. With respect to the moral life, one would need to observe the primacy of the Church's embrace of the natural law doctrine of St. Thomas Aquinas,[7] whose intelligibility itself involves and requires metaphysical judgments.[8] When one treats all these as lacking immutable and naturally intelligible content founded on the reality of things, the Church's own teaching becomes a species of metaphor rather than a doctrine of faith "irreformable by virtue of itself." It is this very thing that made the promulgation of *Dominus Iesus* necessary. The relativization of the content of the secondary object of revelation—of that which is naturally required for the intelligibility of the doctrine of the faith—ineluctably endangers and relativizes the doctrine of the faith itself. This is precisely why overt negation or rejection of the secondary object of

---

[5] Thomas Aquinas, *ST* I, q. 1, a. 7, ad 1.

[6] Thomas Aquinas, *ST* I, q. 45, a. 5, resp.

[7] See John Paul II, *Veritatis Splendor* (Aug. 6, 1993), §44: "The Church has often made reference to the Thomistic doctrine of natural law, including it in her own teaching on morality."

[8] Final cause or *end*, taken as a principle of moral thought, is, of course, part of a teleological account of the moral life. Natural law as a *rational participation* of the eternal law, of course, presupposes the account of the eternal law, which is vouchsafed by the natural intelligibility of the arguments for God as first efficient and last or ultimate final cause. There are, of course, many other illustrations.

revelation (as opposed to simple confusion or ignorance) causes separation from communion with the Church. This is not, of course, to say that every metaphysical unclarity or error is itself immediately a cause of separation from the Church, but only that certain metaphysical truths are required for the intelligibility of revelation, and that, whatever the structure of created being is, it enters into doctrinal consideration and questions of doctrinal development and application pertaining to faith and morals.

The actual being, nature, and substance of created things are real, and supernatural revelation is real. The continuity and relation between these can only be understood, short of the beatific vision, on the basis of metaphysical truth. We cannot start out *within* the beatific vision and see clearly therein or deduce the entirety of divine providence, creation, grace, and revelation. The principle of contradiction in its application to being is one such metaphysical principle; and arguably, it cannot be sustained as applying to many, limited, changing creatures without the real division of being by potency and act because without this division, the limitation, manyness, and change in created being can't be reconciled with the principle of contradiction as a real metaphysical principle. A theologian who wishes to deepen insight into the reality of nature, grace, and revelation, and who absents himself from these principles does so at hazard to the unity and fruitfulness of theology as sacred science.

THE *IMAGO DEI* AND PERSON IN THE HUMAN CREATURE

The teaching of the incorruptibility of the soul is rightly thought of as a preamble of faith. Our Lord is the God of the living, and the creation of the human person according to the image and likeness of God is, as Augustine discovered, not a doctrine of physical similitude or of the containment or trapping of divinity in a human body, but of the analogical similitude of the spiritual principle in the human person with God who is pure Spirit.[9]

In question 93 of the prima pars of the *Summa*, Thomas asserts that the *imago* in man pertains principally and essentially to the intellectual nature and to all else in human existence only by way of "trace"[10] and "accidental qualities."[11] This "trace" is a *signum*, an effect that gives a sign of the divine cause but an effect that does not rise to the level of a specific analogical likeness. A portrait of a person is an image, but the fingerprint of that person, although it is a sign left by that person, is itself only a *trace*, an effect that

---

9 Augustine, *Confessions*, 6.3.4; 8.22.32.
10 Thomas Aquinas, *STI*, q. 93, a. 6, resp.
11 Thomas Aquinas, *STI*, q. 93, a. 3, resp.

bears witness to that person but does not suffice of itself to constitute a likeness of the person as such.

The intrinsically spiritual soul, while limited by *potentia* and accordingly imperfect in its actuality, is nonetheless such as to provide an analogical image of God in the human creature precisely because it is positively immaterial. Without this foundational principle of spirit in the human creature, the elevation of the human person to the beatific vision would be as impossible as the bestowal of the beatific vision to a rock. The rock would need substantially to change into a knowing and loving creature to be susceptible of elevation to the order of grace and the attainment of a union of knowledge and love with God. Owing to the *imago*—the intellectual nature—the human creature does not need to lose humanity (whose formal principle is positively immaterial) in order to be elevated through grace to attain to this vision: under the active agency of God, the natural universality of its intellective power is capable of higher actuation. In *Summa* I, q. 93, a. 2, ad 3, Thomas says that the intellectual nature *alone* is to the image of God ("sola natura intellectualis est ad imaginem Dei")[12] and that it "has a capacity for the highest good" ("quae est capax summi boni"). What kind of capacity is this? Those who know Thomas's teaching realize that he adverts to obediential potency—a passive potency for perfections that may be brought forth in a creature only by an extrinsic active power.[13] The universality of the adequate objects of intellect and will manifests what—consequent on revelation—we realize to be a purely passive capacity for elevation to the beatific vision, a vision toward which Thomas teaches that no creature can move apart from grace.[14]

---

[12] It is noteworthy that Aristotle names God as "thought thinking itself"—as Pure Act and Perfect Intellect. But whence does Aristotle find the analogical foundation for such affirmations save in the evidence of being as irreducible to any genus whatsoever, within which he discerns that analogicity of intellectual nature between man, separated substance, and God, that becomes for Thomas the foundational, essential, and principal reality signified by the *imago dei* in man, the *imago naturae*?

[13] St. Thomas deploys this principle, with respect to infused virtue in Christ and in all those in a state of grace, to the capacity of human nature to be elevated to union with the Person of the Word and generally to infused virtues in the soul. With respect to obediential potency and infused virtue in Christ, see *ST* III, q. 11, a. 3, resp.; with respect to the union of human nature with the Person of the Word, observe his text in *ST* III, q. 1, a. 3, ad 3; and with respect to infused virtue generally, see *Quaestiones disputatae de virtutibus*, q. 1, a. 10, ad 13.

[14] See for example, in *ST* I, q. 62, a. 2. And, of course, for Thomas, desire *is* motion: see *ST* I-II, q. 3, a. 4, resp.: "But it is evident that desire itself of the end is not attainment of the end, but is a movement towards the end." "Manifestum est autem quod ipsum desiderium finis non est consecutio finis, sed est motus ad finem."

In his great work *The Person and the Common Good*, Jacques Maritain wrote of the person as more a whole than a part, and he famously distinguished between the *person* and the *individual*: the former a spiritual whole, the latter, a material part. Yet the human person by nature *includes* bodily nature, not only the *principles* of the sense powers in the soul but these *bodily powers themselves*. Human persons are not merely "spirit," and bodiliness is not an intrinsically spiritual principle and cannot, in and of itself, essentially constitute an analogical image of God. Because at the divine summit of reality, substance and *imago* are substantially one, Maritain seems to identify the integral human person with the *imago dei*.[15] In an opposite direction, one might think that perhaps Karl Barth[16] or Edith Stein[17] implicitly identify the *imago dei* with person *in the other direction*, as implying that the creation of the human person *ad imaginem dei* essentially includes in the *imago* the entire created human nature (e.g., Barth explicating the Pauline account of unilateral uxoral submission by a principal appeal to submission within the trinity; Stein affirming that the sexual difference is originatively and wholly spiritual).

Yet Thomas does not equate the integral human person with the positive immateriality of the *imago,* either by including the entirety of the integral person in the *imago* or by wholly spiritualizing the person. Although the separated soul is personal, it is not for St. Thomas the integral perfection designated by the term "person" (although arguably there is a ground for considering the separated soul to be a person *in virtute* since the *esse* of the separated soul is numerically identical with the *esse* of the whole composite nature complete in its species). For Thomas the *imago dei* in the human creature is an analogical pure perfection variously affirmed of man, angel, and God, and as such is diversified in creation by various limiting potential principles extrinsic to the *imago*. Whereas the completeness of the substance

---

[15] See Jacques Maritain, *The Person and the Common Good*, trans. John J. Fitzgerald (Notre Dame, IN: Notre Dame University Press, 1994).

[16] See Karl Barth, *Church Dogmatics* 4/1 (Edinburgh: T&T Clark, 2010), 201: "His divine unity consists in the fact that in Himself He is both One who is obeyed and Another who obeys"; and on 202: "As we look at Jesus Christ we cannot avoid the astounding conclusion of a divine obedience. Therefore we have to draw the no less astounding deduction that in equal Godhead the one God is, in fact, the One and also Another, that He is indeed a First and a Second, One who rules and commands in majesty and One who obeys in humility." Also, the famed prime advertence to obedience within the Trinity as the model for the unilateral uxoral submission in matrimony is, at least as regards that effort to provide an ultimate reason, seemingly inferior to that of which a serious metaphysically grounded Christian anthropology is capable.

[17] See Edith Stein, *Essays on Woman*, 2nd rev. ed., vol. 2, trans. Freda Mary Oben, ed. Lucy Gelber and Romaeus Leuven (Washington, DC: ICS Publications, 2017).

of the integral human person *includes* the limitation of materiality which, hence, is included within it, the intelligibility of the analogical perfection of the *imago* essentially *excludes* matter.

The specific analogical likeness of the *imago* is *spirit*, found with differing limitations which are *ad extra* in relation to it and are modes of its composite limitation. By way of contrast, the note of analogical pure perfection that pertains to the integral person is *complete substance* of intellectual nature, and here the *completeness* pertaining to human persons intrinsically includes matter and the added real essential perfections of a bodily nature. *In short: the imago dei in man is the formal principle of human nature itself taken in precision from anything other than its positive immateriality, whereas human person entails and implies the integral perfections of bodily nature.* The analogical perfection of the *imago* is the positive immateriality of the intellectual nature as such whereas the analogical perfection of *person* is that of *complete substance of a rational nature*, which thus comprises whatsoever is analogically requisite to that *completeness*. *Contra* Maritain and, perhaps implicitly, *contra* Barth or Stein, the analogical *rationes* of *person* and of *imago dei* are not the same although they are interrelated. In creatures the perfections of *person* and *imago* are not necessarily coextensive.

The susceptibility—the obediential potency—of the human person to be elevated from without by the divine active power is founded initially on the radical spirituality of the human soul capable of intellectual and volitional acts, whose powers may be actuated by God beyond their proportionate objects and ends. So there is a great deal at stake for the understanding of the doctrine of the *imago dei* in the proper understanding of the spirituality of the human soul. I will try with brevity to summarize principal points of St. Thomas's analysis.

ST. THOMAS ON THE HUMAN SOUL

If the *imago* at its root is the intellectual nature as such taken as a pure perfection—the spirituality of the human soul—and this together with its incorruptibility are *preambles of faith*, how is this naturally intelligible? Intellectual activity proceeds through universal concepts and applies to being as such universally, such that a wholly physicalist account by its nature must somehow square the circle and reduce universality to physical particularity. What is at stake is not only the universal mode of conceptual knowledge—already something irreducible to physical particularity and so irreducible to neurophysiology—but also, and even more critically, the adequation or conformability of mind to being.

As St. Thomas puts it, "as sound is the first audible, being is the first intelligible."[18] Thus any denial that being is universally intelligible leaves precisely nothing intelligible since outside of being there is nothing. The logical principle of noncontradiction, according to St. Thomas in *Summa* prima secundae, question 94, article 2, is founded on the metaphysical opposition of *being* and *not being*. Since what does not exist has no real relations, "nonbeing" is not really related to being; but since being *is not* nonbeing, being is itself *really* distinct from nonbeing, owing to its own actuality. Thomas in referring to the logical principle of noncontradiction adds *"quod fundatur supra rationem entis et non entis"*—"which is based on the nature of being and non-being." This is a universal principle pertaining to being as such, and if it were not, then fundamentally there could be no such thing as objectivity because the mind would have no root capacity to conform to what actually exists. But if there is no such capacity to conform our conception and judgment to what is the case, then neither materialist reductionism nor any other account can be known to be true or to have even a verisimilitude of truth. The capacity to conform to any physical structure or state of affairs is not itself merely one physical structure or state of affairs—Thomas's argument in question 75, article 2 of the prima pars of the *Summa*. The capacity universally to conform to what is the case cannot be reduced without remainder to a particular or set of particulars in space and time. As Thomas argues, the perfection of intellectual knowledge exists in inverse ratio to materiality.[19]

---

[18] Thomas Aquinas, *ST* I, q. 5, a. 2, resp. "Unde ens est proprium obiectum intellectus, et sic est primum intelligibile, sicut sonus est primum audibile."

[19] As Thomas puts it, *ST* I, q. 84, a. 2, resp.: "Relinquitur ergo quod oportet materialia cognita in cognoscente existere non materialiter, sed magis immaterialiter. Et huius ratio est, quia actus cognitionis se extendit ad ea quae sunt extra cognoscentem, cognoscimus enim etiam ea quae extra nos sunt. Per materiam autem determinatur forma rei ad aliquid unum. Unde manifestum est quod ratio cognitionis ex opposito se habet ad rationem materialitatis. Et ideo quae non recipiunt formas nisi materialiter, nullo modo sunt cognoscitiva, sicut plantae; ut dicitur in II libro de anima. Quanto autem aliquid immaterialius habet formam rei cognitae, tanto perfectius cognoscit. Unde et intellectus, qui abstrahit speciem non solum a materia, sed etiam a materialibus conditionibus individuantibus, perfectius cognoscit quam sensus, qui accipit formam rei cognitae sine materia quidem, sed cum materialibus conditionibus." "It follows, therefore, that material things known must exist in the knower, not materially, but rather immaterially. And the reason of this is because the act of knowledge extends to things which are outside the knower: for we know even things that are external to us. Now by matter the form of a thing is determined to some one thing. Thus it is clear that knowledge is in inverse ratio of materiality (that the ratio of knowledge of itself is opposed to the ratio of materiality). And consequently things that are not receptive of forms save materially, have no power of knowledge whatever—such as plants, as the Philosopher says (*De Anima* ii, 12). But the more immaterially a thing has the form of the thing known, the more perfect is its knowledge. Therefore the intellect which abstracts the species not

Without the immaterial capacity of human intention to extend universally to being, to conform to that which is, objective knowledge of things is impossible. Even if the neural activity of the human brain were known by God himself to constitute in itself a perfect map of the universe, this would not constitute human knowledge because we would never have direct contact with the thing known but only with our own brain states—which, accordingly, could never adequately be judged as to their capacity to conform to anything at all, even themselves. Only if man possesses the immaterial capacity intentionally to be what he is not—to conform understanding and judgment to real nature—is the problem escaped.[20]

Were brain states simply *identical* with the reality of intellectual knowledge, no labor of correlation would be required. Things are really identical only when everything true of one is true of the other: but the property of a universal concept is not identical with a physical particular; and more importantly, the power of the mind to conform to universal being, a power which must be universal on pain of implying the impossibility of objectivity, *thus* cannot be *identical with* any neural function although it may be *related to it*. Of course there are natural limitations to our knowledge, but these pertain to sense knowledge as our avenue to the potential objects of knowledge and not to any spurious reduction of intellect to material nature.

The formal objects of universal true and universal good that respectively specify intellect and will indicate the positive immateriality of the rational soul. Thomas asserts this judgment: "If the intellectual principle contained a body, it would be incapable of knowing all bodies."[21] Of course, as Thomas teaches (*ST* q. 75, a. 1) the rational soul is the first act of the matter of the human body, but as he observes later: "The human soul, by reason of its perfection, is not a form merged in matter, or entirely embraced by matter.

---

only from matter, but also from the individuating conditions of matter, has more perfect knowledge than the senses, which receive the form of the thing known, without matter indeed, but with material conditions."

[20] The situation with materialism is as if one were locked from birth in a room whose floor were a topographic map of the state where one lived, but one had no contact of any kind with the outside world: one would be in no position to confirm that the floor really *were* a topographic map nor to know its accuracy if it were thought to be one. We are in no position to say that brain states are simply equivalent to knowledge of reality unless we are capable of comparing them with reality, permitting us to judge of the relation between our understanding and the real evidence. This requires a capacity transcending brain states and transcending any particular physical nature. In the absence of such a capacity, it is impossible adequately to know even that there *is* such a thing as a state of the brain much less to know that brain states are adequate to model themselves.

[21] Thomas Aquinas, *ST* I, q. 75, a. 2, resp.: "Si igitur principium intellectuale haberet in se naturam alicuius corporis, non posset omnia corpora cognoscere."

Therefore there is nothing to prevent some power thereof not being the act of the body, although the soul is essentially the form of the body."[22]

The harder argument regards the *subsistence* of the soul because although the rational soul is not a subject of being complete in its species (man is not merely his soul), it still is an incomplete but real *subject of being*. Because the intellectual soul has an act to itself that is not intrinsically conditioned by matter, accordingly it has a *being* to itself that is not intrinsically conditioned by matter. *Operatio sequitur esse.* Operation follows upon being. Our knowledge for Thomas is extrinsically conditioned by our bodily nature and requires sensible contact with the world as our gateway to the real, but we only attain cognition by elevating potentially intelligible objects to actual intelligibility through abstraction from sensible phantasms, after which we may return to sense knowledge of individuals and judge their natures to be thus and so. Thomas concludes that "the intellectual principle which we call the mind or the intellect has an operation per se apart from the body. Now only that which subsists can have an operation 'per se.' For nothing can operate but what is actual."[23] In his reply to the first objection in this article, he identifies two meanings of "subsistence": one extending to any subject of being excluding accident or a form depending on matter to be, and the other entailing *completeness* in specific nature and excluding being "a part." The rational soul subsists in the first way since it *is* a part of human nature. Yet, one must recollect that the rational soul is not *merely* a part—it is in every part of the body—and it communicates *its own existence* to the body. As Thomas observes:

The soul communicates that existence in which it subsists to the corporeal matter, out of which and the intellectual soul there results unity of existence; so that the existence of the whole composite is also the existence of the soul. This is not the case with other non-subsistent forms. For this reason the human soul retains its own existence after the dissolution of the body; whereas it is not so with other forms.[24]

---

[22] Thomas Aquinas, *ST* I, q. 76, a. 1, ad 4: "Humana anima non est forma in materia corporali immersa, vel ab ea totaliter comprehensa, propter suam perfectionem. Et ideo nihil prohibet aliquam eius virtutem non esse corporis actum; quamvis anima secundum suam essentiam sit corporis forma."

[23] Thomas Aquinas, *ST* I, q. 75, a. 2, resp.: "Ipsum igitur intellectuale principium, quod dicitur mens vel intellectus, habet operationem per se, cui non communicat corpus. Nihil autem potest per se operari, nisi quod per se subsistit. Non enim est operari nisi entis in actu, unde eo modo aliquid operatur, quo est."

[24] Thomas Aquinas, *ST* I, q. 76, a. 1, ad 5: "Anima illud esse in quo ipsa subsistit, communicat

As a thing acts, so it is; but the human intellect has an act to itself independent of matter however much this act presupposes extrinsic conditions. One does not lose the *power* of vision in a dark room, and yet he cannot see; likewise during bodily life, the mind when separated from sensible contact with the world by injury or brain damage does not lose the power of intellect but lacks its natural sensible access to potential objects of knowledge, for naturally speaking, understanding requires turning to bodily phantasms. Yet nonetheless, knowing in itself is achieved not by sensing but by intrinsically immaterial cognitive activity irreducible to the physical order.

Because the soul is a real subject of being incomplete in its species and communicates the *esse* in which it subsists to the composite, it is in itself incorruptible. Whereas material forms depend on matter to be and are not the principles of any act rising above materiality, the rational soul is the principle of intrinsically immaterial acts. Thus as a purely and positively immaterial form, it is insusceptible of corruption. God could annihilate it, but this would itself be unbefitting since the rational soul is ordered to receive the gift of existence without material limit; to create it only to annihilate it would be *contra naturam*. In merely material being, the form is the highest part of the whole but subsists only with the existence of the whole because it has no act or being of itself. By contrast, in the human case, the soul communicates the existence in which it subsists to the whole.

THE NATURAL KNOWLEDGE OF THE SEPARATED SOUL

Thomas teaches that the soul subsisting after death exists and understands in a way not natural to it. It is dissevered from the matter of the composite it actuates and has no access to the phantasms from which it naturally abstracts. Yet it can only act as it is, and as its mode of being is now separate in extension from the body, it can only act in this way. Since intelligibility is in inverse *ratio* to materiality, and the soul is not only immaterial but now is separated from its natural union with the matter of the body, it becomes not only a pure intelligible wholly and directly knowable to itself but also enjoys "perfect knowledge of other separated souls"[25] which also are pure

---

materiae corporali, ex qua et anima intellectiva fit unum, ita quod illud esse quod est totius compositi, est etiam ipsius animae. Quod non accidit in aliis formis, quae non sunt subsistentes. Et propter hoc anima humana remanet in suo esse, destructo corpore, non autem aliae formae."

[25] Thomas Aquinas, *ST* I, q. 89, a. 2, resp.: "Modus autem substantiae animae separatae est infra modum substantiae angelicae, sed est conformis modo aliarum animarum separatarum. Et ideo de aliis animabus separatis perfectam cognitionem habet; de Angelis autem imperfectam et deficientem, loquendo de cognitione naturali animae separatae. De

intelligibles (although as Fr. John Wippel observes, Thomas holds that the knowledge of other nobler separated substances—angels—is solely at the discretion of those spirits[26]).

Further, Thomas holds that God bestows to the separated soul species that actuate it apart from its natural mode of knowing. Thomas appears to hold this because he holds that God universally actuates cognitive powers according to their natures and to the way that they exist, and the intellect now existing radically apart from the body is differently actuated not only by the sheer intelligibility of the soul to itself but is also in its separated state able to benefit to some degree from higher species. Such *infused species*, Thomas says, are too exalted and confused for the soul—which is ordered naturally to know *via* sensible experience and abstraction from phantasms— but their infusion still brings about real knowledge. Thomas teaches that intellective memory from this life—as distinct from sensory memory—is retained: "Knowledge, therefore, acquired in the present life does not remain in the separated soul, as regards what belongs to the sensitive powers; but as regards what belongs to the intellect itself, it must remain."[27] This is because the intellect is incorruptible, and there is no contrary to an intelligible intention in the soul as, say, heat is opposed to cold. Thomas argues that even *actual knowledge from this life* is retained (a. 6), as the intelligible species are retained in the spiritual soul.

The principal element in all this is, on the one hand, permanently valid metaphysical principles, and on the other, the doctrine that God illumines all intellects according to their natures and modes of being, thus bestowing a confused but higher natural knowledge upon the separated soul. What is striking is that, on the one hand, Thomas partially prescinds from the large facts of man's ultimate end, and that, on the other, he proceeds from the

---

cognitione autem gloriae est alia ratio." "But the mode of the substance of the separated soul is inferior to the mode of substance of an angel, but is the same as that of other separated souls. Therefore the soul apart from the body has perfect knowledge of other separated souls, but it has an imperfect and defective knowledge of the angels so far as its natural knowledge is concerned. But the knowledge of glory is of another nature."

[26] Fr. John Wippel, "Thomas Aquinas on the Separated Soul's Knowledge," in *Metaphysical Themes in Thomas Aquinas III* (Washington, DC:, The Catholic University of America Press, 2021), 227. Thomas says simply "separated substances," but one might think he refers principally to separate substances that are complete in their species or "such by their complete nature" rather than separate but not complete in their species, as is the human soul. As indicated above, in the *Summa theologiae* he concludes that separated souls enjoy perfect knowledge of other separated souls.

[27] Thomas Aquinas, *ST* I, q. 89, a. 5, resp.: "Quantum ergo ad id quod aliquis praesentis scientiae habet in inferioribus viribus, non remanebit in anima separata, sed quantum ad id quod habet in ipso intellectu, necesse est ut remaneat."

order of the universe with respect to the truth that God moves and actuates all things according to their natures and to the way they exist. The nature of the intellect has not changed, and accordingly, such knowledge is naturally too exalted for the human intellect and is confusedly achieved. But as the soul actually perseveres in existence, consequently at death, its actual mode of intellectual activity is changed: *vita mutatur, non tollitur*. Thomas says, "Nor is the way of knowing unnatural, for God is the author of the influx both of the light of grace and of the light of nature."[28] The grace he speaks of here is not the beatific vision but a grace that consists in a natural good (a higher natural illumination through the divine bestowal of actuating created species). Existence itself is, in this way, a grace, not like sanctifying grace but as an unmerited gift. Limited finite activation of existing intellects seems naturally proportioned to the condition of the separated soul after death and in no way tantamount to the beatific vision or supernatural life as such.

Of course, no pagan held this account although some thought there was likely to be a life of the soul beyond this life and that it was worthwhile to consider in what it could consist. Thomas gives solidity to this natural consideration that only the perfection of metaphysics in the service of theology could provide. God actuates and illumines all intellects according to their natures and to the manner of their existence. This is not in the least naturally unintelligible. In this life, bodily harm extrinsically impedes cognition while yet the actual *extension* of the soul's existence is not changed, and so the soul retains its natural but gravely impeded mode of knowing. But when the extension of the soul's existence is radically altered at death through total deprivation of matter, this causes the subsistent and incorruptible spiritual soul to become to itself a pure intelligible in act, precisely because intelligibility is in inverse ratio to materiality. It is not the integral person, and its state is not natural to it, but the very extent of its deprivation actuates it in a new way, making it wholly intelligible to itself and as an incorruptible principle amenable of further divine activation. This is *praeter* but not *contra, naturam*, and is also something that is suggested by the universality of the divine motion and activation.

The trouble with this teaching is not that it is unthinkable but that, of itself, it might be taken to constitute the full account of the soul after death, which would be catastrophically erroneous. Of itself, the conclusion of this reasoning (as distinct from the entire account engendering it)

---

[28] Thomas Aquinas, *ST* I, q. 89, a. 1, ad 3: "Nec tamen propter hoc cognitio non est naturalis, quia Deus est auctor non solum influentiae gratuiti luminis, sed etiam naturalis."

might be taken as encouraging an overly Platonized account of the human person—although as Thomas's reasoning manifests, this is not the case with respect to his analysis. And as Thomas taught in the *Summa contra gentiles*,[29] the soul's perseverance in being without the bodily life to which it remains essentially ordered following upon the corruption of the body is itself a sign of the fittingness of the Resurrection, since nothing contrary to nature can persist indefinitely.

CONCLUSION

Thomas's analysis constitutes a strong argument rooted in immutable metaphysical principles that the separated human soul—whose immortality is, after all, part of the divine order—is not wholly bereft of all act in its praeternatural state after death. Further, he provides a strong argument of natural fittingness that the separated soul is actuated not alone through complete intuitive self-knowledge, intellective memory, and intuition of other separated souls, but through further species bestowed by God, who illumines every intellect proportionate to its state and manner of existing. Thomas's analysis of the separated soul highlights that limited transcendence of human spirit which is essential to the *imago naturae* in man as an obediential potency for supernatural grace and glory.

---

[29] Thomas Aquinas, *Summa contra gentiles* IV, ch. 79.

Anima mea non est ego:
Thomas, Beatitude, and the Human Person

T. ADAM VAN WART
Ave Maria University, FL

THE GRAMMAR OF HYLOMORPHISM: "MY SOUL IS NOT ME"

Thomas Aquinas maintains that to be a human being is to be a composite creature of a particular kind. And while this composition is multiform, at its most basic are the conjoined realities of an immaterial and rational soul, on the one hand, and a material human body on the other. Only the hylomorphic union of the two constitute a human being as such.[1]

This is largely why, in his commentary on 1 Corinthians, St. Thomas Aquinas opines, "[T]he soul, since it is part of man's body, is not an entire man, and my soul is not me; hence, although the soul obtains salvation in

---

[1] "Man is not a soul only, but something composed of soul and body." *Summa Theologiae* I, q. 75, a. 4, corp. [Unless otherwise indicated, for the sake of non-specialists, all English citations of the *Summa Theologiae* will come from Thomas Aquinas, *Summa Theologica*, 5 vols. (New York: Benziger Bros, Inc., 1981).] This idea is not merely part of Thomistic doctrine but of Church doctrine as well. So, for example, "The human person, though made of body and soul, is a unity." Second Vatican Council, Pastoral Constitution on the Church in the Modern World *Gaudium et Spes* (Dec. 7, 1965), §14. See, too, the Sacred Congregation for the Doctrine of the Faith's *Donum Vitae*, §3, which, quoting Pope St. John Paul II's 1983 address to the World Medical Association, maintains, "Each human person, in his absolute singularity, is constituted not only by his spirit, but by his body as well. Thus, in the body and through the body, one touches the person himself in his concrete reality."

another life, not I or any man."[2] In context, St. Thomas makes this claim—my soul is not me—to counter a potential objection to St. Paul's statement that without the corporeal resurrection of the dead, Christians among all people are to be thought most pitiful (1 Cor 15:12–19). After all, Aquinas suggests, someone might argue against St. Paul that "although our bodies do not possess any good things except in this life, which is mortal, yet according to the soul [Christians] have many good things in the other life [i.e., the life of the postmortem, pre-resurrected soul]."[3] In short, if the human body, being physical, is outfitted to find its fulfillment in the goods of this present life of God's materially mediated presence, and the immaterial human soul is equipped to find its happiness in the good of the immaterially immediate presence of God postmortem, what genuine difference could bodily resurrection make for human beatitude? That is, if the higher part of the baptized human being has reached its maximally elevated end in God's presence once separated from the body, isn't corporeal resurrection superfluous at best with respect to human beatitude?[4]

Given his hylomorphic anthropology, however, for St. Thomas this objection ultimately fails because it suggests parity where, in fact, there is none: a human being's soul is not equivalent to, not the same thing as, a human being as such.[5] To think otherwise is falsely to equate the part with the whole, the instrument with the operator.

Said differently, though Thomas never quite puts it this way, my soul's

---

[2] Thomas Aquinas, *Super I Cor.*, 15, lec. 2, from Thomas Aquinas, *Commentary on the Letters of Saint Paul to the Corinthians*, Latin/English Edition of the Works of St. Thomas Aquinas (Lander, WY: The Aquinas Institute for the Study of Sacred Doctrine, 2012), 349.

[3] Thomas Aquinas, *Super I Cor.*, 15, lec. 2.

[4] For St. Thomas, the human being's ultimate happiness is found in nothing less than the immediate intellectual vision of God. *ST* I-II, q. 3, a. 8, corp.: "[F]or perfect happiness the intellect needs to reach the very essence of the First Cause. And thus it will have its perfection through union with God as with that object, in which alone man's happiness consists."

[5] While Aquinas does affirm that the soul is a substance, the substantial form of the body, he nevertheless maintains in *ST* I, q. 75, a. 4, ad 2: "Not every particular substance is a *hypostasis* or a person, but that which has the complete nature of its species. Hence a hand, or a foot, is not called a *hypostasis*, or a person; nor, likewise, is the soul alone so called, since it a part of the human species." So the "whatness" of the human soul and the "whatness" of the human being whose soul it is are not ontologically equivalent, whatever role the former may play with respect to the latter. What's more, since the human soul is not by nature supposed to exist independently of the body, having come into being simultaneously with it and only separable from it by virtue of sin and its damaging effects, the substantial form any separated soul is must always be *imperfectly* substantial, defective in being the form that it is. Thomas is, of course, correct when he says in *ST* I, q. 90, a. 4, ad 3, "that the soul remains after the body is due to a defect of the body, namely death," but the defect of death is a function of sin and, therefore, not limited to the body alone in its impact. The differences

experience of beatitude is not *my* experience of beatitude because, properly speaking, *I* cease to exist at the moment of death (*"et anima mea non est ego"*).[6] Given that I can only be the human that I am, and what I am is necessarily a union of body and soul, the dissolution of that union means the undoing of the human being I am, and, therefore, the necessary extermination of me.[7] In short, given that human being is only ever constituted by the hylomorphic union of soul and body, the realization of New Testament salvation is an inexorably corporeal affair.[8] As St. Thomas affirms in concert with 1 Timothy 1:15, Christ came to save sinners and not merely their souls.

---

between the respective substances of the human soul and the human being, therefore, are both ontological and hamartiological in character.

[6] In fact, Thomas even suggests here that the very idea of the soul's immortality—a notion frequently taken by many Thomists to be a truth discernable in principle by philosophy or "natural theology"—is undermined to the degree that one denies the resurrection of the body. See *Super I Cor.* 15, lec. 2: "[I]f the resurrection of the body is denied, it is not easy, rather, it is difficult, to sustain the immortality of the soul."

[7] For prolonged meditation on this truth and intriguing speculative thought on its implications for the intermediate state, see Paul J. Griffiths, *Decreation: The Last Things of All Creatures* (Waco, TX: Baylor University Press, 2014), esp. 173–250. Joshua Brotherton has recently offered a critique of Griffiths's speculative thought in Joshua R. Brotherton, "A Response To Paul Griffiths' Annihilationist Proposal," *Modern Theology* 37, no. 1 (2021): 89–113. Over against Griffiths, Brotherton argues, "If the soul is understood, rather, as the subsistent form that gives *esse* to the matter that it actualizes (as body), the separated soul remains the same identical human being as the embodied soul, even though it lacks something proper to its natural state, namely, its *materia quantitate signate*, in Thomist language." Brotherton, "A Response To Paul Griffiths," 94–95. It isn't at all clear to me that Brotherton's criticisms of Griffiths's account, relying on a certain construal of the relationship between act and potency, ultimately succeed, however. After all, it is true that the human soul, the human person/being, and the human body as such all come together in a single act of being (*esse*), an act that mutually constitutes them all. And it is true that, at the moment of death, that same *esse* persists insofar as the human soul continues to exist even after the human body and human person/being unnaturally stop sharing in that *esse*. So, one could argue as Brotherton does that there is a potency in the separated soul and its *esse* for the return of the human body and human person/being to which they appertain. All that may very well be true, so far as it goes. Even so, it doesn't alter the fundamental nonequivalence there is between a soul, on the one hand, and the embodied person whose soul it is, on the other. Potency or not, *these just are not the same thing*. In any case, both Brotherton's engagement with Griffiths and his understanding of Thomas's thought and its deployment are obviously relevant to the topic at hand and, so, included here.

[8] Williamson is exactly right, therefore, when he says, "For many centuries Christian hope has focused on heaven. In contrast, the hope of the early Christians centered on the return of Christ (Titus 2:13), the resurrection of the dead, and the full establishment of God's kingdom as expressed in the Lord's prayer: 'Thy kingdom come, thy will be done on earth as it is in heaven.'. . . [W]e Christians would do well to set our hopes on the full and final establishment of Christ's kingdom on earth." Peter S. Williamson, *Revelation*, Catholic Commentary on Sacred Scripture (Grand Rapids, MI: Baker Academic, 2015), 345. N.

WE SPEAK AS IF IT WERE (THE REALITY OF CONTINUITY)

However, there nevertheless seems to be a tension between Thomas's thoroughly Pauline claims in his 1 Corinthians commentary and many of the arguably more Aristotelian sorts of things he has to say about the soul and human beatitude in the *Summa*. There, though still holding to his hylomorphic anthropology, St. Thomas frequently speaks of beatitude on the supposition that there is an inviolable continuity that exists between the human being who dies (whole) and his separated human soul (part).[9] That he does so is, no doubt, in part a function of longstanding Church practice as grounded in biblical witness.[10] After all, people rightly seek intercession from the separated souls of the saints as if they were entreating the saints themselves.[11] Indeed, it is clearly the saints themselves, and not merely their souls, that the faithful intend when addressing their intercessory petitions. Though "my soul is not me," some sort of connection must remain, therefore,

---

T. Wright makes a similar point, though not in ways obviously compatible with magisterial teaching, in *Surprised by Hope: Rethinking Heaven, the Resurrection, and the Mission of the Church* (New York: Harper One, 2008), 79–186. See also Michael P. Barber, John A. Kincaid, and Brant Pitre, *Paul, a New Covenant Jew: Rethinking Pauline Theology* (Grand Rapids, MI: William B. Eerdmans Publishing Company, 2019), 67–73.

[9] See, for example, *ST* I-II, q. 4, a. 5, ad 2. Of course, the notion that human beings have immaterial souls can no longer be taken for granted. For a particularly interesting and sophisticated set of arguments that we do not have immaterial souls, see Warren S. Brown, Nancey Murphy, and H. Newton Malony, eds., *Whatever Happened to the Soul? Scientific and Theological Portraits of Human Nature* (Minneapolis: Augsburg Fortress, 1998); Nancey Murphy, *Bodies and Souls or Spirited Bodies?* (Cambridge: Cambridge University Press, 2006). See, too, though, Levering's engagement with Murphy's contributions in particular, in Matthew Levering, *Jesus and the Demise of Death: Resurrection, Afterlife, and the Fate of the Christian* (Waco, TX: Baylor University Press, 2012), 97–108.

[10] For engagement with the evidence of the Church's long tradition of seeking the intercession of the saints, see Peter Brown, *The Cult of the Saints: Its Rise and Function in Latin Christianity*, 2nd ed. (Chicago: The University of Chicago Press, 2015), 50–68; Émilien Lamirande, OMI, *The Communion of Saints*, trans. A. Manson, The Twentieth Century Encyclopedia of Catholicism (New York: Hawthorn Books, 1963), 143–52; Jacques Le Goff, *The Birth of Purgatory*, trans. Arthur Goldhammer (Chicago: The University of Chicago Press, 1984), 11–12, 45–46. For a sampling of biblical passages grounding practices like these, see 1 Sam 28; 2 Macc 12:38–45; and Luke 16:19–31.

[11] Indeed, the Sacred Congregation for the Doctrine of the Faith (hereafter CDF) assures that "the Church excludes every way of thinking or speaking that would render meaningless or unintelligible her prayers, funeral rites, and religious acts offered for the dead. All these are, in their substance, *logi theologici*." "Letter on Certain Questions Concerning Eschatology," May 17, 1979, https://www.vatican.va/roman_curia/congregations/cfaith/documents/rc_con_cfaith_doc_19790517_escatologia_en.html.

between the deceased person and his separated soul.[12] So how to account for that connection, particularly with respect to beatitude?[13]

Well, St. Thomas explains, "The human soul retains the being [*esse*] of the composite after the destruction of the body." This is because, he argues, "the being [*esse*] of the form is the same as that of its matter, and this is the same being [*esse*] of the composite."[14]

To understand what this means, we need bear in mind that Aquinas's hylomorphic anthropology is one significantly weighted in deference to the human soul. After all, "The theologian considers the nature of man in relation to the soul; but not in relation to the body, except in so far as the body has relation to the soul."[15] Thomas places the anthropological accent on the soul over against the body for several reasons, but chief among them is that the soul, for St. Thomas, is "the form of the body" because it is what in-forms matter so as to constitute the human being's physicality precisely as human.[16]

---

[12] Helpful here is Joseph Ratzinger, *Eschatology: Death and Eternal Life*, ed. Aidan Nichols, OP, trans. Michael Waldstein, 2nd ed. (Washington, DC: The Catholic University of America Press, 1988), 104–61.

[13] Averring back to what was discussed in n7 above, Daniel Lendman I think very helpfully displays a common Thomistic argument that the continuity between soul and person that the tradition maintains exists must somehow be bound up with the person's coming to be simultaneously with her soul and body at the moment of human conception. See Lendman, "Death, the Last Enemy: St. Thomas's Aristotelian Exegesis of the Soul as *Forma Corporis* in Church Doctrine and What This Implies about the Personhood of the Separated Soul" (PhD diss., Ave Maria University, 2020), 286–98. What's more, since there is an immortality that accompanies the soul that does not accompany the body, Lendman argues, the trace of the person whose soul it is carries forward after death, and so a continuity of a sort in *esse* is maintained between the two postmortem. Lendman characterizes this continuity by maintaining that, while certainly not a proper person, the soul is nevertheless *personal*, "a personal subsistence," or "perhaps a person *in virtue*" (57). I can't help but wonder if language like "the immortality of the soul" doesn't distort just what it is for a separated soul to exist as an exclusively *postlapsarian* phenomenon, but I find Lendman's "personal" versus "person" distinction quite helpful.

[14] Thomas Aquinas, *ST* I-II, q. 4, a. 5, ad 2. This association is, no doubt, why Aquinas manifestly treats "man's happiness" and "the perfect happiness of the intellect" as interchangeable notions, speaking seamlessly of the two in places like *ST* I-II, q. 3, a. 8. But showing that they are not interchangeable notions—*and by Thomas's own lights*—is part of the burden of the current essay.

[15] *ST* I, q. 75, pro.

[16] Some even claim, Thomas seemingly among them, that the soul is, in some respects, incumbered by the body and would be even under the conditions of original justice before sin entered the world to devastating effect (e.g., *ST* I-II, q. 4, a. 6, ad 2). Of course, it is true that the soul needs the body for the concrete, sensible phantasms requisite for the formation of linguistically mediated concepts. But understanding and contemplation, for Thomas, take place irrespective of sensation as these acts of the (person by way of her) intellect traffic in abstract universals which extend beyond the concrete particulars delivered in phantasms.

The human being's soul serves, therefore, as the unifying integrative principle of the human body, which is why, metaphysically speaking, at the moment of death (i.e., the soul's separation from the body), bodily disintegration inevitably follows.

Unlike the body, however, and though it comes into being concomitantly with it, "the soul subsists in its own being."[17] In fact, St. Thomas says, in light of the above, "It follows . . . that after being separated from the body [the soul] has perfect being [*esse*], and that, consequently it can have a perfect operation, although it has not the perfect specific nature." So given that "beatitude belongs to man in respect of his intellect," and "since [as a function of the soul] the intellect remains" and "can have a perfect operation" after death, it follows that "[the soul] can have beatitude."[18]

Aquinas goes on to say that the body is certainly not unimportant to beatitude. Indeed, "bodily good can add a certain charm and perfection of beatitude."[19] But "after the body is resumed [in resurrection], beatitude increases not in intensity but in extent."[20] Even though a human person is

Consequently, though in this life the soul requires the body and its senses in order to form concepts and know truth, Aquinas has it that the proper object of the intellect is not sensate matter but the metaphysical realties of truth and being. This is why the physical world serves both as a necessary component of the intellect's proper function and a deterrent. On the one hand, it supplies what is necessary for the (person by way of her) intellect to arrive at the contemplation of creaturely being. On the other hand, the physical world and our material needs continually pull us away from that very contemplation (e.g., email inboxes, hunger, and the like). It seems every step up the ladder of ontic contemplation made possible by the material world is inevitably followed by two or more steps back down as a result of the same. But if the intellect as preserved in the separated soul is exposed to the fullness of God's own being, it is seemingly able to realize its contemplative end in superlative fashion. Not only need it no longer fear regress on the ladder of ontic contemplation, it presumably can kick it away altogether for that ladder's having been rendered wholly superfluous. For a characteristically rich account of how the human body, prior to "transfiguration," can be thought to inhibit ultimate happiness, see Matthias Joseph Scheeben, *The Mysteries of Christianity* (New York: The Crossroad Publishing Company, 2006), 666–94.

[17] Thomas Aquinas, *ST* I-II, q. 4, a. 5, ad 2.

[18] Thomas Aquinas, *ST* I-II, q. 4, a. 5, ad 3. By Thomas's lights, the soul is roughly equivalent to "the intellect or mind." See *ST* I, q. 1, a. 2, corp. See also *ST* I, q. 75, a. 2, corp.: "The intellectual principle which we call the mind or the intellect has an operation per se apart from the body. Now only that which subsists can have an operation per se. . . . We must conclude therefore that the human soul, which is called the intellect or mind, is something incorporeal and subsistent."

[19] Thomas Aquinas, *ST* I-II, q. 4, a. 6, ad 1. For more on this, see Reinhard Hütter, *Bound for Beatitude: A Thomistic Study of Eschatology and Ethics*, Thomist Ressourcement Series 12 (Washington, DC: The Catholic University of America Press, 2019), 387–445, esp. 425–36.

[20] Thomas Aquinas, *ST* I-II, q. 4, a. 5, ad 4. Indeed, "because of the beatitude of the soul there

precisely not a human person until the postmortem soul and body are joined at the resurrection, so long as the separated human *soul* experiences the beatific vision of God, post-resurrection or not, it seems the full capacity for human beatitude is essentially realized. The body is simply drawn into what is already fully in act: intellectual beatitude.

At this point, however, one might begin to wonder if Thomas hasn't functionally wound up assuming the very position of the objector he opposed in his commentary on 1 Corinthians 15. After all, given Thomas's claims that "the human soul retains the being [*esse*] of the composite after the destruction of the body," and that "the separated soul is entirely at rest as regards the thing desired,"[21] what happiness could ever be possessed by the resurrected person that the separated soul of that person didn't already have? In his attempt to account for the connection of deceased person and separated soul, has Thomas not conflated the beatitude of the soul and the beatitude of the person, and, with them, the respective bearers of that beatitude?[22]

There are several ways one might respond to such questions.

THE "AS IF"

One approach might be to say that while Thomas is correct to insist that "my soul is not me," perhaps we should read Thomas to say that nevertheless my soul is, in comparison with the body, mostly me (or mostly what makes me me).[23] We spoke previously of the asymmetrical functional relationship that

---

will be an overflow on to the body so that this too will obtain its perfection." *ST* I-II, q. 4, a. 6, corp.

[21] Thomas Aquinas, *ST* I-II, q. 4, a. 5, ad 2.

[22] It seems to me that Thomas, indeed, often conflates "soul" and "person," at least in what we find in the *Summa Theologiae*. See n14 above. To the degree that his position insufficiently distinguishes the two, therefore, I think it to be deficient in all the ways I outline here and, thus, not ultimately sustainable theologically. It remains the case that insofar as the human soul and the human being/person are not identical, the beatitude of the former simply cannot be identical to the latter even if the latter's beatitude comes by way of the (instrumentality of the) former or the *esse* of both is the same. The object of both is certainly identical for Aquinas (i.e., the divine essence), but the subjects of perfection, and thus their respective beatitudes, are not.

[23] Lendman, "Death, the Last Enemy," 318, argues for something along these lines, concluding, "The separated soul is not an indifferent 'part' of the human person. Rather, since the soul is the place of intellect and will, it is the most formal and constitutive element of the person." As is clear in the following paragraphs, I remain unconvinced of this. Nevertheless, I think Lendman, in denying that one's separated soul is flatly equivalent to the person whose soul it is, is quite right to identify the soul as *personal*. Time does not permit elaboration along these lines, but Lendman's work makes a significant contribution to this conversation. See n13 above.

exists between soul and body in constituting the human person. On the basis of that asymmetrical functional relationship, therefore, one might go on to suggest that this asymmetry isn't merely functional but ontological as well. Though the soul alone does not constitute the person, properly speaking, it is functionally most responsible through its unique contribution in constituting the human person. And so, the argument might go, ontologically the soul, even in death, is still quantitively and qualitatively *mostly* the person to whom it belongs. Though to be a human being is to be a rational animal, we are *more* rational than animal, on this reading, which is why Thomas so frequently uses "rational natures" interchangeably with "human beings," and perhaps most fully accounts for his claim that "the human soul retains the being [*esse*] of the composite" in death. So, the (separated) soul *technically* is not the same as the person (it once constituted), but it may as well be because it's the bit of us that most counts and disproportionately so.

But this approach carries with it several less than salutary implications and, I would argue, significant logical difficulties.[24]

SEVERAL DIFFICULTIES ACCOMPANY THIS "AS IF"

To begin, it is not clear that the proposition that the rational bit of us is more human than the animal bits of us is logically coherent. This is because existence as a particular substance—to exist as a human being, for example—is ostensibly a toggle concept. A given *suppositum* either substantially is a human being or it is not. Human being, in other words, is not obviously a concept that, properly speaking, admits of degrees. Indeed, it is precisely just this truth that underlies the Church's stance against abortion, euthanasia,

---

[24] Some of the unfortunate implications of construing human being in ways that deprecate the significance of embodiment might conceivably involve the following: Since being embodied is essential to distinguish us from the angels, we must be careful that we don't so stress the intellectual aspect of our being that we functionally portray human beings as a(n inferior) sub-species of angel. Moreover, precisely as a critical aspect of our uniquely imaging God, we mustn't forget that our being embodied allows us to join with God in bringing new rational life into the world while exercising dominion over it. Animals can bring new life into the world. Angels can exercise governance. But only humans, by virtue of being both spiritual and physical, are capable of doing both, partnering uniquely with God is his work of creation. Finally, God the Son became flesh—joined the ranks of human being—to obtain our salvation. God the Son is, therefore, always and forever after human (and so compositely material) because of his Incarnation. This, too, means that our conception of what beatitude ought look like cannot effectively treat the body as ancillary or merely decorative (either with respect to the full implications of the Incarnation for human flesh, in general, or our engagement with Christ in the availability of his flesh, in particular).

and so on.[25] Being human is an either/or proposition, and so it makes no sense to say that a human being is mostly his or her soul. Human beings as such cannot more or less be.[26]

Granted, human being is composite, and the soul, as the form of the body, does play a unique role in determining or informing matter so as to constitute a human being as such. Functionally, then, there is indeed an asymmetrical relation of the soul and body in human formation. But it doesn't follow from this that a human being *is* more soul than body. By way of example, one might say that clearly the head is more important to a given human's ongoing existence than, say, one's eyes. But neither head nor eye suffice to constitute a human being as such and, while functionally asymmetrical, neither one nor the other makes one more or less human. It doesn't make sense, consequently, to say a human is more head than eyes.[27] Similarly, two hydrogen atoms may contribute more to the formation of a water molecule than oxygen, but it would be a mistake to say that hydrogen is more water than oxygen.

So whatever else a separated soul may be capable of, it is not capable of being a human person.[28] Not even of mostly being a human person since being a human, however constituted, does not admit of gradation.

---

[25] So, for example, the CDF's *Dignitas Personae* (Dec. 8, 2008), §5 insists, "Indeed, the reality of the human being for the entire span of life, both before birth and after birth, does not allow us to posit either a change in nature or a gradation in moral value, since it possesses full anthropological and ethical status." Consider also John Paul II, The Gospel of Life *Evangelium Vitae* (March 25, 1995), §2, which teaches, "Life in time, in fact, is the fundamental condition, the initial stage and an integral part of the entire unified process of human existence."

[26] It seems to me one can affirm this and still make ongoing, salutary use of the Augustinian insight that evil of whatever sort (i.e., endured or enacted) is in some sense a privation of being. In so doing, one would simply have to distinguish between differences in, say, plenitude versus differences in kind. By way of illustration, there is a difference between saying Michael Jordan is more of a basketball player than Lebron James, on the one hand, and Michael Jordan is a more of a basketball player than Benjamin Franklin, on the other. In the first instance, both Jordan and James are undeniably basketball players, so the "more" in this case serves to signal Jordan's greater standing (plenitude) as a basketball player. But the difference between Jordan and Franklin with respect to basketball is a difference in kind, as basketball was invented a century after Franklin's death. The difference between a separated human soul and a human being is a difference in kind, even if a uniquely existing one. The introduction of evil corresponds to a difference in plenitude *within* a shared category of kind.

[27] It is true that human being's creation in the divine image uniquely implicates the rational soul, but it may well be that imaging God involves more than the soul and, in any case, it doesn't obviously make the notion of being more or less human any more coherent.

[28] Here we might note the CDF's teaching in "Letter on Certain Questions Concerning Eschatology" that "a spiritual element survives and subsists after death, an element endowed

Secondly, and as a result, ordinary language makes plain that the sorts of things we can say about humans and the kinds of things we can say of intellectual souls are not wholly coextensive. For example, it is clear, so far as Thomas is concerned, that human beings attain knowledge instrumentally by way of their intellectual souls.[29] By extension, then, it is true to say that the intellectual soul attains knowledge. But surely it is only on the basis of human beings coming to know that we can speak of the intellectual soul's coming to know. After all, it would make for an especially strange

with consciousness and will, so that the 'human self' subsists. To designate this element, the Church uses the word 'soul.'" Does our above claim stand at odds with this teaching? I don't think so. Firstly, a clear distinction is made in the text immediately preceding the above citation between "the whole person" as the subject of resurrection and the soul as the "spiritual element" of human beings that survives and subsists in a postmortem state prior to resurrection. We clearly, then, have official recognition of both the difference between whole and part with respect to the human composite and the non-interchangeability of the two. Secondly, while the document maintains that "the 'human self' subsists" after death as a function of this surviving "spiritual element," it isn't obvious what "human self" here means. After all, the critical terms are in quotation marks, indicating a certain recognized ambiguity as to what exactly is in view by way of the designation "human self." For a helpful summary of the differing modern conceptions of the "self" that may or may not fit the bill, see Fergus Kerr, OP, "The Modern Philosophy of Self in Recent Theology," in *Neuroscience and the Person: Scientific Perspectives on Divine Action*, ed. Robert John Russell et al., Scientific Perspectives on Divine Action 4 (Vatican City State: Vatican Observatory Publications, 2002), 23–40. What's more, the language of subsistence is somewhat slippery as well, and, it seems to me, intentionally used precisely for this reason. For example, famously, in *Dominus Iesus* (June 16, 2000), §17, the CDF underscored *Lumen Gentium* (Nov. 21. 1964), §8's teaching that "the unique church of Christ . . . subsists in the Catholic Church, which is governed by the successor of Peter and by the bishops in communion with him." But in its intention to provide greater specificity as to what "subsists in" means with respect to the teachings of *Lumen Gentium*, the CDF notably refrained from flatly *equating* the church of Christ with the Catholic Church. And one needn't bother getting into issues of ecclesial division or ecumenism to see why. Jesus's own instruction regarding the wheat and the tares, for example, clearly implies that even *ad intra* "subsists in" cannot be understood to mean "wholly identical with" in this case (Matt 13:24–30). So, if this is true with respect to the church of Christ and its subsistence in the Catholic Church, presumably it is as well with respect to a human being and her postmortem soul, that in which "the 'human self' subsists." Thirdly, and finally, CDF, "Letter on Certain Questions Concerning Eschatology" under discussion later says that "the Church excludes any explanation that would deprive the Assumption of the Virgin Mary of its unique meaning, namely the fact that the bodily glorification of the Virgin is an anticipation of the glorification that is the destiny of all the elect." It isn't difficult to imagine that a case could be made that those who functionally equate the separated soul's experience of beatitude with the resurrected human person's experience of beatitude actually work against this Marian affirmation thereby; Mary, whose existence in glorification precisely as a human being makes her experience of beatitude qualitatively and crucially different from that of the separated souls of the saints.

29 See, for example, *ST* I, q. 85.

anthropology wherein the intellectual soul itself first came to know and then passed that knowledge on to the human who subsequently likewise knows. What could the receptivity of knowledge on the part of the human even be in such a scenario? By nature, then, the soul is a "means by which," not a "that which." Persons and their souls are not two different things of the same kind but two different things entirely and differently dependent upon each other.[30]

There is, then, not simply an important but a crucial difference between saying the *person* knows and wills by way of her soul and the *soul* knows and wills. And, in the state of integrity, there is, properly speaking, only the former. The soul is an instrument of the person's knowledge and desire, but it is the person who knows and wills.[31]

It is, of course, numbered among the defined truths of the Church's teaching that the separated soul is rightly said to know and will.[32] But these

---

[30] Even though both come into being simultaneously, the human being depends on the soul in her constitution as a hylomorphic human being, both in coming to be and in her ongoing existence as such. Conversely, the soul depends on the human being for its coming to be but seemingly not its ongoing existence. At least, this is true in a certain sense. A separated soul, after all, while being continuous with the integrative soul it was before death, nevertheless lacks substantially precisely as a function of its being separated, and this in arguable parallel with how human flesh differs from a corpse. This is why, as we have already noted, Aquinas identifies the separated soul as an "imperfect substance."

[31] Perhaps it is at this juncture that we should offer the additional reminder that the separated soul is, at root, inherently a mystery to us. That it is a mystery can be shown in numerous ways, but certainly one of them is bound up with the soul's unique role in humanity's imaging of God. After all, if the soul is the primary means by which we image God, and if that which is being imaged is wholly unknown to us (see Thomas Aquinas, *ST* I, q. 3, pro.), then the image *qua* image of the ineffable must itself likewise be beyond our ability to conceive. In any case, we can't properly know what it is for a human intellect and will to exist and operate independently (unnaturally) of any human being, as such. That we claim that they do so is, I would argue, a feature of God's revelation of just this mystery to us. That we have difficulty accounting for the soul's role in one's postmortem personal subsistence, therefore, is wholly to be expected and perhaps a signal that we are operating under conceptual constraints it would be unwise to deny or attempt to transgress. As with all divinely revealed mystery, the point of one's theology that flows therefrom is not to solve the apparent riddle but to add greater clarity in specifying just what the mystery is. For more on this, see T. Adam Van Wart, *Neither Nature nor Grace: Aquinas, Barth, and Garrigou-Lagrange on the Epistemic Use of God's Effects* (Washington, DC: The Catholic University of America Press, 2020), 258–81.

[32] In the decrees of the Council of Vienne (AD 1311–1312) and in Pope Benedict XII, *The Beatific Vision of God Benedictus Deus* (AD 1336), the tradition formally affirms what Aquinas himself puts forward, the Council laying the anthropological groundwork for the more straightforwardly theological claims of the following bull. So, citing the former, "We reject as erroneous and contrary to the truth of the catholic faith every doctrine or proposition rashly asserting that the substance of the rational or intellectual soul is not of itself

activities of the separated soul must be a different sort of thing than the knowing and willing of the person because that which is doing the knowing/ willing is different in each case. Consequently, whatever account of beatitude we put forward, either on the part of the soul or the person, needs to be very carefully considered and distinguished with respect to this difference.

In short, if we want to maintain the hylomorphic truth that "my soul is not me," and yet likewise want to insist on an ongoing connection between the separated soul and the person to whom it belongs, particularly with respect to beatitude, any metaphysical account of the soul that wants to treat it as quantitatively or qualitatively equivalent to the human person simply won't do.[33]

---

and essentially the form of the human body, or casting doubt on this matter. In order that all may know the truth of the faith in its purity and all error may be excluded, we define that anyone who presumes henceforth to assert defend or hold stubbornly that the rational or intellectual soul is not the form of the human body of itself and essentially, is to be considered a heretic." From Norman P. Tanner, SJ, ed., *Decrees of the Ecumenical Councils*, vol.1 (Washington, DC: Georgetown University Press, 1990), 361. *Benedictus Deus* clearly builds on this, holding that "[redeemed] souls . . . have been, are and will be with Christ in heaven, in the heavenly kingdom and paradise, joined to the company of the holy angels. Since the passion and death of the Lord Jesus Christ, these souls have seen and see the divine essence with an intuitive vision and even face to face, without the mediation of any creature by way of object of vision; rather the divine essence immediately manifests itself to them, plainly, clearly and openly, and in this vision they enjoy the divine essence. Moreover, by this vision and enjoyment the souls of those who have already died are truly blessed and have eternal life and rest. Also, the souls of those who will die in the future will see the same divine essence and will enjoy it before the general judgment. Such a vision and enjoyment of the divine essence do away with the acts of faith and hope in these souls, inasmuch as faith and hope are properly theological virtues. And after such intuitive and face-to-face vision and enjoyment has or will have begun for these souls, the same vision and enjoyment has continued and will continue without any interruption and without end until the last Judgment and from then on forever." In Heinrich Denzinger et al., eds., *Compendium of Creeds, Definitions, and Declarations on Matters of Faith and Morals*, 43rd ed. (San Francisco: Ignatius Press, 2012), *1000. It is, of course, somewhat strange that *Benedictus Deus* should use the Pauline language of "face to face" (1 Cor 13:12) given the by definition facelessness of separated human souls. And while it seems to me Paul intends "face to face" in a real, physical, and resurrected sense, the Church is certainly right to assert and affirm the accompanying spiritual thrust of Paul's language, as it does here. See, though, Barber, Kincaid, and Pitre, *Paul, a New Covenant Jew*, 212–16.

[33] Several other objections might be raised, though. Firstly, there is the fact that we are not merely rational beings but essentially embodied ones. The soul is the form of the body, but it is not the form of the human. Rational animality is the form of the human; neither rationality nor animality alone are ontologically sufficient unto themselves. Secondly, the soul apart from the body is imperfect, not fully what it is supposed to be. The soul never comes into being without the body, and, were there no fall into sin, presumably never would have existed apart from it. That soul and body are separable at all is a function of the devastation wrought by sin, and so the separated soul of necessity exists in a state of lack. In parallel

"IT IS NOT I WHO LIVE, BUT CHRIST WHO LIVES IN ME."

But perhaps a less metaphysically based argument and a more straightforwardly theological one could be made for the separated soul's experience of beatitude; an argument that both maintains that the soul is not me (its realization of beatitude is not my realization of beatitude), and which accounts for the connection between soul and self so as to provide for the intelligibility of the intercession of the saints.

We've only time to sketch it briefly here, but it might run roughly as follows.

Let us affirm, firstly, St. Paul's teaching that, at the moment of baptism, a human person as such (body and soul) is united to Christ and made a member of Christ's own Mystical Body in a real and intimate way.[34] This incorporation takes place because, by Christ's own institution, through baptism a person is sacramentally joined to Jesus's own death and raised to new life with him such that St. Paul can even say in Galatians 2:20, "It is no longer I who live, but Christ who lives in me."[35] Indeed, the baptized person is intimately united to Christ (and his Mystical Body) as a bride is joined to her husband, the two becoming one "flesh," as it were.[36] And though the

---

with the body of the annihilated human person, the soul of the no longer extant person undergoes experiences that are of necessity unique to the isolable part that it is. What was a human body becomes a corpse and, as we've said, begins to suffer radical disintegration, eventually being reduced to its most basic material elements. The soul of the human person likewise becomes something less than what it was, but, unlike the body, is not subject to decay (even though diminished). Rather than decomposition, the realities it experiences are of a different and mysterious sort, though Scripture as understood through tradition does offer us some small guidance on how we should imagine such experiences. In fact, it is here where the relationship of the soul to the self becomes especially difficult to untangle. Thirdly, and again, at the moment of death, when soul and body are separated from each other, properly speaking the human person whose body and soul have been divided ceases to be. This is the necessary logical entailment of the hylomorphic principle. The soul and body become, to borrow from Griffiths, "traces" of a person who no longer exists and won't again until the event of the resurrection and New Creation.

[34] This idea permeates Paul's writings, as can be seen in places like Rom 6, 8; 2 Cor 5; Gal 2:20; and Col 2:9–15; 3:1–4.

[35] See also Romans 6 and 8. On this, see Barber, Kincaid, and Pitre, *Paul, a New Covenant Jew*, 21–23, 67–73. For a fascinating theological exploration of what it means to die with Christ vis-à-vis the New Creation, see Herbert McCabe, OP, *The New Creation* (London: Continuum, 2010), 121–38.

[36] Ephesians 5:21–33; Paul's claim seems to be that the natural institution of marriage exists first and foremost for the sake of anticipating and typologically manifesting the sort of intimate union Christ desires for his Church. This is presumably why, *per* Matthew 22:30, there is no marriage or giving in marriage in the New Creation (the wedding feast of the Lamb having displaced natural marriage similarly to how the New Law of the New Covenant displaces the ceremonial and dietary laws of the Old Covenant). And this is why the

complete outworking of one's already enacted personal union with Christ awaits one's resurrection and glorification, nevertheless, such a one, Paul says, is already in some sense a new creation in Christ, already a(n eschatological) participant in the New Creation of the New Covenant.[37] So, the baptized person becomes supernaturally united to the person of Christ by means of that self-same baptism, and, moreover, this is a durative union of sufficient strength that not even death itself can dissolve it.[38] "So then, whether we live or whether we die, we are the Lord's. For to this end Christ died and lived again, that he might be Lord both of the dead and of the living."[39]

Let us maintain, secondly, that since the unity of the person *qua* human being is constituted by the union of body and soul, death's dissolution of that natural union means an unnatural end to the human person as such. As argued above, whatever the relation of the soul to the body or the person constituted by the union of the two, *anima mea non est ego*.

Perhaps we might, then, posit, thirdly, that the natural unity of the person dissolved by death is nevertheless still supernaturally retained by

---

Song of Songs has been read by the Church Fathers not as curiously canonized Hebraic *erotica* but as a description of the nuptial bliss, the ultimate satisfaction of *eros*, that is realized in the Bridegroom's spousal unity with his bride, the Church and her members. On this, see Paul J. Griffiths, *Song of Songs*, Brazos Theological Commentary on the Bible (Grand Rapids: Brazos Press, 2011), xxiii–xlii.

[37] There are grounds here to answer objections to Hütter's arguments that those who adhere to what he calls the "total-death theory" (i.e., those who hold that death dissolves the human person/being as such) unwittingly turn resurrected humans into mere copies of the annihilated selves that no longer exist. See Hütter, *Bound for Beatitude*, 54–55. But if baptism *already* in some sense makes one a new creation, as St. Paul says, and death is, for such a one, *already* in some sense defeated in Christ, then the (hamartiologically wholly unnatural) "natural" dissolution of the person in death is somehow nonetheless still supernaturally preserved through that person's sacramentally acquired unitive membership in/as Christ's body prior to death. Resurrection, then, is not the creation of an altogether new person to replace the one who was previously annihilated at death. Rather, it is the consummation of the abundant, Christic life that already began by way of sacramental grace.

[38] See Rom 8:38–39.

[39] Rom 14:8–9. Interestingly, it is perhaps plausible to read Aquinas himself as occasionally gesturing towards the sort of intimate union I'm entertaining. In *Ad Gal.* 2, lec. 6, for example, he says, "Strictly speaking, things are said to live which are moved by an inner principle. Now the soul of Paul was set between his body and God; the body, indeed, was vivified and moved by the soul of Paul, but his soul is [vivified and moved] by Christ. Hence as to the life of the flesh, Paul himself lived and this is what he says, namely, 'but that I now live in the flesh,' i.e., by the life of the flesh; but as to his relation to God, Christ lived in Paul. Therefore he says, 'I live in the faith of the Son of God,' through which he dwells in me and moves me: 'but the just shall live by faith' (Hab 2:4)." Thomas Aquinas, *Commentary on the Letters of Saint Paul to the Galatians and Ephesians*, Latin/English Edition of the Works of St. Thomas Aquinas (Lander, WY: The Aquinas Institute for the Study of Sacred Doctrine, 2012).

means of the person's having been previously united to Christ and his body in baptism. More simply put, let us suppose that, given the Christian's having been mystically joined to the person of Christ himself, what *de*sists in death *per*sists in Christ.[40] As St. Paul says, "For you have died, and your life is hidden with Christ in God. When Christ who is your life appears, then you also will appear with him in glory."[41] The ongoing subsistence of the deceased person's soul finds its continuity with the person of which it was a constitutive part from both having already been mystically joined to Christ's own person.[42] The souls of the faithful would find their composite personal union through having already been mystically joined to Christ's own body in baptism, as members of he who died once for all that death itself might die. In such a scenario, the soul's experience of beatitude would be distinct from the person's experience of beatitude which would await the resurrection as the final consummation of what began for one in baptism. But the supernatural retention of the person as an already conjoined member of the Mystical Body of Christ would allow for the intelligibility of practices like seeking the intercession of the saints which suppose some sort of underlying continuity between annihilated persons and their subsisting souls.

No doubt this more theological approach would, once fleshed out, entail its own attendant difficulties.[43] But perhaps it offers a more salutary forward than a strictly metaphysical analysis alone.

---

[40] Hans Boersma has recently offered an intriguing account of the beatific vision that, with Christological sympathies much the same as my own, seeks to offer a thoroughly Christocentric account of ultimate human happiness. Especially illuminating for our purposes here is his juxtaposition of Aquinas's and Jonathan Edwards's respective speculations on that in which the beatific vision consists. For that, see Hans Boersma, *Seeing God: The Beatific Vision in Christian Tradition* (Grand Rapids, MI: William B. Eerdmans Publishing Company, 2018), esp. 354–84.

[41] Col 3:3–4.

[42] To anticipate at least one objection, Thomas in *ST* III, q. 50, a. 4, corp., recognizes that even the Incarnate Logos ceases to be a human being (though without nullifying his assumption of human nature) during the three-day period between Christ's death and Resurrection: "It belongs to the truth of the death of a man or animal that by death the subject ceases to be man or animal; because the death of the man or animal results from the separation of the soul, which is the formal complement of the man or animal. Consequently, to say that Christ was a man during the three days of his death simply and without qualification is erroneous." But, as Leontius of Byzantium helped the tradition to articulate, since the person who the human being Jesus is always already exists as the eternally begotten Son of the Father, the personal continuity of the human being Jesus is preserved by virtue of Christ's divine nature. Aquinas affirms this several places throughout his *corpus*, including in his recitation of John Damascene in *ST* III, q. 50, a. 3, ad 4, who makes the same point.

[43] For example, what of the souls of the damned, assuming the traditional view that there are any? Or what of the souls of those Old Testament saints who died prior to the institution of sacramental baptism and its resulting effects?

CONCLUSION

In the above we explored an apparent tension in Aquinas's writing about human beings/persons, separated souls, and beatitude. On the one hand, St. Thomas affirms the logical consequence of his hylomorphic anthropology wherein any soul that is separated from the human person and body to whom it belongs is not identical to the human being from which it is separated: *anima mea non est ego*. On the other hand, Aquinas places such anthropological weight on the human soul in composing the human person that, when the separated soul experiences the beatific vision of God, it seems everything necessary for human happiness is already attained in full, the resurrected body only serving to extend what cannot be improved upon thereby.

Given this tension, we evaluated one possible metaphysical means of redress wherein the functional asymmetrical relationship of the soul to the body in constituting the human person might be used in an attempt to render the distinction between separated soul and human being largely irrelevant. Though my soul isn't technically me, it is *mostly* me such that *its* experience of beatitude is, for all intents and purposes, equivalent to *my* experience of beatitude. But this, we argued, was an avenue that leads us nowhere in the end. Even supposing the logical possibility that what it is to be a human being could meaningfully be scaled by terms like "mostly" or "lesser" (there is no such logical possibility), nevertheless, a human soul can no more be equivalent to the human being whose *esse* it shares than any part can be identical to the whole. The soul apart from the body is in no sense a living human being; it is part of a dead one. How, then, to make intelligible the Church's teaching regarding beatific continuity?

It was here where we turned to Christology and the gifts to be found in the Sacrament of Baptism as a potential means of divining a more viable way forward, seeking in theology what we could not (hope to) find in metaphysics. Perhaps, we suggested, a person's being baptized into Christ and his body effects a mystical union of such significance that what desists in death (the baptized human person) persists in Christ, membership in the body of Christ serving as a means of personal continuity for the human soul as it awaits the proper reconstitution of the person to whom it belongs at the *parousia*, when one *truly*, at long last, can see the Lord face-to-face. This theological approach, we suggested, would certainly raise its own questions in need of answer. But perhaps it contains the resolution we seek. [44]

---

[44] This essay benefited immensely from my exchanges on this topic with Michael Dauphinais, Danny Houck, Daniel Lendman, Steve A. Long, Ladislav Sallai, Michael and Susie Waldstein, and Jeff Walkey. I am grateful for their feedback, their friendship, and the spirit in which both are consistently offered.

Hope, the "Behovely," and the Doctrine of Eternal Hell:

The Thomism of Julian of Norwich

TAYLOR PATRICK O'NEILL
Thomas Aquinas College, CA

INTRODUCTION

We are told that Julian of Norwich, the English-speaking world's most famous mystic-contemplative, is a harbinger of hope, especially and famously because she tells us that "all shall be well." Unfortunately, today Julian is lost to two gross perversions of her work. One is to reduce Julian to a Hallmark card version of Christian mysticism. Her words live on in a near-infinite number of saccharine, superficially therapeutic quotation images on Facebook, superimposed over some slightly blurry image of daffodils or a sunset.

Less comical but no less absurd is the common academic and theological reception of Julian. This corruption often twists Julian's fecund contemplation of providence and hope into a perfunctory defense of universalism. But, as we shall see, Julian explicitly affirms the reality of eternal hell. According to either popular image of Julian's thought, this would render her to be uninteresting and even a harbinger of outdated and monstrous (so-called) infernalism, thus neutering her ability to be a font of hope at all. Julian the dissenting Pollyanna or nothing.

However, it is possible, and indeed necessary, to escape between the horns of this false dilemma. A clear and honest look at Julian of Norwich forces us to wrestle with the fundamental question of how the Christian can maintain both that God gains an exhaustive victory over evil while simultaneously recognizing that some souls are forever lost. In fact, this is *precisely* the insight which makes Julian so important. Far from Julian's orthodoxy regarding hell and damnation making it impossible that all shall be well, it helps to explain it. What shall be argued here, then, is two-fold: First, that Julian's uniting of these two seemingly disparate truths is fundamentally rooted in Catholic orthodoxy and is heavily complementary to the teaching of the Angelic Doctor. Second, that Julian's poetic-mystical language, due to its complementarity with the teaching of St. Thomas, provides a unique insight into providence and evil. In other words, if the theologian aims at some degree of understanding of how all shall be well alongside the reality of sin and final impenitence, then he ought to study Julian of Norwich seriously, for she articulates the parameters of this mystery exceptionally by describing the meeting place of these two truths with her insight that "sin is behovely." That sin is behovely is the gravamen of Julian's theology, and, by unpacking exactly what it means for sin to be behovely, we can recognize just how perdition does not negate that "all shall be well, and all shall be well, and all manner of things shall be well."[1]

JULIAN AND UNIVERSALISM

The temptation to read universalism into Julian begins with two presuppositions, and we shall take them both in turn. First, it presumes that God *can* save all and, indeed, that God could have created a universe without any sin at all. As we shall soon see, Julian's entire contemplative project rests upon her acknowledgement that this would be possible. Indeed, without the possibility that there could be no sin at all, the question of *why* sin should exist could not at all arise; it would be a mere necessity, an unavoidable fact of a universe inhabited by free creatures. But Julian does not maintain this understanding of human freedom, nor does she endorse anything like the free will defense for evil.[2] Denys Turner puts this well:

---

[1] All Julian citations are from the Long Text of her *Revelations of Divine Love*, ed. Grace Warrack (London: Methuen & Company, 1901), here 56, https://www.gutenberg.org/files/52958/52958-h/52958-h.htm. I have updated a word here or there to a more contemporary English rendering.

[2] See Denys Turner, *Julian of Norwich, Theologian* (New Haven and London: Yale University Press, 2011), 32–35. For more on the free-will defense itself, see Alvin Plantinga, *God, Freedom, and Evil* (Grand Rapids, MI: Wm B. Eerdman's Publishing Company, 1977).

For it would amount to little more than paganism to maintain that the providential outcome of salvation history is a post-factum business of God's making the best of what happens—as if maintaining a sort of herding cats notion of providence wherein God has no causal role in the making of human choices but awaits their outcome, and then herds them as best as he can. It is certainly not Julian's belief. She tells us that she "saw truly that God doeth all-things, be it ever so little."[3]

And this is precisely what we also see in St. Thomas Aquinas, for whom the notion that Pure Act could be somehow passively responsive to that which he alone causes would be absurd. St. Thomas says that all things fall under divine providence[4] and that nothing happens outside of the divine government and the universal causality of God.[5] Certainly what it means for God to be the First and Universal Cause is that all other causation, including free human acts, are radically contingent upon the ontologically antecedent causality of God.[6]

The second presupposition on which Julian's supposed universalism is grounded is that, given that God can save all, he must then be under some kind of obligation to do so. Perhaps it is not an obligation imposed from without, for nothing lays claims on the divine nature but an obligation imposed from within, as it were. In other words, it would be incompatible with who God is for God to permit final impenitence. *Deus caritas est* is taken here to mean "God *will* save all." This is the backbone of David Bentley Hart's recent defense of universalism. For Hart, universalism doesn't just *happen* to be true. It must be true given what God has revealed about Himself. Hart appeals to the analogy of a father to defend his thesis. He states:

> Christ instructs his followers to think of God on the analogy of a human father, and to feel safe in assuming that God's actions toward them will display something like—but also something far greater than—paternal love. . . . We can then at the very least gain some sense of what not to expect from God. . . . One who surrenders his child to fate, even if that fate should consist in the entirely "just" consequences of his child's own choices and actions, is an

---

3   Turner, *Julian of Norwich*, 54.
4   *ST* I, q. 22, a. 2.
5   *ST* I, q. 103, a. 7.
6   *SCG* III, chs. 66 and 67; *ST* I, q. 22, a. 2, ad 1.

altogether unnatural father—not a father at all, really, except in the most trivial sense.[7]

In sum, the sort of God that would permit damnation, even as understood as self-damnation, could not truly be called a father. But the Christian God is called a father. Therefore, the Christian God does not permit damnation.[8] As we shall see, though this argument is formally valid, the Thomist would reject the major premise—that is, that God can only be called a father if he saves all. Yet, we can see that this is the presupposition which animates most contemporary Julian scholarship. All is not well unless all are saved.

The examples of this in recent Julian scholarship are almost too many to count. The number of books published on Julian of Norwich in the last ten years is striking, and *almost* all of them are united in linking the happiness or the goodness of all things to the non-existence of eternal damnation. For example, medievalist Robert Sweetman states:

> The reality of hell is deeply rooted in the traditional understanding of God's revelation and its implications for our lives and destinies. Nevertheless, we can hope, indeed, we have a Christian obligation to live in the hope that it is or shall be an empty place, so that in the end, as Julian never tired of saying—all shall be well.[9]

One assumes, therefore, since "that all shall be well" is here intrinsically linked with hell being empty, that, if it turns out that hell indeed is not empty, apparently *all shall be pretty horrible.*

Duke Divinity theologian Amy Laura Hall, who explicitly calls Julian a universalist,[10] admits that Julian's universalism may not be explicit but comforts the reader by stating that "her [Julian's] use of what may be seen as

---

[7] David Bentley Hart, *That All Shall Be Saved: Heaven, Hell, and Universal Salvation* (New Haven and London: Yale University Press, 2019), 53–54. For a strong argument against this dismantling of the *anologia entis*, see Brian Davies, *The Reality of God and the Problem of Evil* (London and New York: Continuum, 2006), especially ch. 4. Hart explicitly references and responds to Davies's argument in *That All Shall Be Saved*, 56–61.

[8] In traditional logic, this would be referred to as a CESARE syllogism.

[9] Robert Sweetman, "Sin Has Its Place, but All Shall Be Well: The Universalism of Hope in Julian of Norwich," in *All Shall Be Well: Explorations in Universal Salvation and Christian Theology from Origen to Moltmann*, ed. Gregory MacDonald, (Cambridge: James Clarke and Co., 2011), 66–92, especially 90–91.

[10] Amy Laura Hall, *Laughing at the Devil: Seeing the World with Julian of Norwich*, (Durham and London: Duke University Press, 2018), 3: "A woman, a visionary, a universalist, a writer from long ago: Julian of Norwich is by many different categories easy to dismiss."

tentative language [regarding universalism] could be in part her deference to Church authorities."[11]

Nor does this corruption of Julian remain merely at the level of commentary and secondary sources. Mirabai Starr has abused Julian's words themselves in her own translation of Julian's sole written work, *The Shewings*. Therein she unscrupulously translates "those who will be saved" as "all beings"! Starr writes in her introduction that any hints of loyalty to the Church's teaching on eternal damnation are due to Roman Catholicism being "the only religion she [Julian] knew."[12]

This is, of course, a completely demeaning reading of Lady Julian. Julian, like any faithful Catholic, understands that the Church is not merely some institution of power which arbitrarily meddles in the soul's pursuit of God; rather it is indeed Christ's body, and the gift of faith is delivered to us in and through the Church. This love and loyalty for the Church, contrary to the wishful thinking of many contemporary Julian scholars, is evident throughout Julian's writing. For example:

> In all things I believe as Holy Church believes, preaches, and teaches. For the Faith of Holy Church, which I had beforehand understood and, as I hope, by the grace of God, earnestly kept in use and custom, standing continually in my sight: I willed and meant never to receive anything that might be contrary thereunto.[13]

Moreover, consider again Hall's claim that there is a slight tentativeness to Julian's universalism and juxtapose that with Julian's own words on hell. For example:

> And yet in this I desired, as [far] as I dared, that I might have full sight of Hell and Purgatory. But it was not my meaning to ask for proof of anything that belongs to the Faith: for I believed truly that Hell and Purgatory are for the same end that Holy Church teaches. . . . I saw that the devil is reproved by God and endlessly condemned. In which sight I understood the same for all creatures that are of the devil's condition in this life, and therein they end.

---

[11] Hall, *Laughing at the Devil*, 14.

[12] Mirabai Starr, *The Showings of Julian of Norwich: A New Translation*, trans. Mirabai Starr (Charlottesville, VA: Hampton Roads Publishing Company, 2013), xviii.

[13] Julian, *Revelations*, 21.

. . . I knew in my Faith that they were accursed and condemned without end.[14]

Those who claim that Julian is a universalist have twisted the text beyond all of its original meaning with the motive of making her a champion of a position which is explicitly rejected by her. It is eisegesis of the worst kind.[15]

Yet, there is one way in which we ought not (and indeed cannot) reconcile damnation and the goodness of providence—that is by appealing to some sort of inevitability of sin which extends beyond the reach of God's providential governance. If God is omnipotent and therefore possesses complete governmental control over his creation, then the notion that his will is sometimes defeated or overcome simply—by the very creatures upon which he bestows causal act at all—is metaphysically impossible. As we have already illustrated, this is not a tenable position for Julian, the Thomist, or even the classical theist. And this very justifiable concern over passivity in God or overthrowing the divine plan indeed motivates at least some of the defenses of universalism. For Hart, the permission of final impenitence would be tantamount to divine defeat, which is a contradiction in terms. He says, "The ultimate absence of a certain number of created rational natures would still be a kind of last end inscribed in God's eternity, a measure of failure or loss forever preserved within the totality of the tale of divine victory."[16] Here, the Thomist must emphatically agree that *no failure can be ascribed to an omnipotent and all-wise God.* This would be tantamount to claiming that some secondary cause could escape the universality of the first cause, which would be not merely infelicitous or philosophically awkward but would indeed be metaphysically impossible, an absurdity.

On the surface of things, then, universalism can actually seem to be a very rational way to answer the question of evil. If I could imagine, for example, a perfect day, it would certainly be perfect in every part. A perfect day does not include a trip to the doctor or a flat tire or a faculty meeting. It's good from start to finish. The only reason that I do not actually live a perfect day is because it is beyond my capacity. But a perfect universe is not beyond the capacity of God. So why should God include all of the difficult bits in

---

[14] Julian, *Revelations*, 68. The quote ends, "except those who are converted by grace."

[15] Fortunately, though they are comparatively rare, there are more nuanced and faithful interpretations of Julian's work to be found on the contemporary landscape. The best of these is, without doubt, Denys Turner, *Julian of Norwich, Theologian.* Another fair assessment on Julian and universalism can be found in Philip Sheldrake, *Julian of Norwich: In God's Sight: Her Theology in Context* (Hoboken, NJ: Wiley Blackwell, 2019), 132–36

[16] Hart, *That All Shall Be Saved*, 87.

the final story of the universe? Why should there be areas of shadow rather than uniform light?

SIN, THE BEHOVELY, AND DIVINE PROVIDENCE

For Julian, for sin to exist, God must permit it. And if God permits sin, given his infinite and sublime wisdom, he must permit it *for some reason*. And since sin itself is fundamentally irrational, its permission must be for the sake of some other and higher good. That is, the reason for permitting the irrational must be itself rational and for the sake of a higher good, which renders the permission itself *to be good*. *This* is what Julian means when she says that "sin is behovely." We don't use the word *behovely* in English often today, but we do use the related term "behoove," as in, "It would behoove me to check in with my wife before heading off to the pub." In short, the word means neither necessary nor unnecessary but rather a middle term between the two—that is, the advantageous or the useful. Or, as Denys Turner has argued so well, in the language of the scholastic theologian, the behovely is the *conveniens*, that which is *fitting*. For example, Turner says, "The Incarnation was neither a necessity imposed upon God, nor just a divine whim. It was meet and just, conveniens—or, had you been writing in Julian's Middle English, behovely."[17]

But this still leaves the question of how sin could be behovely or fitting. Surely sin is the least fitting or useful or behovely thing of all. There is nothing *less* fitting than sin since it departs from the reality of what is and descends into the unreality of what is not.

For Julian, sin *in and of itself*, sin *qua sin*, is evil, or as she says "viler and more painful than hell, without likeness: for it is contrary to our nature."[18] As such, Julian is at first startled and bewildered that God should permit evil at all. She says:

> If sin had not been, we should all have been clean and like our Lord, as He made us. And thus, in my folly, before this time I often wondered why sin was not stopped [letted] by the great foreseeing wisdom of God; for then, all should have been well. . . . But Jesus . . . answered by this word and said: It behoved that there should be sin, but all shall be well, and all shall be well, and all manner of thing shall be well.[19]

---

[17] Turner, *Julian of Norwich, Theologian*, 40–41.
[18] Julian, *Revelations*, 157–58.
[19] Julian, *Revelations*, 55–56.

Note here that both of the following statements are true for Julian: sin is evil—that is, it ought not to exist—but also it is good that it does exist, making explicit reference to it occasioning the coming of Christ.[20] In another place, Julian tells us that Christ reveals to her:

> Adam's sin was the most harm that ever was done, or ever shall be, to the world's end. . . . Furthermore He taught that I should behold the glorious Satisfaction: for this Amends-making is more pleasing to God and more worshipful, without comparison, than ever was the sin of Adam harmful. . . . For since I have made well the most harm, then it is my will that thou know thereby that I shall make well all that is less.[21]

This is the *felix culpa* theology at the heart of the Catholic tradition. Sin is neither beyond God's control nor permitted meaninglessly. St. Thomas puts it quite clearly when he says, "God therefore neither wills evil to be done, nor wills it not to be done, but wills to permit evil to be done; and this is a good."[22] Moreover, he says:

> As Augustine says (Enchiridion xi): "Since God is the highest good, He would not allow any evil to exist in His works, unless His omnipotence and goodness were such as to bring good even out of evil." This is part of the infinite goodness of God, that He should allow evil to exist, and out of it produce good.[23]

St. Augustine says that "in the universe, even that which is called evil, when it is regulated and put in its own place, only enhances our admiration of the good; for we enjoy and value the good more when we compare it with the evil."[24] Similarly, St. Thomas teaches us that there would indeed be many

---

[20] Julian, *Revelations*, 71: "I say not that any evil is worshipful, but I say that sufferance of our Lord God is worshipful."

[21] Julian, *Revelations*, 60.

[22] *ST* I, q. 19, a. 10, ad 3: "Deus igitur neque vult mala fieri, neque vult mala non fieri, sed vult permittere mala fieri. Et hoc est bonum."

[23] *ST* I, q. 2, a. 3, ad 1: "Ad primum ergo dicendum quod, sicut dicit Augustinus in Enchiridio, Deus, cum sit summe bonus, nullo modo sineret aliquid mali esse in operibus suis, nisi esset adeo omnipotens et bonus, ut bene faceret etiam de malo. Hoc ergo ad infinitam Dei bonitatem pertinet, ut esse permittat mala, et ex eis eliciat bona."

[24] St. Augustine, *The Handbook on Faith, Hope, and Love (The Enchiridion)*, in Philip Schaff, ed., *Nicene and Post-Nicene Fathers*, first series, vol. 3, trans. J. F. Shaw (Buffalo, NY: Christian Literature Publishing Co., 1887), https://www.newadvent.org/fathers/1302.htm.

goods of a higher order that would be missing from the cosmos without the permission of sin. He says:

> Since God, then, provides universally for all being, it belongs to His providence to permit certain defects in particular effects, that the perfect good of the universe may not be hindered, for if all evil were prevented, much good would be absent from the universe. . . . There would be no patience of martyrs if there were no tyrannical persecution.[25]

Of course, like Julian, for St. Thomas, the chief and highest good obtained by the permission of sin is the Incarnation and the salvific mission of Christ, which is the motive for God's permission of sin.[26] And here we return to the language of the *conveniens*. The very first article in the *Tertia Pars* and the first article in the *Summa Theologiae* to deal with the Incarnation is specifically an article on the *fittingness of the Incarnation*. And indeed, St. Thomas mentions the Easter Exultet explicitly here. He says, "But there is no reason why human nature should not have been raised to something greater after sin. For God allows evils to happen in order to bring a greater good therefrom; hence it is written (Rom 5:20): 'Where sin abounded, grace did more abound.' Hence, too, in the blessing of the Paschal candle, we say: 'O happy fault, that merited such and so great a Redeemer!'"[27]

Creation is fundamentally Christological. The Incarnation is for the created order as a whole, and the created order is for Christ. A corollary of

---

[25] *ST* I, q. 22, a. 2, ad 2: "Cum igitur Deus sit universalis provisor totius entis, ad ipsius providentiam pertinet ut permittat quosdam defectus esse in aliquibus particularibus rebus, ne impediatur bonum universi perfectum. Si enim omnia mala impedirentur, multa bona deessent universo, non enim esset vita leonis, si non esset occisio animalium; nec esset patientia martyrum, si non esset persecutio tyrannorum. Unde dicit Augustinus in Enchirid. Deus omnipotens nullo modo sineret malum aliquod esse in operibus suis, nisi usque adeo esset omnipotens et bonus, ut bene faceret etiam de malo."

[26] *ST* III, q. 1, a. 3: "Hence, since everywhere in the Sacred Scripture the sin of the first man is assigned as the reason of the Incarnation, it is more in accordance with this to say that the work of the Incarnation was ordained by God as a remedy for sin; so that, had sin not existed, the Incarnation would not have been."

"Unde, cum in sacra Scriptura ubique incarnationis ratio ex peccato primi hominis assignetur, convenientius dicitur incarnationis opus ordinatum esse a Deo in remedium peccati, ita quod, peccato non existente, incarnatio non fuisset."

[27] *ST* III, q. 1, a. 3, ad 3: "Nihil autem prohibet ad aliquid maius humanam naturam productam esse post peccatum, Deus enim permittit mala fieri ut inde aliquid melius eliciat. Unde dicitur Rom. V, ubi abundavit iniquitas, superabundavit et gratia. Unde et in benedictione cerei paschalis dicitur, o felix culpa, quae talem ac tantum meruit habere redemptorem."

this truth is that the created order is ordered not as so many disparate parts, nor is it merely an arena for God to perfect each individual creature. Rather, providence *governs the particulars for the sake of the whole* (and not the other way around). God governs it holistically, toward a truly common good and not merely a long list of disparate and private goods.

This is a constitutive element of St. Thomas's theology of providence. He says, "Every evil that God does, or permits to be done, is directed to some good; yet not always to the good of those in whom the evil is, but sometimes to the good of others, or of the whole universe."[28] Often when St. Thomas addresses providence and its end, he cites Proverbs 16:4, "The Lord hath made all things for Himself." And elsewhere, "Thus He is said to have made all things through His goodness, so that the divine goodness might be represented in things."[29] *This*, we must not forget, is the *reason* for the universe. God does not create in order to make the best of all possible worlds in the sense that all individuals and particulars are as perfect as possible. Similarly, the healthiest family is the one ordered toward familial, communal happiness and flourishing rather than the compartmentalized and individualized good of each member. It is the *whole* which is the chief object of divine providence, and the parts are objects of divine providence only secondarily, that is, governed as they are insofar as they relate and are ordered to the whole. In other words, the primacy of the common good applies *to the whole of the created order.*

ETERNAL HELL, THE BEHOVELY, AND HOPE

If this is true of the diversity and disparity of the parts, then it must also be true *even for the fundamental eschatological disparity between the blessed and the damned.* In some way, even hell serves the whole. St. Thomas associates this truth with the variety of things in the natural world, a variety rooted in the gradation of goodness in created things.[30]

---

28 *ST* I-II, q. 79, a. 4, ad 1: "Ad primum ergo dicendum quod omnia mala quae Deus facit vel permittit fieri, ordinantur in aliquod bonum, non tamen semper in bonum eius in quo est malum, sed quandoque ad bonum alterius, vel etiam totius universi."

29 *ST* I, q. 23, a. 5, ad 3: "Sic enim Deus dicitur omnia propter suam bonitatem fecisse, ut in rebus divina bonitas repraesentetur."

30 *ST* I, q. 23, a. 5, ad 3: "Thus too, in the things of nature, a reason can be assigned, since primary matter is altogether uniform, why one part of it was fashioned by God from the beginning under the form of fire, another under the form of earth, that there might be a diversity of species in things of nature. Yet why this particular part of matter is under this particular form, and that under another, depends upon the simple will of God; as from the simple will of the artificer it depends that this stone is in part of the wall, and that in

St. Thomas also tells us that both justice and mercy exist in God.[31] In the predestination of the elect and the reprobation of the damned, we find the manifestation, therefore, not of God's justice to the exclusion of his mercy or his mercy to the exclusion of his justice, but rather both are made manifest.[32] And yet, we have to admit that *precisely what that means escapes us.* We can say that the end of the created order is to manifest or to express God's nature in some way, but since God's nature is unknowable to us as wayfarers, *precisely* what God means to do with the created order is also unknowable to us. What we do know is that he shall, because he is good, order all things to the good, an unthinkable tapestry of unimaginable beauty. Therefore, *if we can see ourselves not as the end of our own universe but rather as a part of a whole ordered and perfectly fitted to the glorification and manifestation of God*, then we can see things rightly. And then we shall be filled with hope, for hope is based fundamentally on the ability to recognize that which is the one truth undergirding all truths—namely, that God *is* and that all that is *is good.*

But the myopic nature of the sight of the wayfarer is what makes hope necessary. The flames of God's love, which engulf and consume all things, *are hidden from us.* The hopeful are those who "apprehend happiness as a future possible thing."[33] Obviously that begins with the potential for eternal life for the individual,[34] but St. Thomas teaches that this blossoms out into a hope for the other. Insofar as man possesses "a union of love with another, a man can hope for and desire something for another [man], as for himself."[35] Man is called to love *the entire created order* as himself, for man is called to love God and all things in light of God, and the created order is God's art; it is that which God loves and makes just so—that is, *conveniens* or behovely.

Our hope is rooted in God as understood by Julian and St. Thomas. Only the radically transcendent Creator can derive something from nothing, and only an omnipotent will ordering the universe exhaustively and infallibly could order evil, when all is said and done, *to have been for the good.*

---

another; although the plan requires that some stones should be in this place, and some in that place."

[31] *ST* I, q. 24.

[32] *ST* I, q. 23, a. 5, ad 3. It should be noted that, though the elect chiefly manifest God's mercy and the reprobate chiefly his justice, insofar as even the elect are punished for sins and the reprobate are bestowed many graces, God's justice and mercy are manifested in both the elect and the reprobate, though in varying degrees. See *ST* I, q. 21, a. 4, ad 1.

[33] *ST* II-II, q. 18, a. 3: ". . . apprehendunt beatitudinem ut futurum possibile."

[34] *ST* II-II, q. 17, a. 3.

[35] *ST* II-II, q. 17, a. 3: "Sed praesupposita unione amoris ad alterum, iam aliquis potest desiderare et sperare aliquid alteri sicut sibi."

Indeed, since only a God of infinite power and wisdom could effect such a universe in which evil is turned to good, we might well wonder if this was not, at least partly, God's reason for doing so. In other words, as St. Thomas teaches us, God creates in order to communicate to us, to manifest to creatures, the splendor of the divine nature. What manifests or communicates that splendor more efficaciously than the *power* to bring beauty from ugliness and the *goodness* to actually do so?

I think that this is something like what Herbert McCabe was trying to get at when he said:

> It is one thing to know that the proposition that some creatures are evil is not incompatible with the proposition that the Creator is omnipotent and good. It would be quite another thing to understand the mysterious goodness of the Creator. When all is said and done, we are left with an irrational but strong feeling that if we were God we would have acted differently. Perhaps one of his reasons for acting as he did is to warn us not to try to make him in our own image.[36]

We asked earlier why light and shadow instead of merely uniform light? Well, it would seem that, by including shadow, *there is* universal light. This is, of course, a paradox but not one which is *entirely* outside of human understanding. We have all heard a piece of music which included portions of dissonance that, nevertheless, added to the beauty of the piece as a whole.

Still, it is indeed mostly outside of human understanding and, particularly because the way in which the shadow and light fit together to form a perfect *whole*, is as yet unseen to us. We are in the middle of the novel, awaiting to see how the author resolves all of the conflicts. The ending is important not just because it comes last but because, in a very real sense, it rewrites everything which came before. A final cause is most formal. That tragedy in chapter four which seemed meaningless at the time is now shot through with beauty, re-defined by my understanding of its place within the whole. Julian speaks of a "great secret" which reveals the behovely nature of sin in general and every sin in particular. This great secret is not some new or particular *datum* but is rather the comprehensive vision of the whole, known only by God and, perhaps, by the blessed.[37]

---

[36] Herbert McCabe, "On Evil and Omnipotence," in *Faith Within Reason* (London and New York: Continuum, 2007), 93.

[37] See Turner, *Julian*, 81: "The secret, which cannot be known until the end of time, is the story within which alone sin's being behovely could be understood, if only we knew it—which,

This is why the nice and neat answer of the universalists, while being aesthetically pleasing on the surface, is self-defeating. We should be wary of an answer to the mystery of evil which just explains away the mystery. The answer requires a holistic vision of the entirety of the cosmos. One might debate whether such a vision is knowable even to the blessed but surely is not possible for the wayfarer. So any total answer given by the wayfarer must be fool's gold, a façade of an answer, or what C. S. Lewis called, "soft soap and wishful thinking."[38] Turner puts this well. He says, "Julian is the theologian that she is because she knows that theology is writing as penultimate, and she refuses Hume's easygoing and yet preemptory closure. For writing that is pretentiously 'finished' is not theological, it is parody, it is Jeremy Bentham's 'nonsense parading upon stilts,' the ridiculous parading as the sublime."[39] Or, Turner points out, it is like Gabriel Marcel's entreaty never to turn a mystery into a problem. Turner says wisely, "It is not the likes of Thomas but the heretics who want to reduce the mysteries to problems."[40]

The permission of evil *is a mystery*. It transcends human reason. But like all things which flow from the *Logos*, it is not unreasonable. Yet the reason is beyond our scope *hic et nunc* precisely because we see through a glass darkly. Julian is a true mystic not simply because she tells us *that all shall be reconciled in the end* but also because *she makes no pretenses to knowledge of how that might actually happen*. She does not just know that she doesn't know, but she knows that she cannot know, at least not yet. Julian's "sin is behovely" does not give any indication as to how the story will end. It is merely a way of saying that it will end well.

CONCLUSION

This is the provenance of authentic Christian hope. All shall be well not because God undoes evil in the way that one erases a mistake on a page. Indeed, sin is permitted sometimes for the sake of our own personal growth, and the same is true on the cosmic scale. Our hope rests in the God who is not beholden to sin nor incapable of making anything meaningful out of sin. Our hope rests in the God who instead *turns evil to good*, both now and

---

to be sure, we cannot know, not prematurely, not before the beatific vision. Nor, she adds, should we strive to know it."

[38] C. S. Lewis, *Mere Christianity* (San Francisco: HarperCollins), 32.

[39] Denys Turner, *God, Mystery, and Mystification* (Notre Dame, IN: University of Notre Dame Press, 2019), 23.

[40] Turner, *God, Mystery, and Mystification*, 35.

forever more. The universe is just as God wills it, and God always wills the good. In the end, no matter what happens in the middle chapters of the story, we can let go of all anxiety because we *know* that all shall be well, and all shall be well, and all manner of things shall be well.

The Consummation of the World:

St. Thomas Aquinas on the Risen Saints' Beatitude and the Corporeal Universe

BRYAN KROMHOLTZ, OP

Dominican School of Philosophy and Theology, CA

IN THE CATHOLIC TRADITION, the object of human hope is offered as bodily resurrection from death, and "the life of the world to come." Implicit in that short phrase from the Nicene-Constantinopolitan Creed is that this "life" is understood to be life in communion with God, knowing and loving him without end, for "this is eternal life: that they know you, the only true God, and Jesus Christ, whom you have sent" (John 17:3). Pope Benedict XII's encyclical *Benedictus Deus* (1336) states dogmatically that the souls of the saints enter immediately into beatitude—perfect beatitude—constituted essentially by the vision of God "face to face."[1] God, as the Source of all being, all truth, all goodness, and all beauty, perfectly and superabundantly satisfies every human longing.[2]

---

[1] Heinrich Denzinger, *Enchiridion Symbolorum: Compendium of Creeds, Definitions, and Declarations on Matters of Faith and Morals*, ed. Peter Hünermann and Helmut Hoping (43rd Latin ed. [DH]), English ed. Robert L. Fastiggi and Anne Englund Nash (San Francisco: Ignatius Press, 2012), nos. 1000–1002, esp. 1000.

[2] Reinhard Hütter, *Bound for Beatitude: A Thomistic Study in Eschatology and Ethics*, Thomistic Ressourcement 12 (Washington, DC: Catholic University of America Press, 2019), has recently offered a thoroughly documented, penetrating treatment on God as final end of

Such a conception of the object of our hope may leave one wondering: since God is, indeed, all that one could ever want—which we have no intention of denying here—what will the rest of creation be for the blessed who partake of the vision? If we are blessed to be counted among those resurrected to glory, what will it matter to us (1) that we will be risen bodily, (2) that others will be there with us, including (3) the angels, and (4) that there is also to be a renewed world, a "new heavens and a new earth"? The first two parts of this question have received a fair amount of attention, including discussions over the relation of bodily resurrection to beatitude, as well as reflections on the eschatological nature of the Church.[3] Here, we will limit ourselves to considering the fourth of those parts, namely, how and why we are to look forward to the life of the *world* to come. In this regard, we can ask: is the "world" of the creed merely a shorthand for "the way things will be" after the resurrection? Does it instead mean that the new heavens and new earth are also, in some way, to be awaited, hoped for, by humanity?

Our study will consider the respects in which this latter question can be answered positively, particularly according to the teaching of St. Thomas.[4] We will consider what precisely the role of non-human material creation may be—that is, of the non-human animal, vegetable, and mineral world—for human beatitude and eternal life, for St. Thomas.[5] In doing so, we will first briefly consider those other questions, particularly regarding the role,

---

humanity. The present essay is intended to complement that project, albeit modestly, by fleshing out one aspect related to human finality that is not considered extensively in it.

[3] How communion with the blessed angels in praising the eternal God might relate to human beatitude may deserve more attention than it has received of late, but that will not be our task here.

[4] The Latin texts of the works of St. Thomas Aquinas cited in this article are as follows: *Summa theologiae* [*ST*] is taken from the edition by the Institutum Studiorum Medievalium Ottaviensis (Ottawa: Studium Generale O.P., 1945); *In sententiarum* is taken from vol. 7.2 of the Parma edition (1858); *Summa contra gentiles* [*SCG*], *De veritate*, *De potentia*, *Super Iob*, and *Compendium theologiae* [*CT*] all are taken from the Leonine edition; *Super Eph*, *Super Ioan*, and *Super Matt* are all taken from the Marietti edition. English translations of *ST*, *SCG*, and *CT* (modified, in some cases) come from, respectively: the *ST* translation by the Dominican Fathers of the English Province; *Summa contra Gentiles: Book Four: Salvation*, trans. Charles J. O'Neil with introduction and notes (Notre Dame, IN: University of Notre Dame Press, 2012 [orig. 1957]); and *The Compendium of Theology*, trans. Cyril Vollert (St. Louis, MO: Herder, 1947). All other English translation, unless otherwise attributed, is original to this article.

[5] The scope of the present study allows us to explicate only cursorily the role of heavenly bodies relative to final human beatitude. On the celestial bodies in St. Thomas's work, see Thomas Litt, *Les corps célestes dans l'univers de saint Thomas d'Aquin*, Philosophes médiévaux 7 (Louvain: Publications Universitaires; Paris: Béatrice-Nauwelaerts, 1963).

in the post-resurrection world, of the body and of other risen human persons, by way of comparison and contrast, in order the better to illuminate Thomas's teaching. What I intend to argue is that Thomas teaches that the eschatologically transformed, non-human material creation does not contribute to the beatitude of the saints, although it does offer them something, namely, the conditions of their existence, as well as an enjoyment of that creation as a kind of expression of the glory of God. I will also argue that—perhaps surprisingly—this does not derogate from the dignity of material creation but should instead further our appreciation to God for providing it.

It is evident why such questions should be worthy of attention, for anyone interested in the faith—whether because they share that faith or because they want to know how those sharing it might address them. After all, the world that God created is believed to be "very good" (Gen 1), the very place in which God has placed us, upon whose creatures we depend for life itself. Furthermore, the creatures in the world provide us innumerable indications of him and his goodness constantly. That there will be a "new heavens and a new earth" (2 Pet 3:10–13; Rev 21:1) is a matter of faith and also an indication of God's regard for his own creation—it will not be left behind in the world to come, but will come to its own perfection. This perfection or finality of the world, with its nearly endless and wondrous variety of creatures, and its relation to our own finality, should always be of at least some interest to us.

Beyond such a general and perennial interest, there are also certain recent developments in reflection upon the faith and matters allied to it that indicate that these questions are particularly timely. One of them would be (1) the increasing attention paid globally toward care for the environment, and the need for persons of faith and the Church as a body to contribute to that care in ways consistent with and even animated by that faith. This can be seen in the relatively recent development of more extensive teachings by the magisterium on the question of the eschatological fate of material creatures. While the official teaching office of the Church had not pronounced much of moment on the topic before the Second Vatican Council, certain teachings from two of the four most prominent documents from the Council itself, in addressing matters of the end, briefly consider the final renewal of the heavens and the earth.[6] Even more recently, *Laudato Si'*, Pope Francis's 2015 encyclical on care for creation, offered certain reflections on

---

[6] See Second Vatican Council, Dogmatic Constitution on the Church *Lumen Gentium* (Nov. 21, 1964), §§5–112, esp. §48, and Pastoral Constitution on the Church in the Modern World *Gaudium et Spes* (Dec. 7, 1965), §§1025–120, esp. §§38–39; see also *Catechism of the Catholic Church*, §§1042–44, 1046–50, and 1060, and Nathan W. O'Halloran, "'Each

the final end of non-human material creation, suggesting possibilities for further theological consideration and development. While a cursory reading of the document might suggest that it has little to say about creation's final end, there a few passages that are readily construed as eschatological (§§83, 99–100, 237–44). And parts of those few passages are suggestive for a theological consideration of the ultimate fate of animal, plant, and mineral beings. One states that "all creatures are moving forward with us and through us" towards God (§83), while another notes that "the Son will deliver all things to the Father" at the end of time, even mentioning in that context the very flowers and birds that Christ saw while on earth (§100; citing Col 1:19–20 and 1 Cor 15:28).[7] While these teachings are not presented as dogmatic definitions, they nevertheless invite theologians to consider the final fate of material creatures more deeply.[8]

Another set of relevant discussions would be (2) efforts to re-think what constitutes human eschatological fulfillment, with some proposals leaving aside the possibility of any beatific vision and suggesting that it would rather be an endless passing from one fulfillment of desire to another, one action to another, each surpassing the last in an ever-increasing passage from glory to glory, forever. Others question whether such construals of the ultimate end of human persons really allow for the attainment of an eternal life that can properly be considered ontologically perfective, final, and deifying—as truly uniting the blessed with the one God.[9] Clarifying Thomas's position

---

Creature, Resplendently Transfigured': Development of Teaching in *Laudato Si'*," *Theological Studies* 79, no. 2 (2018): 376–98, esp. 379–91.

[7] See O'Halloran, "'Each Creature, Resplendently Transfigured,'" 392–98, who considers Pope Francis's encyclical "an important new development in the teaching on New Creation," representing "a significant development in the church's eschatological teaching" (377–78). See also: Anthony J. Kelly, "Eschatology and Hope for Nature," *Pacifica* 28, no. 3 (2015): 256–71; Stephen N. Williams, "*Laudato Si'* and the Environmental Imperative: A Compelling Theology for our Times?," *European Journal of Theology* 28, no. 2 (2019): 144–53, esp. 149.

[8] For some recent theological speculation on the ultimate destiny of non-human creatures, barely predating *Laudato Si'*, see Paul J. Griffiths, *Decreation: The Last Things of All Creatures* (Waco, TX: Baylor University Press, 2014).

[9] It would be outside the scope of the present paper to enter into an evaluation of such efforts or their reception. Briefly, we will mention in particular Hütter, *Bound for Beatitude*, 416–25, which discusses and critiques (aptly, in my opinion) the proposal of Germain Grisez that the final end of humanity should be considered the Kingdom of God, rather than God himself; see Grisez, "The True Ultimate End of Human Beings: The Kingdom, Not God," *Theological Studies* 69, no. 1 (2008): 38–61. Hütter notes briefly that such proposals are not unique to Grisez but are "encountered widely in contemporary Protestant, and especially Evangelical theology" (*Bound for Beatitude*, 422n54), mentioning N. T. Wright, *Surprised by Hope: Rethinking Heaven, the Resurrection, and the Mission of the Church* (New

on the role of created material things in human beatitude can contribute in an ancillary way to such considerations, showing where Aquinas's teachings give a proper place to some kind of human participation in a renewed creation without denying the primacy of man's close relation to God for his happiness. Thus, the present article is relevant to at least these two sets of discussions and reflections of current interest.[10]

Our work will proceed as follows. Having introduced our topic, we will offer in the next section a brief overview of some relevant texts by the Common Doctor on our theme of how material creatures can or cannot contribute to the final beatitude of risen human persons. We will note his rather consistent position that such creatures will not contribute to human beatitude in the new heavens and earth, after the resurrection, but that they will nevertheless have a role in the eternal life of those raised to glory. The section will conclude with a consideration of how to interpret Thomas's teaching in a way that allows it to be rightly received in the face of our antecedent expectations and academic habituations—emphases in previous considerations of the question that may help us see some things and miss others. In our conclusion, we will discuss how these interpretations might offer some resources for the discussions we just mentioned above.

THOMAS'S TEACHING

We will look first at the section of St. Thomas's writing that is best known, and rightly so, for its consideration of human beatitude: the first five questions of the *prima secundae* of the *Summa theologiae* [*ST*], his mature work

---

York: HarperOne, 2008). See also J. Richard Middleton, *A New Heaven and a New Earth: Reclaiming Biblical Eschatology* (Grand Rapids, MI: Baker Academic, 2014).

[10] Of relevance also is a third current area of inquiry—albeit more tangentially related—which concerns the nature of Christ's causality of the beatific vision, including how Thomas considered it, or might consider it, in view of the overall structure and content of his thought. Essentially, the question concerns whether, in Aquinas's account, Christ has any ongoing role in any given saint's beatific vision. For Thomas, is Christ merely a kind of "means" for the saints to arrive at the end of seeing God himself, after which the humanity of Christ (at least) is no longer needed? See Hans Boersma, "Thomas Aquinas on the Beatific Vision: A Christological Deficit," *TheoLogica* 2, no. 2 (2018): 129–47; Boersma, *Seeing God: The Beatific Vision in Christian Tradition* (Grand Rapids, MI: Eerdmans, 2018); Simon Gaine, "Thomas Aquinas, the Beatific Vision and the Role of Christ: A Reply to Hans Boersma," *TheoLogica* 2, no. 2 (2018): 148–67; Gaine, "Thomas Aquinas and John Owen on the Beatific Vision: A Reply to Suzanne McDonald," *New Blackfriars* 97, no. 1070 (2016): 432–46; Gaine, "The Beatific Vision and the Heavenly Mediation of Christ," *TheoLogica* 2, no. 2 (2018): 116–28; and Michael Root, "The Christological Character of the Beatific Vision: Hans Boersma's *Seeing God*," *The Thomist* 84 (2020): 127–51.

of (and on) *sacra doctrina*, a work both systematic and unfinished (lacking, alas, a section planned on the end, including general resurrection, judgment, and the like). In that section on beatitude, Thomas states that ultimate human beatitude, which comes to those who love God, consists solely in the intellectual vision of the divine essence (not by bodily eyes), which is an operation of the intellect, resulting in delight in the will. The souls of the saints are introduced to this beatific vision immediately upon death, and it continues after the common resurrection at the end of the world, at which time the renewal of the world will also occur.

Now, as we mentioned in our introduction, it will be instructive for our purposes to consider also what Thomas says about the potential contribution to a risen saint's happiness by the saint's own risen body and by interaction/communion with other blessed, risen human persons. Regarding the risen body, we may wonder what it might contribute to a beatitude that the human soul has already reached, because Thomas clearly states that souls need not await the resurrection for perfect beatitude.[11] Citing St. Paul (2 Cor 5:6–8; Phil 1:21–23), he states that "the souls of the saints, separated from their bodies, are in God's presence."[12] He also claims this is evident also by appeal to reason, since "the intellect does not need the body for its operation except on account of the phantasms, wherein it looks on the intelligible truth," and that "the Divine Essence cannot be seen by means of phantasms." Thus "since man's perfect Happiness consists in the vision of the Divine Essence, it does not depend on the body." Nevertheless, the body does contribute to beatitude, in a certain way:

> Something may belong to a thing's perfection in two ways. First, as constituting the essence thereof; thus the soul is necessary for man's perfection. Secondly, as necessary for its well-being: thus, beauty of body and keenness of perception belong to man's perfection. Wherefore though the body does not belong in the first way to the perfection of human Happiness, yet it does in the second way.[13]

---

[11] When we speak of final human beatitude as perfect, we are not suggesting a beatitude perfect in itself (which would be proper to God), but perfect for man. See: *In II sent.*, d. 1, q. 2, a. 2, ad 4; *ST* I, q. 26, aa. 1 and 4.

[12] *ST* I-II, q. 4, a. 5, corp.

[13] *ST* I-II, q. 4, a. 5, corp.: "Ad perfectionem alicuius rei dupliciter aliquid pertinet. Uno modo, ad constituendam essentiam rei, sicut anima requiritur ad perfectionem hominis. Alio modo requiritur ad perfectionem rei quod pertinet ad bene esse eius, sicut pulchritudo corporis, et velocitas ingenii pertinet ad perfectionem hominis. Quamvis ergo corpus primo modo ad perfectionem beatitudinis humanae non pertineat, pertinet tamen secundo modo."

The body is not necessary to the essence of beatitude, but to its well-being or *bene esse*, the way, as Thomas says, a horse is needed for a journey: not absolutely needed, but needed according to some consideration:

> Something is said to be necessary with respect to an end in two senses. In one sense, as that without which an end cannot exist, as food is necessary for human life. And this is unqualifiedly necessary for the end. In the other sense, that without which the end is not so fittingly attained is called something necessary, as is a horse for a journey. But this is not, simply speaking, necessary for the end.[14]

Thus, for a resurrected saint, that saint's own risen and glorified body belongs in some way to his or her beatitude, but not as an essential element of it (although the body is an essential element of the risen saint's humanity)—in Thomas's mature view, as seen here.[15] Thomas says something similar about the fellowship of friends in this beatitude, this state of glory. He states that "the fellowship of friends is not essential" to this ultimate happiness, since "man has the entire fullness of his perfection in God. But the fellowship of friends conduces to the well-being of Happiness."[16] Notice that this fellowship of friends makes a real contribution to this ultimate human happiness, being positively part of it, but not necessary to it.

There is a notable contrast when Thomas takes up the question as to whether "external goods," such as "food and drink, wealth and a kingdom" (*ST* I-II, q. 4, a. 7, obj. 1), are necessary for perfect happiness:

> Such goods as these are in no way [*nullo modo huiusmodi*] necessary for perfect Happiness, which consists in the vision of God. The

---

[14] *ST* III, q. 65, a. 4, corp.: "Necessarium respectu finis . . . dicitur aliquid dupliciter. Uno modo, sine quo non potest esse finis, sicut cibus est necessarius vitae humanae. Et hoc est simpliciter necessarium ad finem. Alio modo dicitur esse necessarium id sine quo non habetur finis ita convenienter, sicut equus necessarius est ad iter. Hoc autem non est simpliciter necessarium ad finem."

[15] It is well known that Thomas's teaching on this point seems to have undergone a development. In one of his earliest works, he taught that the separated soul's beatitude would increase both extensively and intensively after the addition of the body (at the glorious resurrection). See: *In* IV *sent.*, d. 49, q. 1, a. 4, qa. 1, corp. and ad 4, esp. in contrast with *ST* I-II, q. 4, a. 5, ad 5. See also Bryan Kromholtz, *On the Last Day: The Time of the Resurrection of the Dead according to Thomas Aquinas*, Studia Friburgensia 110 (Fribourg, Switzerland: Academic Press Fribourg, 2010), 472–82.

[16] *ST* I-II, q. 4, a. 8, corp.: "Si loquamur de perfecta beatitudine quae erit in patria, non requiritur societas amicorum de necessitate ad beatitudinem, quia homo habet totam plenitudinem suae perfectionis in Deo. Sed ad bene esse beatitudinis facit societas amicorum."

reason for this is that all such external goods are required either for the support of the animal body, or for certain operations that belong to human life, which we perform by means of the animal body: whereas that perfect happiness which consists in seeing God, will be either in the soul separated from the body, or in the soul united to the body then no longer animal but spiritual. Consequently, these external goods are in no way [*nullo modo huiusmodi*] necessary for that Happiness, since they are ordained to the animal life.[17]

We ought to take note when Thomas makes a strong denial. Such does not happen so often, but here it is—twice. Unlike the fellowship of friends, and unlike the perfection of one's own body, which is part of one's own nature, external goods are not to be necessary in any way to beatitude, because they are necessary only for animal-level operations. They are not needed in any way for helping one participate in knowing God, whether as a separated soul or as a risen human person, along with other risen persons.

However, let us notice also what St. Thomas does *not* say. He does *not* say that the risen man *cannot* look at, or consider, or do something with such external goods. And he does not say that there will be no positive relation between risen man and the new heavens and new earth. So, we will now consider some texts where Thomas says that the risen man may look upon the transformed world, and some where he states that there is a close relation between the two. To do this, it is helpful to review, all too briefly, how Thomas sees the relation between man and the non-human material world.

Thomas holds that all bodily creatures, including heavenly bodies, were made for the sake of man.[18] This anthropocentric aspect of his cosmology is found within an even more fundamental theo-centrism, since it is God who orders "lower things through higher ones," including ordering "bodily

---

[17] *ST* I-II, q. 4, a. 7, corp.: "Ad beatitudinem perfectam, quae in visione Dei consistit, nullo modo huiusmodi bona requiruntur. Cuius ratio est quia omnia huiusmodi bona exteriora vel requiruntur ad sustentationem animalis corporis; vel requiruntur ad aliquas operationes quas per animale corpus exercemus, quae humanae vitae conveniunt. Illa autem perfecta beatitudo quae in visione Dei consistit, vel erit in anima sine corpore; vel erit in anima corpori unita non iam animali, sed spirituali. Et ideo nullo modo huiusmodi exteriora bona requiruntur ad illam beatitudinem, cum ordinentur ad vitam animalem."

[18] See: *In II sent.*, d. 1, q. 2, a. 3; *In IV sent.*, d. 47, q. 2, a. 1, qa. 1, corp.; d. 48, q. 2, a. 2, ad 8; a. 3, ad 3 ad 6; a. 4, corp.; *SCG* IV, ch. 97, no. 1; *De veritate*, q. 5, a. 9, obj. 13; *De potentia*, q. 5, a. 9, corp.; *CT* I, ch. 148; *Super Ioan* 6, lec. 5 (no. 940); on John 6:44b); *Super Eph* 1, lec. 3 (no. 29; on Eph 1:10); *ST* I-II, q. 2, a. 1, corp. See also *ST* I, q. 73, a. 1, corp., which says that the perfect beatitude of the saints is the purpose of the entire universe; and Kromholtz, *On the Last Day*, 152–64. See also Emmanuel Cazanave, "L'Église et le bien de l'univers: une lecture de la *Summa contra Gentiles*," *Revue Thomiste* 120 (2020): 309–30.

things through spiritual ones."[19] Yet even as human persons are subject in a bodily way to the heavenly bodies (which themselves are believed to be of a higher kind of material), they share in governance due to their intellectual nature.[20] Though they are subject to heavenly motion, that motion is for the sake of humanity, a motion that is ultimately directed by God.[21]

In this light, Thomas considers, then, in his commentary on Peter Lombard's *Sentences*, what corporeal beings, which were made for human beings, can do for risen and *glorified* human persons:

> All bodily things are believed to have been made for man; hence all things are said to be subject to him. Now they perform services of two kinds for him. One is for the sustenance of his bodily life; the other is for the advancement of his knowledge of God, inasmuch as man perceives the invisible things of God through the things that are made, as is said in Romans 1. Now glorified man will not need the first of these services of creatures in any way, since his future body will be incorruptible in every way, because the divine power will make it that way through the soul, which it glorifies immediately. Man does not need the second service either, so far as his intellectual knowledge is concerned, because the saints will see God with such knowledge immediately according to his essence. But the eye of the body will not be able to attain this vision of essence; and thus, so that it may be provided with the comfort of the vision of God that is fitting to it, it will observe the Godhead in its corporeal effects, in which indications of the divine majesty will appear clearly, primarily in the flesh of Christ, and then also in the bodies of the blessed, and finally in all other bodies. Thus even these other bodies ought to receive a greater influx from the divine

---

[19] *SCG* III, ch. 83, nos. 2–3. For Thomas, the end of all things (including man) is the divine goodness; see *In* II *sent.*, d. 1, q. 2, a. 2; *ST* I, q. 65, a. 2. See also: *In* IV *sent.*, d. 48, q. 2, a. 3, ad 6; *SCG* III, ch. 17, no. 2; *De veritate*, q. 5, a. 9, ad 13; *De potentia*, q. 5, a. 4, corp.; *ST* I-II, q. 1, a. 8, corp.

[20] *SCG* III, ch. 78, nos. 1 and 5.

[21] See *De veritate*, q. 5, a. 9. For Thomas, there is a more fundamental theo-centrism that goes beyond the anthropocentric aspect present in his understanding of creation. All creatures are ordered *by* God, *to* God. It has been noted that in this way, Thomas (like Bonaventure) attenuated an exaggerated anthropocentrism found in Peter Lombard's *Sentences*. See Richard Schenk, "Der Mensch—die Dornenkrone der Schöpfung? Umweltzerstörung aus theologischer Sicht," in *Nachhaltigkeit in der Ökologie: Wege in eine zukunftsfähige Welt*, ed. Luca Di Blasi, Bernd Goebel, and Vittorio Hösle (Munich: C.H. Beck, 2001), 151–74, 276–82 (notes), esp. 165–68.

goodness, not changing their species but adding the perfection of a certain glory; and this will be the renewal of the world. Thus, at the same time, the world will be renewed and man will be glorified.[22]

Somehow, in this text, we see how corporeal things—renewed by God—can serve risen, glorified human persons: comforting the bodily eye, in a way proportioned to it, so that they may participate in perceiving God, not only through seeing Christ and the saints bodily, but also by seeing the world.[23] In the same article, the final objection effectively asserts that since non-sensate creatures will not have merited anything, they ought not be renewed. The response is particularly relevant, helping show how the world can serve humanity in the next life:

> Although non-sensate bodies will not have merited that glory, properly speaking, man will have merited in such a way that this glory will be bestowed on the whole universe, insofar as this results in an increase of man's glory, just as a man merits being clothed with more richly adorned clothing, whereas the clothing in no way merits the adornment.[24]

---

[22] *In* IV *sent.*, d. 48, q. 2, a. 1, corp.: "Omnia corporalia propter hominem facta esse creduntur; unde et omnia dicuntur ei esse subjecta. Serviunt autem ei dupliciter. Uno modo ad sustentationem vitae corporalis; alio modo ad profectum divinae cognitionis, inquantum homo per ea quae facta sunt, invisibilia Dei conspicit, ut dicitur Rom. I [Rom 1:20]. Primo ergo ministerio creaturarum, homo glorificatus nullo modo indigebit, cum eius corpus omnino incorruptibile sit futurum, virtute divina id faciente per animam, quam immediate glorificat. Secundo etiam ministerio non indigebit homo quantum ad cognitionem intellectivam; quia tali cognitione Deum sancti videbunt immediate per essentiam. Sed ad hanc visionem essentiae oculus carnis attingere non poterit; et ideo, ut ei solatium congruens sibi de visione Divinitatis praebeatur, inspiciet Divinitatem in suis effectibus corporalibus, in quibus manifeste indicia divinae majestatis apparebunt, et praecipue in carne Christi; et post hoc in corporibus beatorum; et deinceps in omnibus aliis corporibus; et ideo oportebit ut etiam alia corpora majorem influentiam a divina bonitate suscipiant; non tamen speciem variantem, sed addentem cujusdam gloriae perfectionem; et haec erit mundi innovatio; unde simul mundus innovabitur, et homo glorificabitur."

[23] See also: *In* IV *sent.*, d. 44, q. 2, a. 3, qa. 2, corp.; d. 49, q. 2, a. 2, corp. and ad 6; *Super Matt* 5, lec. 2 (no. 434; on Matt 5:8). In *Super Iob* 19. Thomas gives the end of Augustine's *De civitate Dei* as a source for this notion (Leonine ed., 26:117, lns. 302–34, esp. 327–31; on Job 19:26–27). See Augustine, *De civitate Dei* 22.29, in *The City of God against the Pagans*, ed. and trans. R. W. Dyson (Cambridge: Cambridge University Press, 1998), 1171–78.

[24] *In* IV *sent.*, d. 48, q. 2, a. 1, ad 5: "Quamvis corpora insensibilia non meruerint illam gloriam, proprie loquendo; homo tamen meruit ut illa gloria toti universo conferretur, inquantum hoc cedit in augmentum gloriae hominis; sicut aliquis homo meretur ut ornatioribus vestibus induatur, quem tamen ornatum nullo modo ipsa vestis meretur."

We can notice how closely this places the renewed world in association with risen humans. Of the many possessions that might have been discussed, clothing in particular is the possession in this life that is most closely identified with humans and is literally closest to the body. Accordingly, the type and appearance of clothing worn symbolizes the identity of the wearer. Thomas is saying that the transformed world is like transformed clothing for a glorified humanity. For risen persons, the world ought to "suit" them; it ought to "fit" them, like good clothing does. And notice that it is men that may *merit* (through Christ) the renewal of the world, which shows in yet another way the close relation of humans to the world: the very effects of their salvation and glorification are to extend beyond their persons to the world.[25] The glorification of the world happens in response to the glorification of humanity and for the sake of humanity. We can see something similar in a passage from the end of the *Summa contra gentiles*, which notes that "because the bodily creation will in the end be ordered to be in harmony with the state of man, since men, of course, will not only be freed from corruption, but also clothed with glory . . . it must be that even the bodily creation will achieve a kind of radiance of glory in its own way."[26] Because of the change that happens to humanity, the world is to be changed also, in order to be "in harmony with the state of man." Similarly, in the *Compendium theologiae*, we have a text indicating the ordering of things to man:

> But the four elements—namely, fire, air, water and earth—are ordered toward man not only regarding the utility of corruptible life, but also regarding the composition of his body, for the human body is made up of these elements. Thus, the elements have an essential ordination to the human body. Hence when man reaches his consummation in body and soul, it is fitting that the elements remain also, but changed to a better disposition.[27]

---

[25] Elsewhere, Thomas says that the elements of the world will be given "radiance" (*claritas*) when they are renewed at the end of the world, because the elements composing the human body will be glorified (*In IV sent.*, d. 48, q. 2, a. 4, sc 3).

[26] *SCG* IV, ch. 97, no. 7: "Quia igitur creatura corporalis finaliter disponetur per congruentiam ad hominis statum; homines autem non solum a corruptione liberabuntur, sed etiam gloria induentur, . . . oportebit quod etiam creatura corporalis quandam claritatis gloriam suo modo consequatur."

[27] *CT* I, ch. 170: "Quatuor vero elementa, scilicet ignis, aer, aqua et terra, ordinantur ad hominem non solum quantum ad usum corruptibilis vitae, sed etiam quantum ad constitutionem corporis eius: nam corpus humanum ex elementis constitutum est. Sic igitur essentialem ordinem habent elementa ad corpus humanum; unde homine consummato in

Here, Thomas says that it is fitting that the elements remain because they will be included in the composition of humans. It is not asserted that they must remain *only* within human bodies, but that it is fitting, appropriate that those elements themselves be renewed. Of course, Thomas holds that the elements will indeed compose the risen human body.[28] Yet their renewal is to occur for both the parts that compose human bodies and those that do not. In the same chapter of the *Compendium*, then, the Angelic Doctor goes on to consider whether, in the renewed world when man is in the state of perfection, the material world can offer indications of God, or will need to do so:

> In that state of perfection man is not led to the knowledge of God by a consideration of sensible creatures, since he sees God in himself; it is nevertheless enjoyable and pleasant for one who knows the cause to consider how its likeness shines forth in the effect. Thus, it will give joy to the saints to consider the refulgence of the divine goodness reflected in bodies, and particularly the celestial bodies, which appear to have a preeminence over other bodies. Heavenly bodies also have an essential ordination in a certain manner toward the human body under the aspect of efficient causality, just as the elements have under the aspect of material causality: "for man—and the sun, also—generates man": thus, for this reason also, it is fitting that the heavenly bodies remain in existence.[29]

Yes, bodily creatures can and will continue to manifest their Creator, in some way, as his effects—although human persons will not need them for that service. Even though risen persons will have the direct vision of God in himself, without the help of the indications of God available through sensible creatures, it will be "delightful" and "pleasing" (*delectabile* and *iucundum*)

---

corpore et anima, conveniens est ut etiam elementa remaneant, sed in meliorem dispositionem mutata."

[28] *In* IV *sent.*, d. 44, q. 2, a. 1, qa. 1; d. 47, q. 2, a. 1, qa. 1; a. 2, qa. 2–3; a. 3, qa. 2, ad 3; d. 48, q. 2, a. 4, sc 3; *De potentia*, q. 5, a. 7, corp., ad 9 and ad 10; a. 8, obj. 8; a. 9, ad 9; a. 10, corp. and ad 7. See also *ST* III, q. 54, a. 2, ad 2.

[29] *CT* I, ch. 170: "In statu perfectionis illius homo ex creaturis sensibilibus in Dei notitiam non adducatur, cum Deum videat in se ipso, tamen delectabile est et iucundum etiam cognoscenti causam, considerare qualiter eius similitudo resplendeat in effectu: unde et sanctis cedet ad gaudium considerare refulgentiam divinae bonitatis in corporibus, et praecipue caelestibus, quae aliis praeeminere videntur. Habent etiam corpora caelestia essentialem quodam modo ordinem ad corpus humanum secundum rationem causae agentis, sicut elementa rationem causae materialis: 'Homo enim generat hominem et sol'; unde et hac etiam ratione convenit etiam corpora caelestia remanere." The quotation is from Aristotle, *Physica* 2.4.194b13.

to them to see God in his creatures. The direct vision of God, although perfect, does not exclude other possible kinds of perception of him, nor does it exclude taking a kind of joy in that lesser form of consideration of God.[30]

That part of the *Compendium* then goes on to mention another way in which the universe relates to man, although it also offers a reason why the universe should continue in itself:

> Since man is a part of the corporeal universe, it must remain when man is brought to his final consummation; for a part does not seem complete if it should exist without the whole. Now the corporeal universe cannot remain in existence unless its essential parts remain. Yet its essential parts are the heavenly bodies and the elements, such that the whole world system is made up of them; but other bodies do not appear to pertain to the integrity of the corporeal universe, but are rather for its adornment and beauty, which is fitting to its changeable state in the sense that, with a heavenly body acting as efficient cause and with the elements as material causes, animals and plants and mineral bodies are generated. But in the state of final consummation another kind of adornment will be given to the elements that suits their condition of incorruption. Accordingly, in that state, men, the elements, and the heavenly bodies will remain, but not animals or plants or mineral bodies.[31]

---

30 The "joy" that such sensible perception of God's creatures might afford, coexisting with the beatific vision but distinct from it, would likely fall under the category of those delights that follow human reason but do not arise from nature; see *ST* I-II, q. 31, a. 3, corp. That the risen saints' beatific vision would not interfere with certain natural human operations such as natural human reason and sensation—and vice versa—is held throughout Thomas's work, consistent with his view that not only grace but even glory does not destroy nature, but elevates it and perfects it. See: *In IV sent.*; d. 49, q. 2, a. 3, ad 8; *ST* II-II, q. 26, a. 13, sc. On angels' nature, see *ST* I, q. 62, a. 7, sc, corp., and ad 1. I thank Matthew Ramage for prompting me to offer some clarification on this point.

31 *CT* I, ch. 170: "Cum enim homo pars sit universi corporei, in ultima hominis consummatione necesse est universum corporeum remanere; non enim videtur esse pars perfecta si fuerit sine toto. Universum autem corporeum remanere non potest nisi partes essentiales eius remaneant. Sunt autem partes essentiales eius corpora caelestia et elementa, utpote ex quibus tota mundialis machina consistit; cetera vero ad integritatem corporei universi pertinere non videntur, sed magis ad quendam ornatum et decorem ipsius qui competit statui mutabilitatis, secundum quod ex corpore caelesti ut agente, et elementis ut materialibus, generantur animalia et plantae et corpora mineralia. In statu autem ultimae consummationis alius ornatus elementis attribuetur qui deceat incorruptionis statum. Remanebunt igitur in illo statu homines et elementa et corpora caelestia, non autem animalia et plantae et corpora mineralia."

Since human persons are a part of the universe, the universe must remain if human persons are to be raised. Yet the completeness of the universe itself is also invoked. For the world to continue to exist, it must have all its essential parts, including the heavenly bodies and the elements.[32]

We can now summarize what we have reviewed. Though the body and the fellowship of friends can each conduce to the well-being (*bene esse*) of final human happiness, external goods are in no way (*nullo modo huiusmodi*) necessary for that perfect happiness. Yet after the general resurrection, the bodily eye of the risen person will observe the Godhead in its corporeal effects. Furthermore, man will have merited in such a way that this glory will be bestowed on the whole universe, insofar as this results in an increase of man's glory. Bodily creation will in the end be ordered to achieve a kind of radiance of glory. The elements will be changed to a better disposition. It will give joy to the saints to consider the refulgence of the divine goodness reflected in bodies, and particularly the celestial bodies.[33] Since man is a part of the corporeal universe, it must remain when man is brought to his final consummation; and the corporeal universe must remain in its essential parts: men, the elements, and the heavenly bodies.

What must be noticed is the sharp denial by the mature Thomas of any contribution of external goods toward ultimate happiness. Thomas is insistent that it is not through lower things that human fulfillment can come. Yet there are ways in which there is a relation of the world to human beatitude. In fact, the relation is reversed from our original question. It is not the case that man attains or enjoys his end through material creatures, but rather that the material world somehow reaches *its* end, a higher state for itself, through man having reached his. Because the just have been raised and glorified, the creation, too, shares in that renewal and in its way shares in a radiance of glory. Human persons do not depend on mere material creatures for their beatific operation; rather, the world, in some lesser way, participates in human beatitude—or even receives its own perfection in its own way, for all things are ultimately made by God and for God.

This means that the material creation of which we are speaking, on Thomas's view, is not to be considered merely as a means by which humans reach their end, but also as having a more limited but real creaturely

---

[32] One aspect of Thomas's teaching on the "new earth" that we will not be able to address here is his position that plants and non-rational animals will have no place in it.

[33] We noted above that that the *Summa theologiae* remained unfinished—notably, finally lacking the planned section on eschatology. This work seems to lack any mention of the possibility of the risen saints' sight of non-human material creation as providing some indication of God or delight to them; however, it does not deny that possibility.

participation in final perfection. In places, Thomas speaks of glory as a kind of "overflowing" from the soul to the body (and not vice versa).[34] Similarly—extrapolating, as it were—we might say that it is consistent with Thomas's thought to suggest a kind of overflow to the material creation from man, coming down the hierarchy of being. Yet there is also on occasion room for considering material creation as having its share in final perfection in its own right, directly from God.

IMPLICATIONS FOR SOME CURRENT DISCUSSIONS

It is this nuanced and potentially varied consideration of the relation between the material universe and risen and glorified man that may make some contribution to the kinds of discussions considered early in this presentation. The effort in *Laudato Si'* to bring a theological consideration of ecology to that of the common good (such that the natural moral law is extended to include ecological considerations) could be aided by a further application of the eschatological categories it suggests—aided in particular by St. Thomas's teaching on the new heavens and new earth. If, as I have said St. Thomas implies, other creatures' eschatological end is in some way dependent on that of the just, this suggests a deeper human responsibility for the world than perhaps is instinctively felt by someone in the Western world, accustomed to use and control of the world, rather than to seek a kind of solidarity with the rest of creation, at least insofar as all creatures look toward a final renewal (Rom 8:19–23). In this, there may be potential for reviving the kind of connection with the divine that a sense for natural law can help foster. Further reflection will be needed on the kind of eschatology that, on the one hand, allows for both an appreciation of creation and an appropriate stewardship of it and yet, on the other hand, opposes both an idolization of that creation and any abusive exploitation of it.

As for those seeking to reimagine the afterlife as including so much more than "merely" the beatific vision of God, they may do well to recognize that the goodness of all creatures need not require them to contribute by necessity to the end of humanity. It may even be possible that the very quality of *not* being necessary for human beatitude can make the promised eschatological renewal of creatures act as a salutary reminder that there is a higher purpose to the ontological universe than serving us—for God himself is that purpose. On the other hand, Thomas's sharp insistence that human happiness cannot be achieved through material creation points us

---

[34] *ST* I-II, q. 3, a. 3, corp.

rightly toward the One on whom our attention should be fixed even in this life, and away from any idolization of economics, acquisition, production, or consumption, or the control of goods, whether public or private—without denying the necessity of a proper ordering of worldly affairs in this life.[35]

For St. Thomas, then, in the glorious resurrection—if, as we pray, we may be a part of it—material creatures will not contribute directly to our union with God, nor even to the fellowship we will have with others in concert with that union, nor in our own integral unity as soul-body creatures. Yet in that renewed heavens and earth, we may engage with what God has created, for all of it will continue to exhibit his wisdom, goodness, and beauty. It may not be the case that the new heavens and the new earth are going to help us see the face of the living God. But they may continue to reflect the divine goodness to us, whether this be by reflecting the glory refracted through ourselves by the grace of Christ, or bestowed upon them directly by their Creator. This is something to await with eager expectation.[36]

---

[35] Discussions over whether Thomas's account of beatific vision is sufficiently Christological, as we mentioned above in note 10, may be enriched by considering how Thomas's teaching allows for the simultaneous operations of various kinds in a single human person: a risen saint can intellectually see (and voluntarily love) God in the beatific vision while also being perfected bodily and being in fellowship with other risen human persons, while perceiving the world with the bodily eye (and even choosing to do things in it), a world that itself is clothed in a radiance due to the just by their merit in and through Christ. What role, for example, would the humanity of Christ play in each of these modes of knowing (and choosing)?

[36] A version of this essay was originally delivered as a lecture (remotely via electronic link), under the title "The Consummation of the World: The Beatitude of the Saints and the Corporeal Universe, according to St. Thomas Aquinas," for the conference "Hope & Death: Christian Responses," hosted by the Aquinas Center at Ave Maria University, Ave Maria, FL, held February 11–13, 2021. Another version with the same title (and virtually identical content) as the one in this volume appeared in *Nova et Vetera*, English edition, Vol. 19 no. 4 (2021): 1271–1287. I am grateful to the organizers of the conference and to the editors of *Nova et Vetera* for allowing this arrangement.